Adrian Guelke is Professor of Comparative Politics at Queen's University, Belfast. He is the director of the Centre for the Study of Ethnic Conflict (within the School of Politics). He was the Jan Smuts Professor of International Relations at the University of Witwatersrand, Johannesburg in 1993, 1994 and 1995. He has been the editor of *The South African Journal of International Relations* since 1995. Publications include *The Age of Terrorism and the International Political System* (I.B.Tauris), *Northern Ireland: The International Perspective,* (with John Brewer, Ian Hume, Edward Moxon-Browne and Rick Wilford) *The Police, Public Order and the State* and (editor) *New Perspectives on the Northern Ireland Conflict.*

International Library of African Studies
Series ISBN 1 86064 078 8

SOUTH AFRICA

IN

TRANSITION

The Misunderstood Miracle

Adrian Guelke

I.B.TAURIS *Publishers*
LONDON ● NEW YORK

Published in 1999 by I.B.Tauris
Victoria House, Bloomsbury Square, London, WC1B 4DZ
175 Fifth Avenue, New York NY 10010

In the United States and Canada distributed by St. Martin's Press
175 Fifth Avenue, New York NY 10010

ISBN 1 86064 343 4   ·

A full CIP record for this book is available from the British Library
A full CIP record for this book is available from the Library of Congress

Library of Congress catalog card: available

Typeset by The Midlands Book Typesetting Co, Loughborough, Leicestershire
Printed and bound in Great Britain by WBC Ltd, Bridgend

Contents

TO BRIGID, JOHN AND KATE

Preface

The inauguration of Nelson Mandela as President of a democratic South Africa on 10 May 1994 stands out as one of the epic moments of the second half of the twentieth century, on a par with the breaching of the Berlin Wall on 9 November 1989. But unlike the fall of Communism in Eastern Europe which took place suddenly, the triumph of democracy in South Africa was a culmination of a longer process. Its obvious starting point was the announcement by President F.W. de Klerk on 2 February 1990 of the unbanning of the African National Congress (ANC) and other prohibited organisations. The tale of South Africa's transition has been told in a number of books and television documentaries. It is not my intention to produce another version of what happened, but rather to attempt to explain why the transition took place.

However, it is scarcely possible to do that without at the same time throwing a somewhat different light on what happened than that given by popular accounts of South Africa's liberation from apartheid. Exploration of the reasons for the transition has entailed highlighting some events that took place before and during the transition that other accounts have glossed over. The search for explanations of why De Klerk initiated the transition and why it followed the path it did has led me to concentrate on what have seemed to me to be the most fruitful lines of inquiry. Readers should not expect a comprehensive account of all that happened in South Africa between 1990 and 1994. However, by giving an account of why the transition occurred and comparing it to the passage from white minority or colonial rule to African majority rule elsewhere in Africa, I hope to have illuminated the nature of contemporary South African politics, so that the reader comes away with a better understanding of the problems of post-apartheid South Africa. These are likely to come under the spotlight during the course of South Africa's general elections in 1999.

As of late 1998 it appears likely that these elections will take place against a backdrop of low economic growth, in part, but by no means entirely the product of the negative influence on South Africa as a developing market of the crises in Asia and Russia. South Africa's economic woes have led to noticeable discontent with the post-apartheid era compared to the high hopes that accompanied voting in 1994. African dissatisfaction is with the pace of change and has been directed at those they perceive as opposing transformation, generally whites. White disillusionment is a reflection of many factors, including the high crime rate and fear that in future their children will be discriminated against as a result of the passage of far-reaching legislation to promote affirmative action.

The National Party appears likely to suffer reverses in the 1999 elections, partly because white voters have blamed the party in retrospect for the terms of the country's political settlement. Hoping to benefit from the sour mood of white voters is the Democratic Party of Tony Leon, which has positioned itself on the right. However, the party presents no threat whatever to the dominance of the ANC, with its electoral base among the country's African majority. The main challenge to the ANC comes from a new party, the United Democratic Movement, launched at the end of September 1997 and led by Bantu Holomisa (a former ruler of the Transkei, who was expelled from the ANC) and Roelf Meyer (the former National Party negotiator). Support for the new party seems unlikely to prevent an ANC victory in the 1999 elections, though it may be sufficient to prevent the ANC from gaining two-thirds of the vote and consequently the capacity to amend the constitution without the support of other parties.

Race remains an important source both of identity and division in South Africa, as even the positive description of Archbishop Tutu of the country as a rainbow nation acknowledges. I have generally employed the terms, white, Coloured, Indian and African to describe the four-fold racial division of the country's population. I have avoided (except where it occurs in quotations) the term, black (or Black), as some writers mean by this term, African, while others mean African, Coloured and Indian. A few employ capitalisation to distinguish between the two meanings, a usage liable to confuse readers, especially as publishers often have their own conventions as whether or when to capitalise racial terminology. Of course the use of racial terminology is not meant to imply endorsement of a biological interpretation of these differences. As in the more obvious case of ethnic groups, social construction has played an important role in people's perceptions of the boundaries between racial categories. Further, these categories should not be thought of as fixed. For example, it was common during the 1980s for writers to refer to 'Coloureds' in inverted commas as a way of indicating that 'Coloureds' rejected their classification as Coloureds under legislation enforcing apartheid. Coloured support for the National Party in the elections of 1994 and the evident strength of Coloured identity have led to the disappearance of the inverted commas from writing in the second half of the 1990s. That reflects

both changed political circumstances and evolution in the interpretation of Coloured political attitudes.

This book was not written from scratch. In some of chapters, I make
quite substantial use of work of mine published separately as articles
or chapters in books over the course of the last five years. In particular,
Chapter 2 draws on my article, 'The Impact of the End of the Cold
War on the South African Transition', published in the *Journal of
Contemporary African Studies* (Vol. 14, No. 1) in January 1996; Chapter
4 on a chapter entitled 'The Quiet Dog: The Extreme Right and the
South African Transition' in *The Revival of Right-Wing Extremism in the
Nineties* edited by Peter H.Merkl and Leonard Weinberg (Frank Cass,
London 1997); Chapter 6 on an article entitled 'South Africa's "Peace"
Elections: The Regional Dimension' in *Regional Politics and Policy* (Vol.
4, No.2) in Summer 1994; Chapter 9 on an article entitled 'Dissecting
the South African Miracle: African Parallels' published in *Nationalism
and Ethnic Politics* (Vol. 2, No. 1) in Spring 1996. The section on local
elections in Chapter 8 makes use of material collected for an article
entitled 'Completing South Africa's Democratization: The Local
Elections in KwaZulu-Natal' in *Regional and Federal Studies* (Vol. 7, No.
2) in Summer 1997.

In writing this book I have incurred debts to many people. The
initial research for the book was carried out while I was in
Johannesburg in the years 1993, 1994 and 1995, when I held the post
of Jan Smuts Professor of International Relations at the University of
the Witwatersrand. Nicola Green and Shamrita Singh on Ford
Foundation internships helped me in the collection of material as
did David Burrows, while Rupert Taylor of Wits Political Studies
Department drew my attention to articles that proved important in
the development of my arguments that I might otherwise have missed.
My thanks are also due to Noam Pines of Wits Political Studies
Department for supplying me (and others) information by e-mail on
the latest political developments. The support and help of the staff at
the South African Institute of International Affairs, including at different times, John Barratt, Sara Pienaar and Greg Mills, but especially
its outstanding librarian, Jackie Kalley, also deserves mention, as does
the friendship extended to me and my family in Johannesburg by
John and Judith Kalk and their children.

In the UK my thanks are particularly due to Jack Spence (who read
a first draft) and, at I.B.Tauris, to Lester Crook and Steve Tribe. I also
owe a debt of gratitude to my colleagues in the School of Politics at
Queen's University for allowing me back and for their help and support in the creation of the Centre for the Study of Ethnic Conflict.

Last but not least the book could not have been completed without the support and understanding of my immediate family to whom this book is dedicated since their varying responses to the South African transition helped me in my understanding of this remarkable period.

Adrian Guelke,
Centre for the Study of Ethnic Conflict,
School of Politics,
Queen's University, Belfast.
Autumn 1998.

List of Abbreviations

ACDP	African Christian Democratic Party
ANC	African National Congress
APLA	Azanian People's Liberation Army
AVF	*Afrikaner Volksfront* (Afrikaner people's front)
AVU	*Afrikaner Volksunie* (Afrikaner people's union)
AWB	*Afrikaner Weerstandsbeweging* (Afrikaner resistance movement)
BBB	*Blanke Bevrydingsbeweging* (white freedom movement)
BV	*Blanke Veiligheid* (white safety)
CODESA	Convention for a Democratic South Africa
COSAG	Concerned South Africans Group
COSATU	Congress of South African Trade Unions
DP	Democratic Party
DTA	Democratic Turnhalle Alliance
EPG	Eminent Persons Group
FF	Freedom Front
FNLA	*Frente Nacional de Libertacao de Angola* (National Front for the Liberation of Angola)
GEAR	Growth, Employment and Redistribution
HNP	*Herstigte Nasionale Party* (Refounded National Party)
HRC	Human Rights Commission
ICJ	International Commission of Jurists
IDASA	Institute for Democracy in South Africa
IEC	Independent Electoral Commission
IFP	Inkatha Freedom Party
KANU	Kenya African National Union
KZP	KwaZulu Police
MDM	Mass Democratic Movement
MK	*Umkhonto we Sizwe* (Spear of the Nation)
MPLA	*Movimento Popular de Libertacao de Angola* (Popular Movement for the Liberation of Angola)
NP	National Party
OAU	Organisation of African Unity
PAC	Pan-Africanist Congress (of Azania)

PAGAD	People against Gangsters and Drugs
PLO	Palestine Liberation Organisation
PWV	Pretoria-Witwatersrand-Vereeniging
RDP	Reconstruction and Development Programme
SAAF	South African Air Force
SACP	South African Communist Party
SAIRR	South African Institute of Race Relations
SARFU	South African Rugby Football Union
SWAPO	South West African People's Organisation
SDU	Self-Defence Unit
SPU	Self-Protection Unit
TEC	Transitional Executive Council
TRC	Truth and Reconciliation Commission
TVC	Temporary Voter's Card
UDF	United Democratic Front
UDM	United Democratic Movement
UNITA	*Uniao Nacional para a Independencia de Total de Angola* (National Union for the Total Independence of Angola)
UNOMSA	United Nations Observer Mission in South Africa
UPA	*Uniao das Populacoes de Angola* (Union of Angolan Peoples)
UWUSA	United Workers Union of South Africa

CHAPTER 1

Introduction: The Impasse of the Late 1980s

The subject of this book is South Africa's passage from white minority rule to African majority rule. The justification for such a blunt description of the dramatic events of the 1990s is to convey both the magnitude of the change and the size of the task that faces anyone seeking to explain the change. This is not to deny the validity of the much commoner description of the change as a process of democratisation. This description also has the advantage of locating change in South Africa in the wider context of the triumph of liberal-democratic forms of government round the world in the 1990s. What is more, it may be objected that the racial labelling of majority rule gives too little credit to the non-racialism of the African National Congress (ANC). However, without disregarding the non-racial aspirations of South Africa's political parties, it will be argued in this book that it would be an even bigger mistake to ignore the extent to which South Africa remains a society politically polarised along racial lines.

The book follows conventional usage in describing the change that took place in South Africa in terms of a transition. Transition is defined by O'Donnell and Schmitter in their study of transitions from authoritarian rule as 'the interval between one political regime and another'. More importantly they stress that transition is a period of uncertainty in which

> not only are [the rules of the game] in constant flux, but they are arduously contested; actors struggle not just to satisfy their immediate interests and/or the interests of those whom they purport to represent, but also to define rules and procedures whose configuration will determine likely winners and losers in the future.[1]

1

In South Africa's case, the period between the political system's liberalisation in 1990 and its democratisation in 1994 was a lengthy interval. The question that begs to be answered in this context is: was the outcome of the contest between the ANC and its rivals largely determined in the course of the power struggles in this period? The other term in the title of this book that requires interpretation is miracle.

Stripped of its religious connotations, the term, miracle, refers to an unexpected set of events, with the further implication that the outcome is benign. It is hardly surprising that so many analysts have used the term to describe the South African transition, considering that the process started with President de Klerk's announcement on 2 February 1990 of the unbanning of the ANC and culminated in the inauguration of Nelson Mandela as President of South Africa on 10 May 1994 after democratic elections.[2] The emphasis in books and articles written after Mandela's inauguration has tended to be on the outcome of the transition. And, in fact, a case can be made out for confining the miracle to the events of 1994, when formidable obstacles to the holding of credible elections were overcome in the space of a couple of months. How the process of transition turned out is obviously important, but if the miracle is to be understood, it is just as important to get to grips with what impelled De Klerk to embark on the process in the first place, especially as his need to have done so remains a matter of debate.

In the 1980s few people either inside or outside South Africa anticipated the irreversible liberalisation of the South African polity announced by De Klerk in February 1990, even though it was widely appreciated that South Africa had entered a period of 'unstable equilibrium', as Robin Cohen put it in a book published in 1986.[3] A term commonly used to describe the situation in South Africa by the late 1980s was 'impasse'. John Brewer accounted for the popularity of the use of the term in relation to South Africa in a book published in 1989 as follows:

> Impasse means deadlock and stalemate, and while some situations of impasse seem permanent, there is always a pressure towards flux and change which is absent in situations of amicable (as distinct from enforced) stability. This is because impasse reflects disagreement and incompatibility between opposites, rather than the capitulation of one to the other, and the inability of one to impose upon the other.[4]

By this time the application of the term, crisis, to South Africa's political condition had become a cliché. Further, that description implied the possibility that the instability was temporary and that the government's authority might be restored as had occurred after previous crises. By contrast, the application of the term 'impasse' implied that a more fundamental breakdown of the existing system had taken place, as did increasing reference to the existence of a South African conflict.

Yet, despite the recognition that South Africa by the second half of the 1980s faced a situation qualitatively different from the crisis that had followed the Sharpeville massacre in 1960, this generally did not translate into an expectation of the imminence of fundamental change. Admittedly, some writers did hold out the possibility of the demise of the existing system. Cohen is an example. However, such predictions were usually stated much more cautiously than those of writers who argued on the contrary the paradoxical proposition that the political impasse would prove durable. For example, in *Negotiating South Africa's Future* edited by Hermann Giliomee and Lawrence Schlemmer, which was published in 1989, Simon Jenkins asserted: 'From my observation, South Africa is no more likely to witness a more than cosmetic shift in its fundamental power structure than it was ten or twenty years ago.' [5]

The notion of a miracle carries the further connotation that the events it encapsulates are beyond the realm of rational explanation. This accounts for another dimension of the use of the term, a tendency among social scientists to put the term in inverted commas.[6] Such qualification of the term also usually signals that the writer objects to a common view of the transition that does not go quite as far as to suggest that it lies beyond the bounds of rational explanation, but emphasises the role that a series of lucky accidents played in the transition. Accounts by journalists of the transition tend to stress the role of such contingent factors in the process and in the events that led up to De Klerk's initiative of 2 February 1990.[7] Understandably, there has been a reaction against what seems like a 'Cleopatra's nose' notion of historical development among political scientists studying the transition. But because the word miracle conveys so well the unexpected nature of the transition, they have been hard put to find an alternative description to encapsulate the process.

Expectations of change in South Africa did not remain static. In particular, the sceptical attitude of political analysts to the prospects for fundamental change in the late 1980s stands in marked contrast to the confidence with which predictions of the imminent demise of apartheid had been made in the 1960s. At the same time, there was a recognition of the country's political stagnation so there was plenty of advocacy of the need for far-reaching change. This can be dated back before the late 1980s. It was a reaction in the first instance to the events of 1976 when unrest had followed the brutal suppression of protests by schoolchildren in Soweto over educational policies. By contrast, the expectations of change in the 1960s were not accompanied by much advocacy or exploration of alternatives to the existing system. The assumption then was that South Africa would simply be engulfed by the 'wind of change'[8] sweeping the rest of the African continent and that majority rule would come, whether whites liked it or not.

Part of the reason why analysts were less sanguine about the prospects for either far-reaching or fundamental change in the 1980s was the realisation that it would have to secure white acceptance and that seemed a formidable hurdle to overcome. Part of the explanation for the caution of analysts in the later period was also simply because previous predictions of change had failed to materialise, but more fundamentally it reflected a change in reference points in considering the possibilities for change. Overwhelmingly, decolonisation elsewhere in Africa provided the reference point for those predicting change in the 1960s. Where reference was made to events outside of Africa as the basis for analogy with South Africa, it still tended to be in the context of the fall of empires. For example in his seminal account of South African foreign policy during the early 1960s, J.E.Spence reached the following conclusion:

> South Africa lacks that degree of consensus without which long-term political and economic stability is impossible. Historians in future years may draw an analogy between the present South African situation and that faced by the Austro-Hungarian empire in its declining years, both racked by movements looking for salvation to a powerful ideology that transcended formal boundaries and refusing to recognize the sovereignty of their respective rulers. [9]

By the 1980s the reference points for the prediction of change or the lack of it was no longer Africa, but deeply divided societies elsewhere in the world. Non-African societies beset by conflicts over national identity were seen as providing better models for analysing the South African situation than countries in Africa that had achieved majority rule, including those where this had been in the face of significant opposition from a white settler minority. Reference to societies outside Africa was commonplace among supporters of the South African government and had been so for many years as a way of legitimising the policy of apartheid. For example, Hendrik Verwoerd, Prime Minister between 1958 and 1966, often suggested that the development of the European Economic Community provided a model for future relations among the nations of South Africa.[10] He also drew an analogy between the position of Africans working in 'white' South Africa and that of Turkish *gastarbeiters* (guest workers) in West Germany who similarly had no voting rights where they worked. Interest in political practice elsewhere in the world that might be used to justify South African policies gave supporters of the government an incentive to examine other models than the Westminster parliamentary system. It also formed a useful starting point for *verligtes* (the so-called 'enlightened ones' on the left of the ruling party) seeking modification to the policy of apartheid. The most popular of the external models was the Swiss cantonal system, since it combined a large measure of autonomy for its sub-state units with unquestioned international legitimacy.

In the wake of the Soweto uprising of June 1976 and a consequent loss of confidence within the National Party in the continued viability of the policy of apartheid as it had been developed by Verwoerd, reference to external models by members of the government increased. A conference on the subject of 'Accommodation in Plural Societies' in Cape Town in May 1977 provided the context for introducing South Africa to the work of Arend Lijphart on consociationalism.[11] It also marked the start of Lijphart's long engagement with the problem of South Africa in which he suggested that his prescriptions for divided societies provided an alternative to apartheid, partition or majority rule and yet remained compatible with democracy. One of most *verligte* ministers in the government, Piet Koornhof, gave the conference's keynote address in which he suggested that South Africa should learn from the Swiss example. However, interest in consociationalism was not confined to *verligte* supporters of the government. A significant harbinger in establishing non-African societies as reference points for considering alternatives to apartheid was *South Africa's options: Strategies for sharing power*, which was published in 1979. The authors were Frederik van Zyl Slabbert, who had just become the Leader of the Opposition in the South African parliament as the book came out, and David Welsh, a liberal academic whose field was African politics. The book's point of departure was that South Africa was a divided society and that sustaining democracy in divided societies required special mechanisms.

The authors drew particular attention to the school of political scientists who had devised 'the concept of consociational democracy to account for those cases where a specific type of political system has survived in spite of deep social cleavages'. They went on to discuss the classic consociational democracies of Austria, Belgium, the Netherlands and Switzerland, drawing heavily on the work of Arend Lijphart. The intention was to present South Africa with an evolutionary alternative to apartheid that ideally might secure both white support and acceptance in the international community. They laid special emphasis on the former:

> Anyone who claims that "white politics is irrelevant" in South Africa neither cares for, nor understands the problem of evolutionary change towards a democratic alternative. By evolutionary change we do not necessarily mean a smooth, peaceful transition to a new dispensation. We do not exclude conflict, tension and even sporadic violence. What we do emphatically mean, however, is that whatever constitutional change occurs, or whatever a new democratic South Africa is going to look like, it will come about through the active participation and volition of those who govern in the existing undemocratic dispensation.[12]

Also influential in promoting the relevance of consociationalism to a solution of the South African problem was a book published in an English edition in 1981, *South Africa: the Prospects for Peaceful Change* by Theodor Hanf, Heribert Weiland and Gerda Vierdag. The book had originally been published in a German edition in 1978. It was subtitled in the English edition, *An empirical enquiry into the possibility of democratic conflict regulation.* That reflected the use by the authors of survey evidence to buttress their cautious conclusion that 'peaceful and democratic conflict regulation is still not impossible'.[13] However, the authors argued that the white power-elite would not opt for a consociational solution in the immediate future and they characterised official proposals for constitutional change involving the establishment of Coloured and Indian parliaments alongside the existing white parliament as 'sham consociationalism'.[14] They drew an important distinction between a genuine commitment to consociationalism and the use of the vocabulary of consociationalism to justify proposals designed to perpetuate white supremacy.

Through the 1980s the influence of comparisons outside of Africa grew along with the ideas of Lijphart. Further, with the passage of time, the examples of change in other African societies with large white minorities seemed of less contemporary relevance to the problems of South Africa. At the start of the decade, Slabbert and Welsh's ideas seemed almost impossibly optimistic, except in the sham form that perpetuated white political supremacy, and the authors themselves recognised that by suggesting that the challenge to politics in South Africa was to practise 'the art of the impossible'.[15]However, the liberal distinction between genuine and sham forms of consociationalism did not enjoy universal support outside the ranks of supporters of the South African government. In response to the crisis in South Africa in the late 1970s two conservative Africanists had written a study emphasising the durability of the South African system. They, too, advocated a consociational solution, but one closer to official thinking than that put forward by Slabbert and Welsh. They argued that the best hope for change in South Africa lay in Western support for the *verligtes* within the National Party. The study was expanded into a book and published in 1981 under the title, *Why South Africa Will Survive*.[16] Ten years later Gann and Duignan published a book entitled, *Hope for South Africa?*. They argued:

> For now, a consensus society based on a majority rule is out of the question because whites will not accept it. Conflict will not resolve the country's problems; consensus appears impossible in the short run. Hence, a third way might be tried: a consociational system that would not be based on the majoritarian principle but that would give everyone the vote. In different forms, consociation has operated effectively in countries such as Switzerland, Belgium, and Holland, and at one time in Lebanon.[17]

A measure of the extent of the influence of the comparisons that flowed from the prescriptions of consociationalism was that even radical analysts who cautiously held out the prospect of fundamental change looked to deeply divided societies outside Africa for their analogies. Thus, Cohen's reference points for his assumption that what was being witnessed in the mid-1980s was 'the beginnings of a new long-term unstable equilibrium' were Northern Ireland and Lebanon, though he added 'obviously these analogies do not hold in an exact sense'.[18]

Much more forceful use of such analogies was made by writers who contested the likelihood of fundamental change taking place at all or who disputed the outside world's whole conception of what fundamental change might or should entail. The two cases that were used most frequently in this context were Northern Ireland and Israel/Palestine. Indeed, interest in the two cases was sufficiently strong to provide the basis for the holding of a conference, principally of academics, on the comparisons in Bonn in September 1989. The conference was hosted by the Institute for a Democratic Alternative in South Africa (IDASA), which has been renamed the Institute for Democracy in South Africa, and the Friedrich Naumann Foundation, which provided the funding for the conference and is a body associated with the Free Democratic Party in Germany. A book edited by two well-known South African political scientists, Hermann Giliomee and Jannie Gagiano, based on revised versions of the papers delivered at the conference was published in 1990. In his introduction, Hermann Giliomee described the problem the book posed as follows: 'why are the conflicts in Northern Ireland, South Africa and Israel so intractable and why is the search for peace so elusive?'[19]

In a key chapter in the book, Bernard Crick pronounced the three cases 'insoluble'. He gave two formal reasons for this characterisation of the three situations. The first was 'that no internal solution likely to guarantee peace can possibly satisfy the announced principles of the main disputants'; the second 'that any external imposed solution or enforced adjudication is likely to strengthen the desperation and self-righteousness of the threatened group'. He added a third contingent reason: 'the virtual impossibility of successful armed rebellion against each of the governments concerned'. Crick expressed the hope that a meeting of leaders on both sides might arise out of the very existence of a 'stalemate of subversive terror versus state terror' and concluded: 'concerned persons should be less concerned to predict and support most favoured outcomes and more willing to imagine and to accept many possible and often quite unexpected outcomes.'[20] One of the attractions of comparing the three situations was that it facilitated departure from the zero-sum thinking which had tended to characterise the attitude of the principal conflicting parties in each of the three cases.

The weakening of the influence of the African model on discussion of South Africa's future was reflected by the end of the 1980s in a multiplication of the number of ways in which a resolution of the South African conflict was envisaged. Thus, whereas writers in the 1960s, apart from the most sanguine apologists for apartheid, tended to foresee either majority rule or a failure to resolve the South African situation, by the 1980s, the options seemed both more numerous and less stark. In a memorable phrase, Donald Horowitz noted that there was 'conflict about the conflict'[21] in his book entitled *A Democratic South Africa?*, which was published in 1991, but which reflected the perspectives of the late 1980s when the country's transition to democracy seemed by no means assured. In short, the question mark in the title mattered. The sub-title of the book, *Constitutional Engineering in a Divided Society*, is also important in its reflection of the influence of the comparisons made between South Africa and other deeply divided societies.

In writing of 'the conflict about the conflict', Horowitz drew on a variety of political and academic sources to identify 12 different perspectives on the country's future, involving a wide gamut of diagnoses of, and prescriptions for, the South African condition. The 12 'views' were 'official', 'Charterist', 'alternative Charterist', 'people's democracy', 'Africanist', 'Black Consciousness', 'racial self-assertion', 'two-nationalisms partitionist', 'two-nationalisms accommodationist', 'consociational', 'modified consociational' and 'simple majoritarian'.[22] A brief description of each position is necessary to convey the gist of Horowitz's exposition, especially as some of the labels are not self-explanatory. The 'official' view Horowitz had in mind was the position being taken by the government prior to 2 February 1990 when De Klerk's liberalisation of the political system demonstrated a commitment to the negotiation of a new political dispensation. Broadly, it was the view that the division of society into different racial and ethnic categories or 'population groups' in the language of the government should provide the essential basis for the exercise of political rights.

The label 'Charterist' was a reference to the Freedom Charter adopted by the Congress Alliance (the leading component of which was the ANC) in 1955. The Freedom Charter asserted that South Africa belonged to all who lived in it, 'black and white'. It did recognise the existence of several national groups and held that these were entitled to 'equal rights' in the context of a non-racial democracy. The difference between this view and the 'alternative Charterist view' was the emphasis that the latter placed on the aspiration (and possibility) of South Africa's developing into a common society, with the country's divisions being seen as largely the artificial creation of the policy of apartheid. The 'people's democracy view' with its emphasis on participatory as opposed to multi-party representative democracy stemmed from the influence of Marxist thinking within the anti-apartheid movement within and outside the country in the late 1980s. It also reflected an analysis of South Africa that highlighted the role that class played in the country's political divisions.

The 'Africanist view' of South Africa was that of the country as a colonial society, with apartheid seen as a species of settler colonialism. Reversing the denial of the rights of the indigenous population was a priority for all Africanists, though there were different opinions on what sort of society this implied. The 'Black Consciousness view' differed from the 'Africanist' in the emphasis it placed on colour as the fundamental dividing line in South Africa on the assumption (and objective) of solidarity among all those who had been discriminated against under apartheid, with Coloureds, Indians and Africans collectively being seen as part of an oppressed Black population. What Horowitz meant by the 'racial self-assertion view' was the perspective that saw South Africa as a horizontally divided society dominated by a minority, with change being most likely to take the form of a reversal of roles with a politically dominant majority emerging out of the demise of apartheid. The implication was that such a turning of the tables would prove incompatible with the establishment of a liberal democracy and Horowitz argued that 'since it is extremely unfashionable to eschew democracy in South Africa, this view is rarely, if ever, articulated there'.[23]

The point of departure of the 'two-nationalisms-partitionist view' was that the South African conflict stemmed from the clash between Afrikaner and African nationalism. Their fundamental incompatibility was seen as requiring territorial separation and the creation of at least two states. The 'two-nationalisms accommodationist view' acknowledged the difficulty of reconciling Afrikaner and African nationalism, but saw economic interdependence, among other reasons, as an obstacle to territorial separation and proposed binational institutions as the basis for the accommodation of the two nationalisms. The 'consociational view' was a reflection of the influence that the writings of Arend Lijphart had on South African politics during the 1980s. This perspective accepted Lijphart's prescriptions for the functioning of liberal democracy in deeply divided societies of minority vetoes and mechanisms for extending a maximum amount of autonomy to different ethnic or racial groups. A 'modified consociational view' was to be found among liberals sympathetic in general terms to the analysis of South Africa as a deeply divided society that required special mechanisms to accommodate group differences but who argued for the modified application of Lijphart's model for consociational democracy to South Africa on the grounds that it presented too large an obstacle to the tackling of socio-economic inequalities. Finally, the 'simple majoritarian view' was the straightforward prescription of the extension of the franchise to the country's adult population without reference to group membership.

Horowitz's categories were by no means exhaustive. However, they do convey well the very wide range of possibilities that were seen as salient at the start of the South African transition. From the perspective of the late 1990s, a few of these views appear somewhat naïve or otherwise redundant. Thus, with the collapse of communism in Eastern Europe, the 'people's democracy view' quickly lost much of its resonance, despite the continuing role played by the South African

Communist Party (SACP) within the ANC. But the most common weakness was the overestimation of the power of the representatives of the white minority to shape the basis of the future political dispensation. This applies most obviously to the 'two nationalisms partitionist view'. However, a case can be made that all of the views described by Horowitz played a role of some sort in the actual process of transition, if only in an attenuated form or as a negative model to be avoided.

The quest for a dispensation based on group rights in accordance with the 'official view' was the government's point of departure when it embarked on the transition. The ANC's adherence to a policy of non-racialism and how it was interpreted in policy terms reflected the influences of both the 'Charterist' and 'alternative Charterist' views. Points of reference for what to avoid were provided by both the 'people's democracy view' and the 'Africanist view'. The same could be said of the 'racial self-assertion view'. The polarisation of opinion between the ANC and the National Party provided a measure of vindication for the interpretation of the conflict as a clash of two nationalisms, but much less for the prescriptions based on it. Lijphart interpreted the acceptance of power-sharing, albeit as for a transitional period, as a gesture towards consociationalism, while those who argued for a modified application of the model could take comfort from the absence of minority vetoes even during the transitional period of power-sharing. Finally, the fact that the contest for votes encouraged the parties to project themselves as non-racial in their appeal undercut arguments against the principle of a simple majority.

It is of course open to argument what options really lay open to South Africa at the end of the 1980s. The answers different writers give to this question do depend partly on when they have made their contribution, with greater emphasis tending to be placed on the inevitability of the process in writings produced after the completion of the transition process with Mandela's inauguration as President in May 1994. However, this is a tendency, not a general rule. A number of the most acute observers of the country's politics continue to stress the contingent nature of the transition. For example, Adam, Slabbert and Moodley assert the following in their 1997 book on post-liberation politics in South Africa:

There is very little doubt that if P.W.Botha or Magnus Malan or Gerrit Viljoen had been president in 1990, the National Party would still be in power today and we would still be treated to anecdotes of Afrikaner obduracy and will to self-determination. No doubt, new, innovative and unworkable strategies would have been devised to create the illusion of sharing power without losing any, which is the hallmark of the co-optive domination of the Tri-Cameral Parliament instituted in 1984. There is very little doubt that the Afrikaner minority as represented by the National Party could have dominated into the 21st century if it had so wished. Undoubtedly at considerable cost to the country and region.[24]

The issue of what options were available in the late 1980s is an important one. However, it would be premature to tackle it in detail at this juncture, though the broad terms of the debates are worth identifying at this point. Thus, with the benefit of post-transition hindsight, there continues to be argument over whether De Klerk had been compelled to embark on the liberalisation of the South African political system in 1990. Then there arises the further question as to whether, once the South African political system had been liberalised, a different outcome to the negotiation process itself might have been achieved. Those arguing that majority rule might have been averted before the end of the millennium (for good or ill) generally have based this conclusion on the assumption that the liberalisation of the South African political system might have been delayed rather than that the National Party might have held out for a consociational system or other limitation on an eventual transition to majority rule in the course of the negotiations in 1992 and 1993.

What needs to be underlined at this point is that at the end of the 1980s, the common assumption was that a variety of options was available through negotiations with genuine representatives of public opinion. This perception was important in sustaining a political climate favourable to calls for negotiations. In this context, a distinction was often drawn between substantive negotiations on a new dispensation and the efforts being made by the government to co-opt leaders from the subordinate communities. As early as 1986, Clem Sunter of the Anglo-American Corporation put forward a scenario of South Africa's future that treated this distinction as crucial. Drawing on a model developed by Michael O'Dowd and Bobby Godsell (also of the Anglo-American Corporation), he predicted that negotiations and the forging of political alliances among genuine representatives of the country's population were vital to the country's prospects of achieving economic growth and thence ultimately the means to sustain a democratic form of government.[25]

This 'high road' was contrasted with a 'low road' of authoritarianism and low economic growth that would ultimately turn the country into a waste land. Implicit in this model, as in many other analyses from that time, was that for the country's political leaders to avail

themselves of the multitude of options available required negotiations across the political spectrum and that the liberalisation of the
political system was a pre-condition for making that possible. In short,
without liberalisation, a bleak future was predicted for the polity and
the society. The contrast between these assumptions and those made
after the transition are striking. Once again, the point that is worth
underlining is that the *perception* of the nature of the choice faced by
South Africa itself became a significant factor in influencing opinion
and creating the climate that made February 1990 possible.
Notwithstanding (and perhaps even because of) the free-enterprise
populist ideology that underpinned his presentations, Sunter found
a receptive audience in the white community for his scenarios. Sunter
made very wide use of comparisons with other societies to establish
the credibility of his predictions. In almost all cases he looked to societies outside Africa to provide models of how South Africa might
develop. In the case of the original O'Dowd/Godsell model Sunter
first presented in 1986, the model was Switzerland. In his post-
transition book (*The High Road: Where are we now?*) Sunter explains
the significance of the choice of Switzerland as follows:

> You will see a star adjacent to where we splash down as a developed country
> after emerging from the transition. It is entitled "Switzerland". Again, this
> is a dream because South Africa will never be exactly like Switzerland. On
> the other hand, Switzerland has been home to a wide diversity of people
> who have not fought a war with one another in 700 years. It is therefore a
> good model to aim for.[26]

Predictions that unless the South African government changed course
politically, the country would face revolution or disaster have been
made ever since the National Party came to power (and in the case of
Keppel-Jones's extraordinary book, *When Smuts goes*,[27] published in
1947, even earlier in anticipation of the party's coming to power).
The economic boom of the late 1960s allied to outward political stability had discredited many of the predictions that had been made at
the start of the decade, particularly those that were based on the
notion that had been articulated by the British Prime Minister, Harold
Macmillan, in a speech to the South African Parliament in February
1960, of a 'wind of change' sweeping across the continent of Africa.
The fact that South Africa's development during the 1960s diverged
so clearly from that of the rest of Africa meant that African models
lost much of their relevance for those thinking of the possibilities of
change in the South African case. The remarkable change in South
Africa's fortunes also bred caution among scholars, particularly those

of a liberal disposition whose hopes of change had been dashed in the process. The lesson many derived was that the National Party government possessed the capacity to survive short-term emergencies.

On the precedent of the aftermath of the Sharpeville massacre, the Soweto uprising of June1976 seemed to be just another short-term security emergency resulting from the adoption of particularly insensitive educational policies. In their discussion of the Soweto uprising, Gann and Duignan argued that it presented no real threat to white control. They derided those who portrayed the riots in Soweto as a step towards making South Africa ungovernable as oblivious to the fact

> that similar predictions had been made for a generation; every riot, every commotion had, at the time, presaged similar consequences. Over the last generation, the oppositional literature in South Africa has built up a dream world of its own, a world where time was forever 'running out', where the clock perpetually marked 'five minutes before midnight', where the consciousness of the oppressed eternally experienced new changes of a qualitative kind. [28]

They argued further that the effect of violent outbreaks usually was to strengthen government control because they cemented white unity, while at the same time they tended to open up rifts in the subordinate communities. However, Gann and Duignan were in a minority in denying that the Soweto uprising represented a significant watershed in the country's history, even at the time of the events themselves. Further, the passage of time has tended to enhance the significance of the crisis of 1976.

The obvious reason why the Soweto uprising has tended to be seen as a turning point is the role it played in helping to precipitate a change in direction in the government's policy. At the end of 1976, the Prime Minister, B.J.Vorster, appointed P.W.Botha to chair a special Cabinet Committee of senior party leaders to investigate possible constitutional changes in the light of the crisis. Its recommendations, which included proposals to establish a tricameral legislature, were presented to the National Party caucus in August 1977 and were included in the party's platform for the November 1977 general election. They formed an important element of the reforms introduced by P.W.Botha when he succeeded Vorster as Prime Minister in September 1978 and were embodied in the 1984 constitution. The conflict that implementation of the constitution gave rise to in the mid-1980s spelt the failure of what had been an ambitious attempt to strengthen National Party rule by extending its base through co-option of representatives of the Coloured and Indian communities. The crisis of the mid-1980s demonstrated more generally the failure of the reforms after 1976 to restore political stability. The link between 1976 and what turned out to be apartheid's terminal crisis underscored the importance of the Soweto uprising.

But tempting though it is to construct a narrative of the South African transition showing that De Klerk's initiative of February 1990 followed inevitably from the events of June 1976, it would be misleading. In this context, the similarities between the last years of Vorster's political stewardship of South Africa and those of his successor, P.W.Botha, are worth underlining as they highlight some of the discontinuities in the political process. The Soweto uprising was the culmination of a series of reverses suffered by the South African government under B.J.Vorster, including the failure of South Africa's military intervention in Angola's civil war at independence. Vorster's balancing act between the National Party's factions was exposed as a source of weakness and paralysis. P.W.Botha emerged the victor in a fierce battle to succeed Vorster. His victory had depended upon the damage done to his chief rival, Connie Mulder, by a scandal over the misappropriation of funds by the Department of Information.

Similarly, it was evident by the late 1980s that P.W.Botha's conception of policy – the total strategy to meet the total onslaught South Africa faced – had run its course, with the consequent stagnation of the reform process. The outcome of the battle to succeed P.W.Botha as National Party leader was even narrower, with F.W.de Klerk securing victory in the final ballot by eight votes. At the time of his election in February 1989, it remained unclear what the outcome would be of P.W.Botha's unilateral decision to hold on to the Presidency while giving up the leadership of the National Party. Even on the assumption that the leadership of the country would ultimately go to the new party leader, nothing in De Klerk's past suggested the radicalism of the initiative he would take less than a year after his election. Even after he became President in September 1989, the early indications of his intentions were contradictory. In Chapter 2, the evidence that external factors, most particularly, the collapse of Communism in Eastern Europe played a key role in De Klerk's liberalisation of the South African system, is examined.

While there is no gainsaying the significance of De Klerk's speech of 2 February 1990, it was nonetheless only the start of a process, the outcome of which seemed uncertain almost up to the first day of polling in the April 1994 general election. By that time, admittedly, the political ascendancy of the ANC was apparent, though that had only become unequivocally clear the previous April, following the assassination of the popular South African Communist Party leader, Chris Hani. But, of course, to say that the outcome of the process that De Klerk initiated in February 1990 seemed uncertain is not the same as saying that this perception was correct. Indeed, with the benefit of hindsight, it is possible to conclude that the unbanning of the ANC and the release of Mandela made fundamental change in the South African political system virtually inevitable.

Further, from the perspective of the late 1990s, it is possible to identify structural factors, such as demographic change and economic decline, that underlay the country's political transformation. This is not to deny the validity of the story of the transition as told by journalists, with its emphasis on coincidences and chance encounters. However, it is simply to insist that it is not the whole story and that South Africa's transition can be fruitfully analysed in a comparative perspective highlighting the structural factors involved. What is required is an appreciation of the existence of different levels of explanation. The recording of events can be compared to the detailed charting of the course a river takes to run to the sea. Such an account of every twist and turn in the river's journey is valuable but it is not an explanation of where the water comes from or of its quantity.

In his account of National Party rule from 1948 to 1994, Dan O'Meara takes liberal analysts to task for their tendency to treat ethnic loyalties as primordial and hence as a political given requiring no further examination.

> In this type of analysis, the 'ethnic' character of the National Party (at least until the 1980s) is taken as sufficient both to explain itself and the ethnocentric policies which the party pursued until 1994. How this helps us to explain the (ethnic) NP's abandonment of its ethnically exclusive definition of both itself and the South African nation is less clear in this mode of explanation.[29]

At the same time, O'Meara criticises liberals for misrepresenting Marxist analysis of apartheid when suggesting that it necessarily entails the proposition that capitalists wanted apartheid. Yet O'Meara does concede:

> More than one marxist scholar argued that since capitalism in South Africa took the form of apartheid, the demise of the latter necessarily implied the demise of the former. This has left them peculiarly unable to explain

the current state of affairs in South Africa, except through the lame notion that apartheid (rather than its legacy) is still alive and well under the Mandela government.[30]

These two quotations from O'Meara illustrate some of the difficulties the demise of apartheid has presented for both liberal and Marxist analysts of South African politics, notwithstanding the disrepute Marxist prescriptions have fallen into. The quotations also help to explain the failure of both perspectives to anticipate South Africa's transformation in the 1990s.

However, there is also a danger of exaggerating the extent to which the basic assumptions of either approach have been undermined by the miracle. Racial and ethnic political allegiances did not dissolve in the course of the South African transition. As the evidence in Chapter 6 underlines, race and ethnicity were the major determinants of voting behaviour in the 1994 elections. Similarly, the fact that the demise of apartheid did not coincide with an anti-capitalist revolution should not be taken to invalidate analysis of political change in South Africa on the basis of class interests. In fact, O'Meara's book is a good example of the continuing vitality of Marxist interpretation of the politics of South Africa. His analysis counterposes class and ethnicity in its account of the actions of the National Party during the transition.

In the negotiations leading up to the 1993 adoption of South Africa's interim constitution, the National Party itself jettisoned almost every last element of its own, decades-old ethnic programme and world view. Yet it fought tooth and nail for the retention of a 'colour-blind' free market economy and the class privileges of its leadership. Which leads to a question: what was finally more important to this 'ethnic' party – its Afrikaner ethnic nationalism or the class interests of its leadership?[31]

Set against a static view of the role of race and ethnicity in South African politics, this seems persuasive. But a weakness of O'Meara's analysis is the implication that it cannot have been in the National Party's ethnic or racial interest to have abandoned apartheid (or neo-apartheid). Thus, it is perfectly possible to argue that by the start of the 1990s a negotiated settlement was in white interests as much as it was in those of South African capitalists as a class. To put the point another way, the proposition that De Klerk sacrificed the interests of ordinary National Party voters to safeguard the privileges of its leaders is unconvincing. Given the nature of the South African political system, he could not have afforded to have done so. This issue was, in effect, put to the test in the March 1992 referendum in which De Klerk won an overwhelming endorsement from the white electorate for the continuation of the reform process and the aim of establishing the basis for a new constitution through negotiation.

An important difference between the South African transition and the transition from authoritarian rule in Latin America and Eastern Europe, with which the South African transition is often compared, is the fact that South Africa before 1994 remained to a meaningful degree a democracy for whites, notwithstanding the many authoritarian features of National Party rule. Thus, a major reason why so many analysts in the late 1980s expected a continuation of debilitating political impasse rather than the transformation of the system was precisely the seeming impossibility of getting a majority of whites to accept a radical dilution of their political power. They could cite an abundance of evidence to support this pessimistic conclusion. For example, the most common responses to the prospect of an ANC government in a large survey of white university students in mid-1989 were 'would resist physically' (29.9 per cent) and 'emigrate for political reasons' (34.4 per cent).[32]

It can be regarded as fortunate that the beginning of the transition did not require the prior approval of the white electorate. As it was, in the first significant electoral test of white reaction to De Klerk's initiative, a parliamentary by-election in Umlazi, Natal, in June 1990, there was a massive swing to the extreme right Conservative Party. This of course might be construed as evidence that De Klerk had acted contrary to white opinion (and even interests) in the initiative he took, lending verisimilitude to the explanation advanced by O'Meara. At the least, it underlines the leap of faith De Klerk took that white opinion would eventually come round in response to the lead taken by the government, as indeed it did. His readiness to take such a risk can be seen as the product of a combination of factors, including what he – and, for that manner, his Cabinet colleagues – may have surmised would be the cost of alternative courses of action.

Against this background, the change of white opinion to one of very broad acceptance of the legitimacy of the election of Nelson Mandela as President of South Africa does indeed appear miraculous. It is tempting to construct an answer to this puzzle in terms of change in white hearts and minds effected by the charisma of Mandela and his commitment to reconciliation as a guiding principle. The assumption that this indeed is what happened is one reason why the story of the South African transition has come to be seen so widely as an exemplary tale of the triumph of the human spirit. However, the persistence of racial voting patterns in post-1994 South Africa suggests the limits of this explanation of white acceptance of political change. What exclusive pre-occupation with Mandela's role also most conspicuously leaves out is the role that mass political mobilisation among the disenfranchised played in the transition. This theme is explored in Chapters 3, 4 and 5 examining the part that political violence had in the process.

One of the most common ways in which the South African transition has been presented has been as a pact between political elites. The outstanding example of this interpretation of the transition is Tim Sisk's book, *Democratization in South Africa*. Sisk summarises his explanation of the South African transition as follows:

> As the old order suffered its demise, the realization set in among the major actors that the benefits of a potential positive-sum outcome to the conflict – the creation of a jointly determined set of institutions to govern a future, common, and democratic society – were greater than the costs of continued confrontation in an environment ungoverned by common rules. Once this realization was made among a core set of elites, convergence on exactly what kinds of rules should replace authoritarianism evolved as a result of the strategic interaction among the political parties that committed themselves to a negotiated settlement. This evolution was guided by institutional choice: actors' preferences converged, and are moving toward, a set of democratic institutions that are perceived as *fair* given each party's history, ideology, interests, and power, and the effects of strategic interaction. Moderate parties' positions began to converge on what can be best characterized as a broad-based, multifaceted social contract: a concord among diverse peoples, across class lines, between political leaders and followers, and among the elements of an emerging civil society.[33]

As an ideal model for political accommodation in a deeply divided society, Sisk's description could hardly be bettered. Thus, it could be applied virtually word for word to the basis of the political settlement in Northern Ireland in 1998. It also fits well with the thinking behind the Sunningdale Agreement of December 1993. That attempt to settle the Northern Ireland problem foundered on the failure of Unionist leaders who had accepted power-sharing with nationalists to secure the support of a majority of the Protestant community. Sisk argues 'the conditions that make transition to democracy in a deeply divided society possible include a high degree of interdependence and an approximately symmetrical balance of power'.[34] Although O'Meara does not specifically refer to Sisk's book, his characterisation of the limitations of O'Donnell and Schmitter's theoretical work on transitions from authoritarianism is applicable to Sisk's study. On the question of elite pacting O'Meara concludes:

> In effect, the definition they present is one which mirrors the hopes of the conservative faction, not necessarily the 'revolutionaries' or challengers. One cannot reduce either the process of 'pacting' or its eventual effects to the wish list of the *ancien regime*.[35]

In applying O'Donnell and Schmitter's ideas to South Africa, Sisk is far from alone in presenting a picture of the South African transition in terms corresponding more to the hopes that the National Party had of a negotiated settlement than its actual outcome. In fairness to Sisk, it should be said that the sheer extent of the ANC's dominance of the South African political system only became fully apparent with the implementation of the new constitution, which occurred well after Sisk completed his study.

Thus, while it may be reasonably argued that the ANC has occupied a dominant position within the political system since Mandela's inauguration as President of South Africa in May 1994, this was masked to a degree by the existence of a government of national unity in which the National Party participated under the terms of the interim constitution providing for power-sharing for a period of five years. The reality of ANC political dominance became much clearer in May 1996 when the National Party voluntarily left the Government of National Unity following the adoption of a draft constitution by the Constituent Assembly providing for majority rule after 1999. These issues are discussed in greater depth in Chapter 8. The point that needs to be made in this context is that a major challenge for any explanation of the transition is accounting for the very large shift in political power that took place between 1989 and 1994.

Much of this book is directed towards addressing this puzzle. In particular, with the benefit of hindsight, it is apparent that the fragility of white power in the late 1980s was widely underestimated by analysts of every ideological stripe. The book does not dwell in detail on the negotiations that brought these changes about, in part because these have already been the subject of considerable analysis, but also in part because of the conviction that the power struggles which took place outside of the formal process of negotiation deserve greater attention. This is not to deny how remarkable it was that such fundamental political change should have come about by a constitutional process. It is worth noting that this is different from saying that the changes came about peacefully, which would understate the role that violence played in the transition, even if often in ways contrary to the intentions of its agents. The extraordinary and unexpected transition in South Africa deserves comparison with the sudden collapse of Communism in Eastern Europe. The coincidence between the beginning of the South African transition and the changes in Eastern Europe is the issue addressed next.

Notes on Chapter 1

1   Guillermo O'Donnell and Philippe C.Schmitter, *Transitions from Authoritarian Rule: Tentative Conclusions about Uncertain Democracies*, Johns Hopkins University Press, Baltimore and London 1986, p.6

2   An example is Patti Waldmeir, *Anatomy of a Miracle: The End of Apartheid and the Birth of the New South Africa*, Viking, London 1997.

3   Robin Cohen, *Endgame in South Africa?*, James Currey, London 1986, p.88.

4   John D.Brewer (ed.), *Can South Africa Survive?: Five Minutes to Midnight*, Macmillan, Basingstoke 1989, p.343.

5   Simon Jenkins, 'What Next Out of Africa?' in Hermann Giliomee and Lawrence Schlemmer (eds), *Negotiating South Africa's Future*, Southern Book Publishers, Johannesburg 1989, p.88.

6   Heribert Adam, Frederik van Zyl Slabbert and Kogila Moodley, *Comrades in Business: Post-Liberation Politics in South Africa*, Tafelberg, Cape Town 1997, p.1.

7   See, for example, Allister Sparks, *Tomorrow is another country: The inside story of South Africa's negotiated revolution*, Struik, Sandton 1994.

8   The phrase was used by the British Prime Minister, Harold Macmillan in his historic address to the South African parliament in Cape Town on 3 February1960.

9   J.E.Spence, *Republic under Pressure: A Study of South African Foreign Policy*, Oxford University Press, London 1965, p.128.

10   N.J.Rhoodie and H.J.Venter, *Apartheid*, HAUM, Cape Town 1960, p.250.

11   Arend Lijphart, 'Majority Rule versus Democracy in Deeply Divided Societies', *Politikon*, Vol. 4 No. 2 (1977).

12   F.van Zyl Slabbert and David Welsh, *South Africa's options: Strategies for sharing power*, David Philip, Cape Town 1979, p.166.

13   Theodor Hanf, Heribert Weiland and Gerda Vierdag, *South Africa: the Prospects for Peaceful Change*, Rex Collings, London 1981, p.425.

14   *Ibid.*, p.412.

15   Slabbert and Welsh, *op. cit.*, p.171.

16   L.H.Gann and Peter Duignan, *Why South Africa Will Survive*, Croom Helm, London 1981.

17   L.H.Gann and Peter Duignan, *Hope for South Africa?*, Hoover Institution Press, Stanford 1991, p.167.

18 Cohen, *op. cit.*, p.88.

19 Hermann Giliomee and Jannie Gagiano (eds), *The Elusive Search for Peace: South Africa, Israel and Northern Ireland*, Oxford University Press, Cape Town 1990, p.3

20 *Ibid.*, p.265, p.270, p.271 and p.274.

21 Donald L.Horowitz, *A Democratic South Africa?: Constitutional Engineering in a Divided Society*, Oxford University Press, Cape Town 1991, p.1.

22 *Ibid.*, pp.3–7.

23 *Ibid.*, p.6n.

24 Adam, Schlemmer and Moodley, *op. cit.*, pp.52–3.

25 Clem Sunter, *The World and South Africa in the 1990s*, Human and Rousseau, Pretoria and Tafelberg, Cape Town 1987.

26 Clem Sunter, *The High Road: Where are we now?*, Tafelberg, Cape Town and Human and Rousseau, Cape Town 1996, pp.100–1.

27 Arthur Keppel-Jones, *When Smuts Goes: A History of South Africa from 1952 to 2010 First Published in 2015*, Victor Gollancz, London 1947.

28 Gann and Duignan (1981), *op. cit.*, p.231.

29 Dan O'Meara, *Forty Lost Years: The apartheid state and the politics of the National Party, 1948–1994*, Ravan Press, Randburg 1996, p.421.

30 *Ibid.*, p.425.

31 *Ibid.*, pp.422–3.

32 Jannie Gagiano, 'Ruling group cohesion' in Gagiano and Giliomee (eds), *op. cit.*, p.196.

33 Timothy D.Sisk, *Democratization in South Africa: The Elusive Social Contract*, Princeton University Press, Princeton, New Jersey, 1995, p.13.

34 *Ibid.*, p.15.

35 O'Meara, *op. cit.*, p.465.

CHAPTER 2

The Release of Mandela and the End of the Cold War

Political scientists make poor prophets. A decade ago, few predicted either the collapse of Communism in Eastern Europe or the coming of an ANC-dominated government in South Africa. We are much better at providing explanations of events after they have occurred. In fact, we are quite good at converting impossibilities into inevitabilities. In the process *post hoc* readily becomes *propter hoc*. But, curiously, relatively little has been made of the conjuncture, chronologically speaking, between the East European and South African miracles. The key date in Eastern Europe's transformation is generally taken to be 9 November 1989, the day that the Berlin Wall was breached; that in South Africa's 2 February 1990, when De Klerk announced the unbanning of the ANC and a number of other restricted organisations, including the PAC and the SACP. One can also identify two second watersheds in the two miracles; 22 August 1991, when the coup by hardliners against Gorbachev collapsed, which ultimately led to the break-up of the Soviet Union at the end of that year, and 26 September 1992, when De Klerk and Mandela signed the Record of Understanding, which was to pave the way to the non-racial elections in April 1994.

Admittedly, the conjuncture did inspire a number of writers to compare Gorbachev and De Klerk, among them Allister Sparks in *Tomorrow is Another Country*.[1] Sparks also claims that he had the Gorbachev analogy in mind when he rewrote the last chapter of his book, *The Mind of South Africa*, for its paperback edition. That predicted that the process that De Klerk had unleashed would lead to majority rule by the end of the decade.[2] Norman Etherington made a much more extensive comparison of the two leaders after suggesting that De Klerk might also be compared to Disraeli, Lincoln or De Gaulle. He wrote:

Another frequently drawn comparison, likening De Klerk to Mikhail Gorbachev, is a good test of the premise that a single human being can engineer a revolution from the top, because the two statesmen are exact contemporaries. The comparison is appealing in many ways. Each astounded the world by presiding over fundamental changes in systems which had been thought to be impervious to change except through invasion or violent revolution. Each was subjected to vilification by hardline conservatives and undercut by elements within the police and security forces. Each saw national unity threatened by a Pandora's box of murderous ethnic nationalisms. Each helped pull armies away from debilitating campaigns beyond national frontiers: Gorbachev in Afghanistan, De Klerk in Angola. Each watched with dismay as his state lost the ability to rule in vast regions of the country. Each vigorously promoted the virtues of a competitive market economy.[3]

A Russian example of the comparison of change in the two countries is the small book by Vladimir Tikhomirov, *States in Transition: Russia and South Africa*, though in his case he compared Gorbachev with P.W.Botha.[4] Dislike and suspicion of Gorbachev, an attitude more common in Russia than the West, rather than admiration for the reforms carried out by P.W.Botha explain why he chose this parallel. Comparison inspired by the conjuncture was clearly also in the mind of those who used the term 'the Leipzig way' to describe the strategy of rolling mass action against the government.[5] The analogy here was the manner in which the East German Communist regime was toppled.

However, there is nothing intrinsically remarkable in the comparison of contemporaneous events. Play on the casual juxtaposition of events has long been used by cartoonists to make witty observations about current affairs. The question that needs to be asked is whether there is a stronger basis than the drawing of superficial parallels for analysing the conjuncture. In short, was there any connection between these events? Most attention, such as it is, has been focused on the link between the first two sets of events, the opening of the Berlin Wall and South Africa's political liberalisation. This chapter will follow suit, though brief reference will also be made to the second set of events. However, this will not be for the purpose of tracing the impact of one on the other, but because of what they reveal about the shift in power that the first two had brought about.

To start with, the views of two writers who argue that the opening in the Berlin Wall and its implications for the Communist system in Eastern

Europe was a significant influence on South Africa's transition will be examined. However, it should be admitted that neither example expounds the argument at any great length. That has the advantage that their positions can be expounded quite fully, so there is no danger of distorting their arguments. However, the brevity with which they state their positions might also be seen as having a less helpful implication and that is, that the case for the proposition that the end of the Cold War influenced South Africa's transition is a thin one.

The first example comes from a book entitled, *Transition to Democracy: Policy Perspectives 1991*, edited by Robin Lee and Lawrence Schlemmer. In a chapter entitled 'The Turn in the Road: Emerging Conditions in 1990', Lawrence Schlemmer reviewed the factors and forces that led up to 2 February 1990, while also seeking to provide an explanation of the failure of academics, journalists, and even politicians to predict the scope of President de Klerk's initiative. Schlemmer rejected a single factor explanation of 2 February and suggested that at least a dozen factors played a part in the initiative. He listed them as follows:

> civic resistance; economic stagnation; sanctions; the seepage effects of low-key civil disobedience; the Namibian settlement; the collapse of Eastern Europe; changes in the NP constituency; informal dialogue with the ANC; new kinds of Afrikaner intellectuals; aspects of South Africa's political culture; and the nature of De Klerk as a politician.[6]

He then looked at a number of these in greater depth, starting with international influences under the heading of 'The Eastern Europe collapse and a transformed regional and international context'.

Schlemmer acknowledged that the National Party government exaggerated the external Communist threat in the 1970s and 1980s, but argued that nevertheless the changes in Eastern Europe and their implications for southern Africa as a region allowed 'the security establishment to recalculate the strategic balance in South Africa'.[7] To illustrate his point Schlemmer compared the situation in 1990 with that in 1986 to underline why there was such a favourable scenario for negotiations in 1990 compared to the earlier year. He outlined what he described as 'the boundary effect scenario' for each year. If the government had initiated the transition in 1986, it would have faced the following, according to Schlemmer:

- The ANC/SACP still endorsed Soviet imperialism.
- The Soviet Union, albeit with increasing uncertainty and a crumbling economic base, still pursued strategies aimed at securing at least strategic influence in various international tension zones, including southern Africa.

- The Cubans were ensconced in Angola, and Soviet advisers were building the military technology of Angolan and Cuban forces.
- The ANC/Umkhonto we Sizwe (MK) had functioning base camps in Angola, Soviet military support, and a persisting belief in the inevitable success of the armed struggle.
- Mozambique, while cautious, was still trying to ward off destabilising South African pressure to force it to become neutral and semi-cooperative, like Zimbabwe.
- The effects of new US and international sanctions on South Africa could not yet be calculated.
- South Africa was locked in a war in Namibia in which the ANC was a semi-active opponent.
- Unrest in South Africa had serious revolutionary dimensions which included the possibility of 'ungovernable' townships becoming liberated areas.
- The only relevant models of 'transition' in the region were distinctly unappetizing. Half of the white Rhodesians had fled Zimbabwe, which was starving itself of foreign capital. Lesotho was under military rule. Mozambique and Angola were implementing scientific socialism, re-education camps, and had crude East European equipment which could not be repaired and silted-up, non-functioning harbours. The relative successes of Botswana and Swaziland were too quiet to be noticed.
- The NP voter constituency was still overwhelmingly in favour of political, residential, and educational segregation, maintained in perpetuity. [8]

Schlemmer contrasted this scenario to what he called the 'vastly different' scenario prevailing in 1990 when De Klerk liberalised the South African political system. He highlights the following:

- The Namibian settlement process led to the ANC losing its base camps in Angola. The ANC also faced virtually no prospect of re-establishing them elsewhere in southern Africa. The 'armed liberation' of South Africa became an absurdly remote ideal. The ANC was left with no real option but to seek negotiations in good faith.
- The hugely changed international stance of the Soviet Union, the US-Soviet disarmament talks, the disintegrating Soviet economy and the transformations in Eastern Europe eliminated the threat of Soviet influence operating to the detriment of white establishment interests in southern Africa.
- The Namibian settlement itself had won for the South African

government a large measure of respect in international forums. At least a degree of moral support from abroad could be expected for internal negotiations.

- The US, the Soviet Union, and major Western powers had displayed an even-handed approach in the Namibian settlement.
- Economic factors, the weakening role of the Soviet Union, and the awesome damage attributed to South African destabilization had led to Mozambique unambiguously accepting that it would have to co-operate with the South African government.[9]

Schlemmer sums up: 'A comparison of these two boundary effect scenarios makes it abundantly clear that the strategic balance had shifted in favour of the South African government'. He continues 'Stripped of its Soviet superpower leverage, the ANC could be reassessed as an internal political factor only' and 'in early 1990 government could view the possible outcomes of compromise with the ANC far more positively than at any time since it came to power'.[10] From the perspective of the second half of the 1990s, Schlemmer's argument looks not merely dated, but positively mistaken in its calculation of the impact of the collapse of Communism in Eastern Europe on the South African transition. In particular, it is evident that Schlemmer expected a political compromise much more favourable to preserving the power and influence of the National Party than the eventual outcome was.

Further, his list of the conditions prevailing in 1990 compared to 1986 read more like the rationalisations decision-makers might have advanced to justify their stance on negotiations in the respective periods rather than objective assessments of the realities they faced. Thus, the reference to Soviet imperialism in 1986, despite the qualification added by Schlemmer in his second point, appears anachronistic in the light of the change in Soviet foreign policy that had been initiated by Gorbachev. However, Schlemmer's analysis has not been included simply as a straw man to criticise, but before seeing what might be salvaged from it, it is worth comparing it to a slightly more recent analysis of the South African transition that also includes the collapse of Communism in Eastern Europe as a factor in the process.

The second example comes from an article published in 1995 in *Political Science Quarterly*, the journal of the New York-based Academy of Political Science. The article, 'Democratization in South Africa', was written by Hermann Giliomee, Professor of Political Studies at the University of Cape Town and prolific analyst of Afrikaner nationalism. Giliomee's argument was that the fundamental shift which took place in the government's policy, in particular the decision to open negotiations with the ANC, was the product of debate among the Afrikaner elite, in which three forces received special consideration. They were 'a weakening demographic base, a dramatically different external environment, and economic stagnation'.[11] It is worth mentioning that Giliomee dated the fundamental shift in government policy as taking place at the end of 1989. The conjuncture with the changes in Eastern Europe was not accidental.

Giliomee discussed a variety of factors under the heading of 'A Changing Ideological and External Environment', but he put greatest emphasis on the weakening of the Soviet Union. He argued that the success of the Namibian settlement had played a part in the process, though here it is perhaps worth interjecting that the victory of the South West African People's Organisation (SWAPO) and, perhaps even more significantly, the failure of the Democratic Turnhalle Alliance (DTA) to exploit the fact that SWAPO had fallen short of a two-thirds majority, to insist on power-sharing, had upset some in government and in the security forces.[12] To be fair to Giliomee he did not present the Namibian settlement as an unambiguous triumph for the South African government, but merely argued that it 'made all sides appear winners'. He went on to say:

> Yet De Klerk would not have moved toward negotiations with the ANC as long as it was strongly backed by the Soviet Union. As late as September 1989, De Klerk sent word to his brother to stop talking to the ANC. In his view, this movement could never have a role in negotiations . . . In the last months of 1989, the external environment improved dramatically from the government's point of view. For the first time it considered negotiations a viable option. The crucial development was the severe internal troubles experienced by the Soviet Union. Moscow told the ANC that it was up to the South Africans themselves to reach a political accommodation. At the same time Pretoria believed that without Soviet backing it had a much better chance to contain a legalized ANC.[13]

Furthermore, Giliomee argued that the changed international environment was a decisive factor in the ANC's abandonment of its revolutionary struggle.

> For the ANC the late 1980s also represented a watershed. It had long favoured the nationalization of large sectors of the economy, but it was now confronted with mounting evidence of the malperformance of economies under centralized control in Eastern Europe and Africa. With the South African economy already in trouble, the leadership saw the need for negotiating functional political and economic structures that could deliver on the greatly raised expectations of its followers. Even more

important in its decision to begin negotiations were two major setbacks it received in the form of the New York Accords of 1988 and the collapse of the Soviet Union.[14]

The similarities between Giliomee's and Schlemmer's analysis are striking. Like Schlemmer, Giliomee painted a picture of ANC weakness as the context for De Klerk's initiative. Indeed, he managed to convey the impression that the ANC's entering into negotiations with the South African government represented a concession on its part rather than a long-standing objective of the organisation. Both provide an answer to the question why De Klerk embarked on the transition, or, to put it another way, why he liberalised the South African political system on 2 February 1990. However, their apparent solution of one problem simply creates another. If the ANC entered negotiations from such a position of weakness, how then did it achieve such a position of dominance at the end of the negotiating process?

How Giliomee grappled with this issue in the conclusion to his article is discussed below, but before that it is necessary to outline briefly how he portrayed the transition process itself. Giliomee identified three modes of transition: transition through transformation, transition after regime breakdown, and transition as transplacement. The first two represent opposite ends of the spectrum. In transition through transformation, the existing government basically retains control of the process of change and the transition occurs on its terms. Democratic reform in Taiwan fits this pattern, with the Kuomintang remaining the island's dominant party. By contrast, in the case of transition after regime breakdown, the loss of authority of the old regime is comprehensive and it retains little or no influence over the new dispensation. Notwithstanding the success of post-Communist parties, Eastern Europe generally fits the pattern. The third case of transition as transplacement occurs in situations where there is rough equality between the contending forces and democratisation requires the combined actions of the regime and its opponents. Periods of deadlock frequently occur in this situation prior to democratisation. Giliomee saw the South African transition as fitting this pattern, with the breakdown of negotiations in 1992 representing a period of deadlock prior to concessions by both sides to move the situation forward.

At the end of his article, Giliomee considered the possibility that South Africa might evolve into a system dominated by a single party as a result of what he described as the ANC's 'crushing victory' in the elections in April 1994. The scale of the ANC's victory in the 1994 elections presented a major difficulty for Giliomee, since it ran counter to his assumptions about the political balance of forces existing in the country and his characterisation of the South African case as one of transition as transplacement. Giliomee attributed the one-sided outcome to the elections to the ANC's grip over the townships. In particular, he argued: 'Large-scale intimidation made it nearly impossible for rival parties to campaign in the African townships'.[15] The implication would seem to be that the ANC's domination of the political system stemmed from less than fully free and fair elections. The argument has a number of obvious weaknesses.

Certainly, high levels of political intolerance, particularly in areas where this was reflected in a lot of political violence, did affect opportunities for campaigning at a local level. This was particularly the case in the rural areas of KwaZulu-Natal, where the grip of the Inkatha Freedom Party (IFP) prevented campaigning by the ANC. However, as this example shows, obstacles to electioneering in some parts of the country operated to the disadvantage of the ANC. Further, in any event, Giliomee's argument places too much weight on local electioneering. Radio, television, and the newspapers provided voters with information on the policies of the parties. It is therefore misleading to suggest that the failure of, for example, the National Party to win a larger share of the vote in the townships could be attributed to ignorance of its policies. Finally, the elections did in fact meet two of the most basic criteria for a free and fair election, which is that the overwhelming majority of voters should be aware of, and have confidence in, the secrecy of the ballot. These issues are discussed in greater detail in Chapter 6.

What Giliomee's argument does draw attention to is the relationship between the battle for territory during the transition and the outcome of the 1994 elections. Giliomee attributed the ANC's domination of the decision-making process within the Government of National Unity to the outcome of the elections. His analysis on this point at least was more realistic than Lijphart who concluded after the 1994 elections that South Africa's 'new consociational institutions are just about the best that could have been devised'.[16] In contrast to Giliomee, Lijphart highlighted the ANC's failure to win a two-thirds majority. Giliomee recognised that in practice the ANC had gained a position of predominance and concluded: 'If these trends continue, South Africa may be heading for a one-party dominant system, along Mexican or Taiwanese lines, sooner than most analysts expected'.[17] It was unclear whether the model Giliomee had in mind was derived from the Mexican and Taiwanese past or from their present state of somewhat greater political openness. However, this is a trivial issue compared with the central problem of Giliomee's piece. This is obvious difficulty of reconciling the end of the story with the analysis that preceded it. The fact is that Giliomee is left clutching at straws to explain a far greater shift in power towards the ANC than his analysis would lead one to expect.

It is now perhaps possible to explain why relatively little has been made of the conjuncture of the collapse of Communism and the demise of apartheid. As a factor it seems to point in the wrong direction. In short, what needs to be explained is why there was such a dramatic shift in power in the ANC's favour in the 1990s, while the assumption at the outset of the transition was that the ANC had been handicapped by events in Eastern Europe. A tempting solution to this conundrum would seem to be simply to discount the role of the external environment in the process of change, putting the emphasis squarely on domestic factors, and most particularly on the ANC's mass support within the country. Another way of handling the issue is to tackle it at the level of perceptions. This is essentially what Allister Sparks does in his book, *Tomorrow is Another Country*.

Sparks argued that the changes in Eastern Europe encouraged De Klerk to embark upon the transition.

> But of all the international influences, none was greater than the Gorbachev reforms that began unravelling the communist empire, for they eased Pretoria's phobia that the black struggle against apartheid was a conspiracy directed from Moscow. It took the monkey off De Klerk's back and enabled him to justify to his people what would otherwise have appeared to them a suicidal course of action.[18]

At the same time, Sparks contended that De Klerk did not anticipate the consequences that would flow from his speech on 2 February 1990.

> Just as Gorbachev could not have known that his restructuring of the Soviet system would lead to the loss of his East European empire, the collapse of communism, and the dismemberment of the Soviet Union itself, so, too, De Klerk did not expect his reforms to lead to black-majority rule and the end of Afrikaner nationalism before the end of the decade.[19]

To put it more brutally, Sparks's argument amounted to saying that De Klerk miscalculated. Given what might have befallen South Africa during the 1990s if there had been no initiative to liberalise the system, it may seem very fortunate that he did so, that is, if one accepts Sparks's analysis.

It is not difficult to find evidence to justify the emphasis that Sparks gave to the East European factor. It accords with the emphasis that De Klerk himself gave to the changes in Eastern Europe both in public speeches and in interviews. Thus, in the famous speech of 2 February 1990 itself, De Klerk made frequent references to the changes in Eastern Europe. The section immediately following his introduction was devoted to foreign relations, focusing on the changes in Eastern Europe, and he returned to the issue to justify the lifting of the ban on the ANC and other political organisations. De Klerk identified the four most important facets of advice his government had received in connection with the liberalisation of the political process. The first of these was: 'The events in the Soviet Union and Eastern Europe, to which I have referred already, weaken the capability of organisations which were previously supported strongly from those quarters'.[20]

Of course, it may reasonably be objected that a politician is bound to draw on current events to provide justification for the adoption of a new course of action. Given the links existing between the ANC and the Soviet Union, there were bound to be references to the collapse of Communism in Eastern Europe, just as there would have been to the ANC's links with Gadafy, if there had been a coup in Libya near the time of the speech. However, it would appear from Willem de Klerk's biography that the influence of events in Eastern Europe went deeper than that. Thus, Willem de Klerk recorded that as late as October 1989, he was subjected, along with others, to severe public criticism for his readiness to engage in talks with members of the ANC outside the country. He also had his arm twisted in private.[21] In his 1994 Chatham House discussion paper, *Forging the New South Africa*, James Barber argued that the collapse of Communism in Eastern Europe was one of three factors that determined the timing of De Klerk's initiative of 2 February.[22] The others he identified were the problem of disorder in the townships and continuing economic stagnation.

At this point, it is useful to draw a distinction between two types of explanation of events. It is the distinction between the inside story of events, with its emphasis on personalities and chance encounters as significant in the making of history and the explanation from outside decision-making circles, where the emphasis is on the role of social forces and an attempt is made to identify fundamental causes of change. The distinction is very nicely drawn in Martin Hollis and Steve Smith's book, *Explaining and Understanding International Relations*.[23] They argue that both approaches have utility, though naturally political scientists tend to feel more comfortable with the outsider explanation. The main objection to accounts from inside, such as those by Sparks and Willem de Klerk, is that they provide a persuasive explanation about the manner in which change came about, but say rather less about why it occurred.

However, from both an insider and an outsider perspective, there remain good grounds for not according decisive weight to the role of the changes in Eastern Europe as a factor in the South African transition. The most obvious of these is that, important as De Klerk's speech of 2 February 1990 was as a watershed in South Africa's political development, it did not come entirely out of the blue. Steps in the direction of negotiations had already been taken well prior to the breach in the Berlin Wall. In fact, one reason why Sparks stressed Gorbachev's reforms rather than the East European revolutions as an influence on change in South Africa was because it fitted in better with the chronology of his account from the inside of events leading up to 2 February. That said, there remains considerable justification for treating both the breach in the Berlin Wall and De Klerk's initiative as key junctures. This is because they set in train forces that made far-reaching change inevitable.

The point is underlined by the failure of attempts to limit and control the change, as shown by the collapse of the coup against Gorbachev in August 1991 and by the South African government's abandonment of the IFP in its Record of Understanding with the ANC in September 1992. These two developments indicated just how radical a shift in power had occurred in the two situations and invested the earlier watersheds with even greater significance. In particular, the identification of 1989 with the end of the bipolar system was underpinned, as was De Klerk's initiative with the beginning of South Africa's transition to majority rule.

Admittedly, these comparative points do not help to establish to what extent events in Eastern Europe directly influenced developments in South Africa. But comparison does suggest the need to examine indirect links between the two sets of events. Was it simply coincidence that the two sets of events occurred together or were both products, at least in part, of change within the international political system itself? In this regard, one can point to the difficulty that both the Soviet system and South Africa had in adjusting to the oil crises of the 1970s and to change in the functioning of the international economy as a result of new technology. Similarities between the economic problems that the two countries faced as a result of the projects of Communism and apartheid form a central part of Vladimir Tikhomirov's analysis of the background to transition in the two societies. He argued:

> The impetus for reform in both countries was the realisation by the ruling elites of the need to modernise their economic systems through the improvement of the existing social structures. The absence of modern economic systems was the major stumbling block to further development and the accumulation of capital, which was needed to implement costly social engineering projects.[24]

To put it another way, the market was antithetical to both apartheid and the command economy. As might be expected, Francis Fukuyama, who viewed the revolutions in Eastern Europe as marking the final ideological triumph of liberal-democracy and of capitalism, has adopted a somewhat similar perspective on change in South Africa, while noting parallels in the process of change in South Africa and Eastern Europe. Fukuyama argued:

> If there is any single answer to the question of why South Africa is moving toward full democracy at the beginning of the 1990s, it is because it, like the Soviet Union, China, South Korea, Brazil and Taiwan, has gone through a period of authoritarian modernisation that completely transformed the social and economic character of the country's elites.[25]

A weakness of Fukuyama's analysis was that it relied on the logic of economic development as an agent of universal liberalisation without much reference to more specific trends in the global economy.[26] Norman Etherington in a powerful attack on the assumption of South African exceptionalism, the view that South Africa was immune to the impact of global trends on the rest of the African continent, also related the changes in both the Soviet Union and South Africa to structural economic factors, arguing that neither Gorbachev nor De Klerk were visionaries.

> Each has steadfastly maintained that necessity was the mother of his alleged inventions, and insisted that he could no more stand against the forces of change than Canute could command the waves. These claims should not be dismissed as false modesty. Neither Gorbachev nor De Klerk stepped onto the world's stage as a prophet from the wilderness. Gorbachev had for decades served unobtrusively among the band of brothers who filled the top posts in the Soviet bureaucracy. De Klerk possessed all the usual attributes and attitudes of the Afrikaner *nomenklatura*. When they embarked on new paths, they moved as leaders of packs, not lone wolves. Attempts to turn the clock back by picking off the leaders failed because most of the state apparatus stood firmly on the side of change.[27]

From a very different ideological perspective to that of Fukayama or Tikhomirov, Kathryn Manzo argued that the demise of Communism in Eastern Europe had profound global implications. She identified specific consequences for South Africa as arising from the reassertion of American hegemony and the absence of any apparent alternative to capitalist democracy. These consequences were in addition to the impact on the ANC of the drying up of military support as a result of the fall of Soviet Communism. In a similar vein to Giliomee, Manzo argued:

> Pressure on the ANC for a negotiated settlement has been reinforced by the revolutions in Eastern Europe, from whence a good deal of support came. East Germany, once the major military supplier of Umkhonto (the armed wing of the ANC), ceased supplying aid even before the reunification of East and West Germany; since then all military aid has come to a halt.[28]

She concluded that the Eastern European revolutions had significantly weakened the ANC's position.

> The ANC will almost certainly figure largely at the negotiating table, but unless it can harness the enormous stock of support that it still enjoys at the grassroots level, it will be forced to enter negotiations from an unenviable position – that of a junior and weak partner to the National party.[29]

Manzo's view that the ANC had been adversely affected by global trends was widely held on the Left in the early 1990s. The SACP intellectual, Jeremy Cronin, took a similar view, concluding in his 1992 article with reference to the revolutions in Eastern Europe that 'the world balance of forces that encouraged and sustained mass propelled negotiated transition there, is more or less an entirely unfavourable balance for us here'.[30]

From the perspective of post-transition South Africa, the puzzle remains: if the collapse of Communism in Eastern Europe was so damaging to the ANC because of the support it received from the Soviet Union and its satellites, then how was it that the ANC emerged from the transition in such a dominant position? As suggested earlier, one way of answering this question might be to argue that international factors have been of minimal significance in the transition and that any disadvantages the ANC suffered as a result of changes in the external environment were massively outweighed by the strength of its domestic support. A case might be made along these lines. Indeed, it is argued in Chapter 5 that the effects of the violent battle for political influence between the ANC and the IFP during the transition played an important role in the ANC's ultimate triumph. However, such a line of argument presents problems for the interpretation of South Africa's political transformation as the product of a deal between the elites.

Another line of argument might be that the ANC itself was transformed in the process of the negotiations and that the ANC owes its success to its abandonment of positions it held prior to 1990. Again a case along these lines might be made. Thus, Adam, Slabbert and Moodley characterise the story of the transition as being:

> how an elite conspiracy emerged between both sides, quite willingly, to keep their respective constituencies in the dark about how they were bargaining away fundamental policy positions that they had promised were completely non-negotiable.[31]

Clearly, ANC policy did change to accommodate the new ideological climate. However, such a case is difficult to make without exaggerating the changes in the ANC's policies. In particular, the ANC in power preaching reconciliation and reconstruction is behaving in a very similar way to African nationalist governments in post-independence Kenya, Zimbabwe, and Namibia when they first came to power. Further, the core values of the ANC as expounded by its principal leaders over fifty years do not appear to have changed in any fundamental way, though, of course, external perceptions of the ANC have undergone considerable change

In any event, the discounting altogether of international influences in the context of an increasingly interdependent global economy seems difficult to justify (and to be fair to Adam, Slabbert and Moodley they do not do so). If it is accepted that neither the weight of domestic factors nor changes in ANC policies fully account for the party's emergence from the transition in such a dominant position, then one is driven to conclude that the assumption that the ANC was damaged by the collapse of Communism in Eastern Europe itself needs to be questioned. This is not to discount the importance of the ANC's reliance on the Soviet Union *in the context of the Cold War*. Thus, Soviet fortunes during the course of the Cold War did inevitably affect the ANC. However, the East European revolutions were more than a change within the context of the Cold War. They brought an end to the whole Cold War system and it is the impact of this systemic change on the different parties that one has to evaluate. To calculate this is by no means as simple as it seems. In particular, it clearly cannot be treated as a zero-sum game in which Communist losses produce equivalent gains for anti-Communists. That ignores the interdependence of Communism and anti-Communism. That is to say, anti-Communism requires a Communist threat to legitimise itself.

In the case of South Africa, the National Party government became increasingly reliant on anti-Communism to justify its policies internationally, particularly as any residual sympathy for racial oligarchy in the Western world faded. However, even anti-Communism was of limited help to the government. This was because in general in the West fears of Communist expansion subsided after the Soviet Union backed down during the Cuban missile crisis in 1962. Admittedly, the process was an uneven one. There was a brief period in the late 1960s when Maoism appeared to present a challenge to the West and the fanaticism associated with the Cultural Revolution caused concern, much as Islamic fundamentalism or the resurgence of a politicised Islam does today. The first Reagan Presidency was both a response to, and revived, fears of Soviet imperialism, though outside of Thatcher's Britain, the new American policy won little support in Western Europe. Increasingly Communism came to be viewed by much of public opinion as anachronistic and as no longer a dynamic force. The image of Communist government was of old men clinging to power by methods that involved the suppression of basic human rights.

Further, the failure of the Communist economic model, leading in some cases to its abandonment even by Communist governments, reduced the appeal of Communism as an ideology, despite mass unemployment throughout much of the world. However, in some regions there were deviations from this pattern, reflecting particular local circumstances. The fading of Communism, even prior to its collapse in Eastern Europe, also had an impact on anti-Communist governments. In particular, President Carter's emphasis on human rights in America's foreign policy contributed to the undermining of anti-Communist dictatorships, particularly in Latin America. Even Reagan proved unwilling to back anti-Communist dictatorships unconditionally, as President Marcos of the Philippines discovered.

Nevertheless, prior to the collapse of Communism in Eastern Europe, anti-Communism had some utility for the South African government, not least because the ANC's links with the Soviet Union and its close alliance with the SACP were sources of concern in the West. Naturally enough, the National Party government played up the significance of these points in its efforts to counter the anti-apartheid lobby. In the process, the ANC's dependence on these connections came to be exaggerated right across the political spectrum.

What tended to be underplayed was the leverage the ANC derived as a result of the crisis of governability South Africa had been suffering since 16 June 1976, when the townships first exploded in violence. As was also true of the Palestine Liberation Organisation (PLO) and the intifada in the territories occupied by Israel, the ANC as an organisation played little part in the immediate onset of the crisis, but benefited from it because it was seen to be indispensable to the resolution of the crisis. Because of this, the PLO was able to recover from its isolation as a result of its stance during the Second Gulf War. Similarly, the ANC recovered quickly from blows to its external position as a result of the shifts in the strategic balance in southern Africa that Schlemmer describes. Thus, in the deadlock in the negotiations during 1992, the spectre of political violence and of ungovernability gave the National Party government little option but to seek a partnership with the ANC.

At this stage the ANC's capacity to extract concessions from the government was in practice not adversely affected by the end of the Cold War. This was partly because much of its political strength by this time was derived from its position within the country and not externally to any significant extent. But it was also because there were some advantages to the ANC in the end of the Cold War. In particular, it enabled the ANC in the course of the transition itself to cast off associations that might have weakened its appeal inside the country and generated external opposition to the prospect of an ANC-dominated government. With the demise of the Soviet Union, even the party's continuing close relationship with the SACP lost most of its ideological significance, so that attempts to embarrass the ANC over the relationship by and large fell flat, a reflection of the weakening resonance of anti-Communism.

In a different ideological context, the pressure on the ANC to break with the SACP would have been far greater. Given the importance of the SACP in the projection of the ANC's policies of non-racialism and the SACP's role in the creation of *Umkhonto we Sizwe* (MK), it seems probable that the ANC would have had little choice but to resist the pressure. However, the cost to the ANC of defying the demands of Western governments could have been high, with much greater Western sympathy for efforts by the National Party to construct an anti-ANC coalition. One can surmise that the attitude of Western governments towards violence arising out of rivalry between the ANC and the IFP might have been substantially different if the IFP had been primarily viewed through the lens of its anti-Communism, rather than as an ethno-nationalist movement potentially threatening the country's territorial integrity.

All this is not to say that the impact of the end of the Cold War was of no help to the old South African government. It almost certainly did make it easier for President de Klerk to embark on his major initiative, though admittedly without improving the bargaining position of his government, as he must have hoped and expected. According to Adam, Slabbert and Moodley, De Klerk's liberalisation of the South African political system was based on both a moral shift leap and political expediency.

> Sensing that, because of the collapse of Communism, the ANC had lost a very important resource base and patronage, he thought he could bring them into negotiations in a much weaker state. He certainly developed a vision once he had made the speech on 2 February, but he seriously miscalculated his own and the government's capacity to control the pursuit of this vision. He and his government never dreamt at the outset that everything would be over by 27 April 1994. One of his colleagues told us in confidence that they thought they could keep the ANC negotiating for at least five years whilst the National Party government governed the ANC support base away from them.[32]

However, if De Klerk miscalculated the political consequences of the fall of the Berlin Wall, in his championing of free enterprise he proved more correct about its economic consequences. Not merely was the command economy discredited, but other policies associated with socialism more broadly such as nationalisation and redistribution of wealth lost much of their credibility, as did the notion that the path to development for third world countries lay through policies of self-sufficiency and protectionism. The restricted room for manoeuvre in the economic field of whatever government emerged from the process of democratisation was undoubtedly a factor in allaying white fears of the consequences of political change. Adam, Slabbert and Moodley relate this point, in the manner of Fukuyama, to the growth of white affluence.

> [T]he newly disempowered minority in South Africa still commands vast material and cultural capital that had been accumulated during its previous dominance. The key political question for the future will undoubtedly be: how is the impoverished majority ever to achieve a semblance of equality if the historical discrepancies remain sacrosanct in the name of minority rights? The affluent Afrikaners, led by De Klerk and his negotiators, peacefully negotiated away their position of ethnic dominance on the gamble that these historical discrepancies would be a long time in disappearing and would, in any case, be protected by the rights culture of a

liberal democracy. Given the global predominance of a competitive market economy as the preferred mechanism to generate wealth and the political predominance of liberal democracy, this was not an unreasonable gamble.[33]

This will pass muster as an account of elite attitudes. However, it understates the extent to which the white electorate's living standards had been eroded during the 1970s and the 1980s by the country's low economic growth rate and by the narrowing of the huge disparities in incomes among racial groups that existed by the end of the country's economic boom in the 1960s. Indeed, white acceptance of political change partly reflected the recognition that the continuation of white minority rule in the face of powerful external and internal opposition offered little prospect of an improvement in their circumstances.

When an earlier version of this chapter was published as an article in the *Journal of Contemporary African Studies*, it was accompanied by a critical comment by John Daniel on its central thesis of the importance to the South African transition of the coming down of the Berlin Wall.[34] Daniel argued that it overstated the significance of one event as the decisive catalyst in the thinking of De Klerk and those around him. He saw the breaching of the Berlin Wall and President de Klerk's February 1990 speech as the culmination of processes that went back much further. By tracing these processes to the roots, he argued, the decisive role of the United States in South Africa's transition was illuminated. Like Sparks, Daniel identified Gorbachev's accession to power in the Soviet Union in March 1985 as marking the start of a process of change that was ultimately to culminate in both the coming down of the Berlin Wall and the liberalisation of the South African political system. Gorbachev sought to end the Soviet Union's confrontation with the West and that was reflected in a commitment to the resolution of regional conflicts which came out of the October 1996 summit in Iceland between Gorbachev and Reagan.

From that time on, the United States and Soviet Union worked together to resolve their conflicts over Ethiopia, Angola, Namibia and South Africa. From late 1986, the United States was given *carte blanche* to shape events in southern Africa free from any concern that the Soviet Union might thwart its grand design. That design included getting the Cubans out of Angola, the South Africans out of Namibia and the launch of a democratisation process, or at least a negotiations process involving the ANC and a freed Nelson Mandela, in South Africa. The signing of the New York accords on

Namibia and Angola on 22 December 1988, was a major step in the realisation of these goals and it cleared the way for the heat to be turned on Pretoria.[35]

Further, Daniel claimed on the basis of material that appeared in the bi-monthly journal, *Africa Confidential*, before the Berlin Wall came down, that President Bush had threatened to approve further economic sanctions against South Africa unless the South African government took decisive steps to liberalise the system along the lines of the measures De Klerk actually announced on 2 February 1990. Finally, Daniel suggested that the setback that the South African military had suffered in Cuito Cunavale in southern Angola 1988 had strengthened the hand of those in government who favoured negotiations as a way forward in tackling problems not merely in relation to Namibia but in relation to South Africa's domestic crisis as well. However, none of this alters the fact that De Klerk's actual decision to liberalise the South African system was made in the context of the coming down of the Berlin Wall.

Daniel's arguments do suggest the possibility that the liberalisation of the South African system might have taken place even without the added impetus of events in Eastern Europe. The point is arguable. The fact that consideration had been given by the government to the option of liberalisation prior to the coming down of the Berlin Wall does not prove that such a decision would have been made, given the difficulty De Klerk would have had in justifying it in such different circumstances. As it was, the initial reaction of white opinion to De Klerk's initiative was sufficiently unfavourable that Adam, Slabbert and Moodley include 'the autocratic leadership style of the National Party in power'[36] as a factor in the transition on the grounds that the step De Klerk took would have been impossible if the opinions of the white electorate had had to be canvassed beforehand.

The value of Daniel's arguments lies in the fact that they draw attention to the array of pressures that South Africa faced by 1990 to change course. In a piece published in 1991, Frederik van Zyl Slabbert listed the pressures on the government under the heading of internal and external pressures for transition, which he further sub-divided into the categories of planned and unplanned, on the basis of whether they involved an identifiable agent seeking to bring about or prevent transition. His list of internal pressures include such familiar factors as population growth, urbanisation and the demands of the economy as well as the actions of the political actors themselves. As unplanned external pressure for transition Slabbert listed the changing relationship between the United States and the Soviet Union, the decline of South Africa as gold producer, the decline of Africa as an area of geo-political influence and the collapse of Communism in Eastern Europe. In the planned category he placed the war in Angola, the costs of administering Namibia and sanctions.[37]

Slabbert's listing of the pressures underlines an obvious but important point that it would be a mistake to attempt to explain De Klerk's actions in terms of a single factor. Nonetheless, the passage of time has done little to diminish the impression that the unexpected event of the breaching of the Berlin Wall played a significant role in the unexpected liberalisation of the South African political system. Criticisms of this proposition suggest reasons for examining the connection between them in a larger context of change within the international system over a longer period of time, but do not provide a good reason for ignoring evidence of the link between the two events. Of course, to explain why De Klerk embarked upon the transition is only to account for its beginning. How liberalisation led to democratisation is addressed in the next three chapters.

Notes to Chapter 2

1   Allister Sparks, *Tomorrow is Another Country: The Inside Story of South Africa's Negotiated Revolution*, Struik Book Distributors, Sandton 1994, p.9, p.12, p.98, p.108.

2   Allister Sparks, *The Mind of South Africa: The Story of the Rise and Fall of Apartheid*, Mandarin, London 1991, p.404.

3   Norman Etherington (ed.), *Peace, Politics and Violence in the New South Africa*, Hans Zell Publishers, London 1992, pp.103–4.

4   Vladimir Tikhomirov, *States in Transition: Russia and South Africa*, International Freedom Foundation, Bryanstown 1992.

5   Jeremy Cronin, 'The boat, the tap, and the Leipzig way', *African Communist*, Vol. 23, Third Quarter, 1992, pp.41–54.

6   Lawrence Schlemmer, 'The Turn in the Road: Emerging Conditions in 1990' in Robin Lee and Lawrence Schlemmer (eds), *Transition to Democracy: Policy Perspectives 1991*, Oxford University Press, Cape Town 1991, p.15.

7   *Ibid.*, pp.15–6.

8   *Ibid.*, p.16.

9   *Ibid.*, p.17.

10 *Ibid.*, pp.17–8.

11 Hermann Giliomee, 'Democratization in South Africa', *Political Science Quarterly*, Vol. 110, No.1, Spring 1995, p.86.

12 In particular, South Africa's Administrator-General in Namibia on the eve of the territory's independence expressed disappointment to a delegation of UK-based academics (including this author) that the Democratic Turnhalle Alliance had not insisted on a power sharing government following SWAPO's failure to secure a two-thirds majority in the 1989 elections. He also argued that the danger of placing reliance on a constituent assembly to draw up a constitution was a lesson that South Africa should derive from Namibia's transition.

13 Giliomee, *op. cit.*, p.91.

14 *Ibid.*, p.91.

15 *Ibid.*, p.103.

16 Arend Lijphart, 'Prospects for Power Sharing in the New South Africa' in Andrew Reynolds (ed.), *Elections '94 South Africa: The campaign, results and future prospects*, James Currey, London 1994, pp.230–1.

17 Giliomee, *op. cit.*, p.104.

18 Sparks (1994), *op. cit.*, p.98.

19 *Ibid.*, p.12.

20 *Proceedings of joint sitting, 2 February 1990, Debates of Parliament* (Republic of South Africa) Second session – ninth parliament.

21 Willem de Klerk, *F.W.De Klerk: The Man in His Time*, Jonathan Ball Publishers, Johannesburg 1991, p.55.

22 James Barber, *Forging the New South Africa*, Royal Institute of International Affairs, London 1994, p.6.

23 Martin Hollis and Steve Smith, *Explaining and Understanding International Relations*, Clarendon Press, Oxford 1991, pp.1–3.

24 Tikhomirov, *op. cit.*, p.22.

25 Francis Fukuyama, 'The Next South Africa', *South Africa International*, Vol. 22, No. 2, October 1991, p.80.

26 For a strong attack on Fukuyama's account of South African politics, see the analysis by Rupert Taylor, 'The End of Apartheid as part of "the End of History"?', *The South African Journal of International Affairs*, Vol. 3 No. 1, Summer 1995, pp.22–32.

27 Etherington (ed.), *op. cit.*, p.104.

28 Kathryn A.Manzo (ed.), *Domination, Resistance, and Social Change in South Africa: The Local Effects of Global Power*, Praeger, Westport, Connecticut 1992, p.251.

29 *Ibid.*, p.253.

30 Cronin, *op. cit.*, p.45.

31 Heribert Adam, Frederik van Zyl Slabbert and Kogila Moodley, *Comrades in Business: Post-Liberation Politics in South Africa*, Tafelberg, Cape Town 1997, p.61.

32 *Ibid.*, p.54.

33 *Ibid.*, p.58.

34 Adrian Guelke, 'The Impact of the End of the Cold War on the South African Transition', *Journal of Contemporary African Studies*, Vol. 14, No. 1, January 1996, pp.87–100.

35 John Daniel, 'A Response to Guelke: The Cold War Factor in the South African Transition', *Journal of Contemporary Studies*, Vol. 14, No. 1, January 1996, p.102.

36 Adam, Slabbert and Moodley, *op. cit.*, p.64.

37 Frederik van Zyl Slabbert, 'The basis and challenges of transition in South Africa: a review and a preview' in Robin Lee and Lawrence Schlemmer (eds), *Transition to Democracy: Policy Perspectives 1991*, Oxford University Press, Cape Town 1991, pp.4–10.

CHAPTER 3

Violence and the Transition

Estimates of the numbers killed in political violence in the transition vary among the different monitoring agencies. The monthly totals of fatalities since 1985 as a result of political violence recorded by the South African Institute of Race Relations (SAIRR) are set out in Table 3.1. According to SAIRR figures, in the period from the beginning of February 1990 to the end of April 1994, the months encompassing the transition itself, there were a total of 14,807 fatalities. Even if this is treated as a rough estimate of 15,000 deaths, as it should be, it is evident that the transition was the most politically violent period in the country's history. (Figures of the Human Rights Commission for the period July 1990 to June 1993 are given in Table 3.2 below.) The only other continuous period in which political violence has approached the scale of the political killings that South Africa has experienced since the closing months of 1984 was in 1976–77 following the Soweto riots/uprising of June 1976. According to the government-appointed Cillie Commission 575 people died in the riots between 16 June 1976 and 28 February 1977, while the SAIRR estimate of deaths for the period between June 1976 and October 1977 was 700.[1]

The high level of political violence during the transition raises a whole raft of questions. Who was principally responsible for the violence? Or were all parties more or less equally at fault? Who was blamed for the violence and was that blame deserved? Who benefited from the violence? What part, if any, did violence have in the strategies of the major parties? And what role did it play in the negotiations on democratisation and the new political dispensation? It should be noted at the outset that the high level of political violence presents a

Table 3.1

Monthly Totals of Political Fatalities in South Africa, 1985 to 1996

	Jan	Feb	Mar	Apr	May	Jun	Jul	Aug	Sep	Oct	Nov	Dec	TOTAL
1985	4	35	76	46	66	45	96	163	69	86	101	92	879
1986	105	112	179	145	221	212	122	76	40	16	37	33	1298
1987	40	22	40	40	33	36	39	35	73	93	89	121	661
1988	211	107	62	48	58	76	94	112	108	90	85	98	1149
1989	126	95	89	99	89	38	96	104	135	116	129	287	1403
1990	210	283	458	283	208	150	247	698	417	162	316	267	3699
1991	187	129	351	270	318	150	164	184	282	218	283	170	2706
1992	139	238	348	300	230	324	278	361	339	332	299	159	3347
1993	135	148	143	212	339	309	547	451	425	398	370	317	3794
1994	239	259	537	436	207	119	136	106	109	106	94	128	2476
1995	131	87	79	138	100	82	92	61	69	49	54	102	1044
1996	39	47	59	67	45	53	64	63	81	57	47	61	683

Note: In the months, September to December 1984, there were 149 fatalities.

Source, *South Africa Survey*, South African Institute of Race Relations, Johannesburg 1997, p.600.

serious problem for one of the most common interpretations of the transition as a pact between political elites. Sisk fully acknowledges the difficulty from his perspective of explaining 'the paradox of increased violence following the onset of negotiations' in his book on South Africa's democratisation, which describes 'elite coalescence' as 'the hallmark of the transition'.[2] In particular, he accepts the premise that 'elite-concluded accords do not work unless elites are able to demobilise their own constituencies' and he consequently attributes the failure of the National Peace Accord of September 1991 to the inability of Mandela, De Klerk and Buthelezi to demobilise their constituencies, concluding that '[t]he underlying forces behind the violence were mostly beyond their control'.[3]

Efforts by the political leaders to discourage violence during the transition by their followers can be cited in support of this view. Thus, within weeks of his release from prison Mandela addressing a rally of 100,000 in Durban made a strong appeal for peace:

> My message to those of you involved in this battle of brother against brother is this: Take your guns, knives, and your pangas and throw them into the sea. Although there are fundamental differences between us, we commend Inkatha for their demand over the years for the unbanning of the

ANC and the release of political prisoners, as well as their stand for refusing to participate in a negotiated settlement without the creation of the necessary climate. . . If we do not bring a halt to this conflict, we will be in danger of corrupting the proud legacy of our struggle. We endanger the peace process in the whole of the country.[4]

This speech underpinned Mandela's commitment to peace first given public expression in the statement issued on his behalf following his meeting while still a prisoner with President P.W.Botha in July 1989: 'I would only like to contribute to the creation of a climate which will promote peace in South Africa'.[5] When President de Klerk was accused during the transition of using the security forces to destabilise the ANC following its unbanning, his defenders pointed to the remarkable speech De Klerk had given to senior police commanders days before the unbanning of the ANC in which he had admitted that the police had previously been asked to intervene in matters that had nothing to do with ordinary crime and committed the government to stop using the police for the attainment of political goals.[6] Buthelezi had given his support to a number of peace initiatives in Natal. For example, in a speech in June 1989, he called for an end to violence arguing that its continuance was an obstacle to tackling racial inequality under the law.[7]

Admittedly, the very fact that political violence did continue, some saw as putting in question the good faith of the leaders in relation to violence. However, the ultimate success of the negotiating process many more saw as bearing out their basic commitment to peace. As a consequence, there has been a tendency to discount the role of political violence in the transition. That is reflected in a number of interpretations of the violence which reject the proposition that the violence was a function of political competition at the centre among the major political forces i.e. the ANC, the Inkatha Freedom Party (IFP) and National Party. They generally advance one or more of the following propositions to account for the violence or to rule out the notion that violence played a significant role in the competition for power among the main parties:

1. Violence was a tactic adopted by those seeking to derail the transition.
2. Political violence was a product of local conditions unrelated to the concerns of the national leaders.
3. Violence was a spontaneous reaction to the ending of repression and the liberalisation of the political system.

4. Violence was a product of deprivation, reflecting competition for scarce resources among the poor.
5. Violence was a legacy of the social conditions created by apartheid.
6. The (assumed) fact that the major parties derived no advantage from the violence is evidence that violence was not a part of the national strategy of any of the parties.

Each of these propositions holds good about some of the violence that took place during the transition, but as generalisations none stands up. Firstly, although there were a number of high profile acts of violence explicitly designed to prevent South Africa's passage to majority rule, they formed a very small proportion of the total of political violence. Indeed, the relative quiescence of extreme right-wing whites is a sufficiently important issue as to merit treatment in a separate chapter. Violence perpetrated by the Azanian People's Liberation Army (APLA), the political wing of the Pan-Africanist Congress (PAC) might be classified under this heading as might some security force actions and IFP activity. However, it is probably more accurate to regard APLA and IFP violence, as well as so-called 'third force' violence by agents of the state, as directed towards shaping the outcome of the transition, rather than as having the objective of aborting it altogether. Secondly, while local issues were an independent cause of conflict among the parties, the striving of local leaders for a position of dominance generally had its place in the larger national picture. What is more, the opinions of local leaders influenced the behaviour of national leaders, the most obvious example being Mandela's cancellation of a joint rally with Chief Buthelezi in 1990 on the advice of the leader of the ANC in Natal, Harry Gwala. However, it is true that the statements of local leaders during the transition tended to be more militant and uncompromising than those of national leaders and hence open to the accusation of fomenting conflict when the national leaders desired peace.

Thirdly, while some violence can be regarded as a by-product of the mass political mobilisation made possible by the liberalisation of the political system, the concentration of most of the violence in two arenas of conflict between the ANC and the IFP, the province of Natal and the townships of the East Rand in Pretoria-Witwatersrand-Vereeniging, suggests the limits of that explanation, as the figures given in Table 3.2 underline. Fourthly, while the battle for scarce resources can be shown to have played a part in political violence, the regional pattern of the violence underscores the role of political competition as the dominant factor since deprivation existed across the country and was not a feature that set the areas affected by political violence apart. Fifthly, neither the temporal nor the regional pattern of the violence can be explained by generalised reference to the social conditions created by apartheid. Sixthly, while it is reasonable to assume that parties would not initiate political violence except in the expectation of political advantage, failure to achieve advantage is not proof of the absence of political motivation. Conversely, the fact that a particular party derived benefit from the violence should not be taken as proof that it initiated it. A characteristic of periods of transitions is that the consequences of particular strategies, including the use of violence, are difficult to predict.

Table 3.2

Regional Death Statistics, July 1990 to June 1993

Year	Total	PWV	PWV as %	Natal	Natal as %	Other
1990/1	3190	1982	62.1	1004	31.5	204
1991/2	3039	1688	55.5	1004	33.0	347
1992/3	3096	1086	35.1	1645	53.1	365

Source: Supplement to Special Report SR-13, *Three Years of Destabilisation*, Human Rights Commission, Johannesburg 1993.

The popularity of what might be called non-political explanations of political violence, thereby underlining their paradoxical nature, in part stems from the widespread perception of De Klerk and Mandela as honourable men, reflected in the joint award to them in 1993 of the Noble Peace Prize. There is consequently a strong desire to acquit them of responsibility for the violence. Admittedly, the third party leader, Chief Buthelezi, does not inspire similar respect outside South Africa. Inside the country his reputation has waxed and waned with political circumstances. At present, within the ANC there would seem to be less hostility towards him and the IFP than there is towards the National Party.[8] However, leaving aside Buthelezi's role, the choices facing the analyst are not ones of either questioning the *bona fides* of the National Party or ANC leaders during the transition or opting either for a non-political explanation of the violence or one that focuses on the role of more minor players.

This conundrum can be unravelled simply by the recognition that the parties had very different conceptions of what constituted legitimate political activity in the country during the transition and thus tended to see the actions of the security forces and/or their supporters in an aggressive or defensive light, based on their interpretation of the other side's intentions. It is therefore not surprising that disagreements over political violence played such a central role in the transition, despite the rhetorical commitment of all the major parties to peace. The preoccupation of the parties throughout the transition with the issue of political violence provides reason in itself for rejecting interpretations of South Africa's democratisation that treat the violence as simply a distraction from the constitutional choices that faced the negotiators. In this context two different conflicts during the transition need to be interpreted in the light of the parties' divergent conceptions of legitimate political activity, the conflict between the ANC and the government and that between the ANC and the IFP. The former is discussed below; the latter in Chapter 5. To provide the basis for an understanding of the ANC's perspective on these issues, a brief history of the organisation and the evolution of its strategies for gaining power is necessary.

The ANC was formed in 1912, but it did not become a mass movement until the 1950s. The impetus for the organisation's transformation came from the ANC Youth League formed in 1944 and led by a most remarkable group of people who came to dominate the African nationalist movement. They included Nelson Mandela, Walter Sisulu and Oliver Tambo, to mention some of the best known names. The Youth League persuaded the ANC to adopt a Programme of Action in December 1949 that envisaged civil disobedience, a change from its previous tactics of petitioning and lobbying. This was put into effect in the 1952 Defiance Campaign. In 1955 the ANC and a number of other organisations, which together formed the Congress Alliance, adopted the Freedom Charter as a statement of political aspirations. Leading figures in the movement were charged with treason on the basis of their support for the Freedom Charter, but ultimately were acquitted. Following the Sharpeville massacre on 21 March 1960, when police opened fire on a crowd defying the pass laws, killing 69 of the demonstrators, the government banned the main African nationalist movements, the ANC and the PAC. The PAC had been formed in 1959 by Africanists who rejected the non-racial approach of the Freedom Charter and objected to the extent of influence of white Communists over the Congress Alliance.

After its prohibition the ANC went underground attempting to sustain mass passive resistance and a commitment to non-violent methods, despite being an illegal organisation. Following the failure of a stayaway from work called to coincide with the proclamation of

South Africa as a republic in May 1961, in part due to the savage security measures taken by the government to suppress it but also because of a poor response by its supporters to the call for a strike, discussion began among ANC members on the adoption of a campaign of violence. Discussions on the prospects for such a campaign had already been taking place within the SACP, which had been illegal since 1950. The context was described by Nelson Mandela at his trial in 1964:

> At the beginning of June 1961, after long and anxious assessment of the South African situation, I and some colleagues came to the conclusion that as violence in this country was inevitable, it would be wrong and unrealistic for African leaders to continue preaching peace and non-violence at a time when the government met our peaceful demands with force. This conclusion was not easily arrived at. It was only when all else had failed, when all channels of peaceful protest had been barred to us, that the decision was made to embark on violent forms of political struggle, and to form Umk[h]onto we Sizwe.[9]

Mandela emphasised that one of the purposes of the campaign was 'to canalise and control the feelings of our people'[10] in order to avoid greater bloodshed as a consequence of spontaneous outbursts of anger. He also stressed that the form of violence that MK chose was not terrorism:

> Four forms of violence were possible. There is sabotage, there is guerrilla warfare, there is terrorism, and there is open revolution. We chose to adopt the first method and to exhaust it before taking any other decision. In the light of our political background the choice was a logical one. Sabotage did not involve loss of life, and it offered the best hope for future race relations. Bitterness would be kept to a minimum and, if the policy bore fruit, democratic government could become a reality.[11]

This choice was reflected in the contents of the leaflet MK issued when it launched its campaign on 16 December 1961:

> We of Umk[h]onto we Sizwe have always sought – as the liberation movement has sought – to achieve liberation without bloodshed and civil clash. We do so still. We hope – even at this late hour – that our first actions will awaken every one to the realisation of the disastrous situation to which the Nationalist policy is leading. We hope that we will bring the government and its supporters to their senses before it is too late, so that the government and its policies can be changed before matters reach the desperate state of civil war.[12]

The aim of MK's campaign was to persuade the government to enter into negotiations with leaders of African nationalist opinion. The demand for negotiations was to be a constant factor in the ANC's approach to the conflict. A factor that underpinned this moderate stance was the attitude of its external backers on this issue. States, such as Zambia, that provided sanctuary for the ANC in exile after 1964 were insistent that the offer to the South African government of negotiations should remain open. This position was at the heart of the Lusaka Manifesto of 1969, adopted initially at a meeting of the states of East and Central Africa and then endorsed by the Organisation of African Unity and by the United Nations.

MK's campaign of violence went through a number of phases. The leadership rapidly concluded that sabotage had failed in its aim of inducing a change in the direction of government policy. Analysing the move towards violence from the perspective of the 1990s, the SACP leader, Joe Slovo, argued that 'no-one believed that the tactic of sabotage could, on its own, lead to the collapse of the racist state'.[13] He presented sabotage as marking a decisive break with the previous policy of non-violence and as intended as a form of armed propaganda aimed at encouraging young militants to join the underground.[14] Slovo also made clear that the setting up of MK was a joint decision of the Central Committee of the SACP and 'the Johannesburg Working Group of the ANC'.[15] By the time of the arrest of the principal leaders of the campaign following a police raid on Liliesleaf farm in Rivonia north of Johannesburg on 11 July 1963, preparations were already being made for the start of rural guerrilla warfare. However, the objective circumstances for the waging of any kind of campaign were to prove extremely unfavourable, though that was not immediately apparent at the time.

Trials of the leading figures in the ANC and in MK and a general security clampdown had effectively destroyed the African nationalist movement inside South Africa by the mid 1960s. At the same time, the buffer of white-ruled or colonial states that surrounded the country through the 1960s presented a formidable obstacle to the infiltration into South Africa of members of MK from exile, where the ANC had established camps for the purpose of providing military training to recruits. As an acknowledgement of the ANC's interest in change in the buffer protecting South Africa, MK units fought alongside Zimbabwean nationalists in 1967 and 1968. However, the Wankie and Sipolilo campaigns achieved little politically or militarily either for the ANC or for its Zimbabwean ally. One significant legacy of the campaigns was that a number of individuals enhanced their reputation within the ANC and MK through their participation and survival in battle.

When the ANC met in conference in 1969 in Morogogo in Tanzania, conditions for the advancement of its cause through rural guerrilla warfare either in South Africa or in neighbouring states seemed most inauspicious. This was reflected in a document prepared for the conference, entitled 'Strategy and Tactics of the ANC'.[16] It advocated protracted armed struggle, while emphasising the need for political mobilisation as a precondition for its success. It stressed the revolutionary potential of the urban working class. The nature of the analysis was an indication of the influence of the SACP within the movement at this time. Another was the decision of the ANC in exile to open its membership to non-Africans. In practice, many of those admitted in this way were members of the SACP. However, at this stage, the opening up of membership did not apply to the governing body of the ANC, the National Executive Committee. The conference attracted relatively little interest. The prospect of the ANC's being able to mobilise the masses in South Africa in accordance with the rhetoric of the conference seemed extremely remote.

The situation changed with the Portuguese revolution of 1974, which led to independence for Angola and Mozambique in 1975. Their example inspired opposition to the government inside South Africa. The trigger for revolt was action by the police against a demonstration on 16 June 1976 by 10,000 schoolchildren protesting against a decree that Afrikaans had to be used as one of the languages of instruction in secondary schools. After there was resistance to police attempts to stop the march, the police opened fire on the schoolchildren, killing several.[17] Attacks on government offices in the townships followed. The Soweto Students' Representative Council formed in response to the crisis revived the tactic of the stayaway, using coercion to enforce its strike call for 4–6 August 1976.

> Roadblocks prevented buses and taxis from taking people to town; drivers were threatened; city-bound workers were stoned and forced to turn back; many of the thirteen railway stations in Soweto were blocked off, and trains were stoned.[18]

These methods were repeated in subsequent stayaways, opening up political fissures within the townships that the authorities were able to exploit, with the police encouraging hostel dwellers to attack youths preventing them from earning their living. Whom the populace viewed as the aggressors and whom as defenders depended on perceptions of the relative legitimacy of the combatants. How opinion in the townships divided was open to a variety of interpretations, particularly in the absence of conditions in which the townships residents could express their views freely.

Although the ANC played little part in the events that led up to the violence in Soweto or in the wider revolt against the authorities that followed in townships across the country, it was the major beneficiary of the crisis. The flight into exile of many of the young militants involved in the uprising provided the ANC in exile with a fresh generation of recruits. After a gap of a decade, MK resumed operations inside South Africa in October 1976 with the sabotage of a railway line. Of particular importance in raising the profile of the MK during the late 1970s and early 1980s was a series of spectacular attacks on prestige targets carried out by forces trained for the purpose and organised in a separate Special Operations section of MK headed by the SACP leader, Joe Slovo. For example, on 1 June 1980 an MK Special Operations unit launched an attack on a plant at Sasolburg that produced oil from coal, an important symbol of the country's self-sufficiency and capacity to overcome an oil embargo. The attack caused massive damage to the plant and the smoke from burning fuel tanks was visible the next morning as far as Soweto fifty miles away.

The South African government responded to the challenge presented by the resumption of the MK's campaign by adopting a total strategy including a policy of the destabilisation of neighbouring states designed to punish them for harbouring MK units. However, while massive damage was inflicted on both Mozambique and Angola and in Mozambique's case the pressure persuaded the government to expel the ANC from its territory, the South African government's war against the ANC outside the country was undermined by increasing instability inside South Africa itself as the government lost control of the townships. In September 1984 the Vaal and East Rand townships erupted in protest against rent increases. This was the start of a continuous period of political violence in the country.

The revolt followed the holding of elections to Coloured and Indian chambers of parliament. This was a central part of the government's efforts to strengthen the base of the regime through the cooption of the Coloured and Indian minorities. In seeking to give these elections a measure of international legitimacy, the government had been forced to allow greater political space to its opponents to organise politically and this had been reflected in the creation in August 1983 of the United Democratic Front (UDF). The UDF's endorsement of the Freedom Charter made clear its political alignment to the ANC. It frustrated the government's plans for legitimising the political restructuring of the polity by organising effective boycotts firstly of elections in November 1983 to African municipal authorities and then of the Coloured and Indian parliamentary elections in August 1984. (The township municipalities were intended by the government to provide a measure of political representation for urban Africans in the recognition that they could not be accommodated politically by the homelands.)

By late 1984 the ANC was able to characterise its struggle against apartheid as resting on four pillars: mass mobilisation, armed operations, underground organisation and international solidarity work.[19] ANC rhetoric that it was making the preparations to conduct a people's war no longer seemed incredible, even if the reality was that the organisation in exile had comparatively little control over the militants acting on its behalf in the townships. However, in the eyes of the government and other opponents, the ANC bore responsibility for their actions since in its propaganda it explicitly called for the country to be made ungovernable.[20]

The following year, 1985, saw the first attempts by the government to explore the possibilities for negotiations with leaders of the ANC, including the imprisoned Nelson Mandela. A meeting between Mandela and the Minister of Justice, Kobie Coetzee, in November 1985 initiated four years of secret talks between Mandela and the government.[21] At the start of the year, at the opening of a new session of the South African parliament, President P.W.Botha had offered to release Mandela from gaol if he would renounce the use of violence. Mandela's rejection of this offer was read to a rally of the United Democratic Front by his daughter, Zindzi, in February 1985:

> Only free men can negotiate. Prisoners cannot enter into contracts. . . . I cannot and will not give any undertaking at a time when I and you, the people, are not free. Your freedom and mine cannot be separated.[22]

Mandela also called on Botha to renounce violence, stressing that the ANC had only turned to armed struggle when other avenues of opposition to apartheid had been closed. Two concerns dominated Mandela's discussions with government ministers. The first was the urgency of negotiations between the government and the ANC, given the turmoil in the country. To this end, he had written to the Minister of Justice, Kobie Coetzee, asking for a meeting. The second was that his talks with the government should not in any way undercut the position of the ANC. He was acutely conscious of the danger that the government would attempt to use any talks he had with ministers to drive a wedge between him and the ANC leadership in exile.

In preparation for a meeting with President Botha in July 1989, Mandela drew up a memorandum on the terms of his discussions with the government that was designed to allay any fears that his ANC colleagues had about them. In particular, Mandela was adamant in his rejection of each of what he described as the 'three main demands set by the government as a precondition for negotiations, namely that the ANC must first renounce violence, break with the SACP and abandon its demand for majority rule'.[23] His memorandum concluded by suggesting parameters for the negotiations:

> Two political issues will have to be addressed: firstly, the demand for majority rule in a unitary state; secondly, the concern of white South Africa over this demand, as well as the insistence of whites on structural guarantees that majority rule will not mean domination of the white minority by blacks. The most crucial tasks which will face the government and the ANC will be to reconcile these two positions.[24]

The official position of the ANC on negotiations at this time was set out in the Harare Declaration, endorsed by the Organisation of African Unity in a meeting in Zimbabwe in August 1989. This placed the onus on the South African government to create the climate for negotiations by releasing political prisoners, unbanning organisations, removing troops from the townships, lifting the state of emergency and ceasing political executions.

When De Klerk became President, Mandela wrote to him in advance of their meeting on 13 December 1989, reiterating that the ANC would accept no preconditions for talks, while stressing that the organisation's readiness to negotiate itself constituted a honest commitment to peace. When Mandela was finally released from prison on 11 February 1990, he was aware that in his exploration of the possibility of negotiations he had gone beyond simply stating the official position of the ANC and also that he needed to allay fears of a secret deal with the government. Consequently, in his first speech as a free man, he went out of his way to stress that he was 'a loyal and disciplined member of the African National Congress'[25] and that the purpose of his talks with the government had solely been directed towards paving the way to negotiations between the government and the ANC.

The unbanning of the ANC and the release of Mandela from prison was not immediately followed by negotiations between the government and the ANC. An episode in which the police opened fire on demonstrators delayed a meeting between the two sides to early May 1990. Out of the meeting, which took place over three days, came the

Groote Schuur Minute under which the two sides agreed to a peaceful process of negotiations, the government agreeing to lift the state of emergency, while both sides agreed to establish a joint working group to deal with such matters as the release of political prisoners and the return of exiles. The report of the joint working group established the definition of a political offence and dealt with the question of the release of prisoners, thereby providing the basis for the Pretoria Minute under which the ANC suspended all armed actions on 6 August 1990. The mechanism for the release of prisoners required them to apply for indemnity individually, as provided for in legislation that parliament had enacted. Mandela records that some of the prisoners on Robben Island he visited after his release objected to this procedure as falling short of the unconditional blanket amnesty the ANC had demanded in the Harare Declaration. Mandela told them they were being unrealistic in view of the fact that the government had not been defeated on the battlefield.[26]

According to Mandela's autobiography, the actual decision to suspend the armed struggle was taken by the ANC National Executive Committee at the initiative of Joe Slovo, in advance of its August meeting with the government. Mandela puts the decision partly in the context of the government's discovery in July 1990 of Operation Vula, under which the ANC was continuing to build underground structures and the capacity to sustain a campaign of violence against the state, should the government attempt to reverse its liberalisation of the political system. The discovery of Operation Vula had deeply shocked the government, which presented it as a SACP plot to overthrow the government by force and demanded the SACP's exclusion from the negotiations. Slovo's proposal to suspend the armed struggle, which Mandela supported, led to a lengthy debate within the National Executive Committee before being adopted. The proponents argued that the armed struggle had achieved its aim of bringing the government to the negotiating table. Mandela explains why, nevertheless, the issue proved so controversial as follows:

> Although MK was not active, the aura of the armed struggle had great meaning for many people. Even when cited merely as a rhetorical device, the armed struggle was a sign that we were actively fighting the enemy. As a result, it had a popularity that was out of all proportion to what it had achieved on the ground.[27]

Its popularity was a reflection of the fact that at the level of policy and of rhetoric, MK's armed struggle through all its various phases appeared remarkably principled. The objective of the campaign to achieve inclusive negotiations was clearly a moderate one, from an international perspective. However, it is understandable that this appeared a huge step from the perspective of the South African government. The extension of the franchise to the African majority was unavoidable in any negotiated settlement. Nothing less would be regarded as legitimate by international opinion. This put the ANC in a very strong position given the likely outcome of democratic elections in South Africa. The means employed by the ANC could also be presented as principled, by the standards of modern warfare. When the Geneva Conventions of 1949 were supplemented by the addition of two Protocols in 1977 with the purpose of extending the concept of international armed conflict so as to cover cases of guerrilla warfare, the ANC undertook to adhere to the Convention and its Protocols and took part in a special ceremony at the headquarters of the International Committee of the Red Cross in November 1980 to underline its commitment to the observance of international humanitarian law.

However, the intensification of the conflict inside South Africa in the 1980s put pressure on the stance of avoiding civilian casualties and that was reflected in one of the decisions made by the Kabwe conference in 1985, which came close to a blanket condoning of attacks on soft targets. The resolution stated:

> We can no longer allow our armed activities to be determined solely by the risk of civilian casualties. The time has come when those who stand in solid support of the race tyranny and who are its direct or indirect instruments, must themselves begin to feel the agony of our counter-blows. It is becoming more necessary than ever for whites to make it clear which side of the battle lines they stand.[28]

Further, in practice, the actions of MK members did not always conform to the standards demanded of them by their leaders, as was acknowledged by the ANC in its submission to the Truth and Reconciliation Commission in 1996. The submission discusses examples of breaches of its code of conduct. In particular, there is a reasonably detailed account of the 1980 Silverton Bank siege.

> On January 25, 1980 three MK cadres on their way to carry out a mission realised that they had been spotted and were being tailed by the police. (They) tried to escape almost certain death by entering a bank; they moved all civilians present into one corner in an attempt to ensure that they would not be caught in the line of fire, and held them hostage in support of their demands. The Minister of Police refused to disclose these demands

to the public but it was reported that they wanted to see the Prime Minister, the release of Nelson Mandela and James Mange, and an aircraft to fly to Maputo. A police unit stormed the bank and all three cadres and two civilian women . . . were killed. This was the only incident in which MK cadres, in contravention of ANC policy, seized hostages for political ends.[29]

The submission discusses a number of other instances in which MK operations led to the deaths of civilians, such as the car bomb attack on the headquarters of the South African Air Force (SAAF) in Pretoria in May 1983, in which 19 people were killed (of whom 11 were SAAF officers), and another car bomb attack on two bars in Durban in June 1986, in which three civilians were killed. However, it conspicuously fails to mention others such as the car bomb placed outside the Ellis Park sports stadium in 1988, one of approximately 1,500 attacks attributed to MK between 1977 and 1989. Undoubtedly a factor that contributed to the relatively clean image of MK's campaign[30] was its small scale. Its impact derived from the symbolic effect rather than from any actual damage that it was able to inflict on the South African state, which was very slight, and is why authors such as Stephen Ellis and Tsepo Sechaba characterised the armed struggle as a failure in their 1992 book, *Comrades against Apartheid*.[31] Of course, judged by the utterly unrealistic objective of the military overthrow of the government, it was.

The perception of MK's campaign up to 1989 as ineffective, coupled with the belief that its capacity to sustain the armed struggle had been substantially weakened by the changes in Eastern Europe, contributed to an underestimation of the strength of the ANC's position at the start of the transition. In fact, the presentation of the ANC's entry into negotiations as a compromise forced upon it underplayed how significant a victory that represented for the ANC, especially set in the context of the government's quest for international acceptability. Furthermore, the ANC's bargaining position derived its strength from sources other than the armed struggle, in particular, its identification with political demands seen as legitimate by the international community and the spectre of ungovernability that haunted the country. Within the townships, ANC-aligned self-defence units (SDUs) had sprung up across the country with the growth of unrest in the mid-1980s. However, the SDUs were not formally a part of the ANC or MK, enabling ANC leaders to distance themselves from their excesses. As a matter of fact, the ANC's capacity to control their activities was weak. But critics pointed to the readiness of prominent ANC leaders inside and outside the country to defend atrocities carried out by SDUs in support of the objective of making the country ungovernable, including the use of the 'necklace' against those the SDUs accused of being informers or collaborators. The 'necklace' was a tyre filled with petrol that was placed over the suspect and ignited.

Consequently it is not surprising that MK's suspension of the armed struggle in August 1990 failed to dispose of the issue of violence. As if to underline the point, political violence rose to a peak in the month of its suspension (see Table 3.1). Indeed, the issue of violence was to dominate the transition right up to polling at the end of April 1994. This will be evident from a brief examination of some of the most significant junctures in the chronology of the transition after the adoption of the Pretoria Minute. In January 1991 Mandela and Buthelezi met to sign a declaration calling on their supporters 'to cease all attacks against one another with immediate effect'.[32] That was followed in February by the D.F.Malan Accord between the government and the ANC intended to resolve outstanding issues between them arising out of the interpretation of the Pretoria Minute.[33] Despite these agreements, the violence continued and led the ANC to issue an ultimatum in which it threatened to withdraw from negotiations unless the government took a number of specified steps to control the violence. In July revelations of government funding of the IFP and of parties opposed to the South West African People's Organisation (SWAPO) prior to Namibia's elections in 1989 furthered strained relations among the parties. Another attempt by the parties to reach agreement on rules to govern political mobilisation was made in September 1991 with the signature of the National Peace Accord.[34]

In December 1991, the first set of substantive constitutional negotiations among the parties began with the launch of the Convention for a Democratic South Africa. The government received endorsement of its commitment to reform and the negotiation of a new constitution in a referendum among whites in March 1992. However, the negotiations themselves ended in deadlock in May 1992. Further revelations of security force involvement in ongoing violence intensified ANC distrust of the government. International concern over this issue was reflected in the publication on 10 June of a report by Amnesty International entitled, *South Africa: state of fear – security force complicity in torture and killings, 1990–1992*.[35] The ANC's suspicion that the purpose of the violence was to weaken the ANC's bargaining position in the negotiations was matched by the interpretation placed by its opponents on the ANC's resort to mass action to put pressure on the government. When

IFP-supporting hostel-dwellers massacred 38 people at a shack settlement at Boipatong in southern Transvaal on the night of 17 June 1992, it seemed plausible that the objective of the massacre was to deter township residents from supporting the ANC's campaign of mass action, especially in the light of eye-witness accounts that suggested security force complicity in the killings. Government ministers unwittingly contributed to these suspicions by their attempts to blame the ANC for the violence by constant reference to the climate of tension created by the ANC's campaign of mass action.

The Boipatong massacre created a profound crisis of confidence in the transition, with the ANC breaking off formal contact with the government and escalating its campaign of mass action. At this point the international community intervened through the United Nations (UN) to overcome the political impasse among the parties in South Africa. In July the Security Council gave its approval to the dispatch to South Africa of a special representative of the Secretary-General, an assignment given to a former American Secretary of State, Cyrus Vance. He visited South Africa at the end of July. His mission resulted in the creation of a UN monitoring group in South Africa. Its success in contributing to the restraint shown by all sides at the climax of the ANC's mass action campaign in August 1992 led to the creation of a larger UN monitoring force, the United Nations Observer Mission in South Africa (UNOMSA). Its efforts were supplemented by monitoring groups from the European Community, the Organisation of African Unity, the Commonwealth and the churches. However, all these international monitors proved unable to prevent a massacre of 29 ANC supporters in Bisho on 7 September 1992 by soldiers of the Ciskei Defence Force. The massacre occurred when a group of ANC radicals led a section of the crowd towards the town in violation of an agreement to confine the demonstration to the stadium on its outskirts. Despite the aspect of provocation and Ciskei's nominal independence, world opinion blamed the South African government for the massacre, putting further pressure on the government to change course. At the same time, ANC leaders were perturbed by the spectre of loss of control over its conduct of the mass action campaign.

The conjuncture created the basis for a deal, resulting in the signature of a Record of Understanding between De Klerk and Mandela on 26 September. The agreement underlined the priority each leader gave to reaching a negotiated settlement with the other. It established concord on four key issues: the broad parameters of a new constitution, including the creation of an interim government of national unity; the release of prisoners convicted of politically motivated offences before October 1990; the fencing of hostels; and prohibition on the carrying of dangerous weapons in public places. The fury with which the leader of the IFP, Chief Buthelezi, reacted to the agreement underlined its significance, the fact that it signalled the final abandonment of the National Party's efforts to construct an alliance to defeat the ANC. There was some criticism of De Klerk within the National Party over this change in direction, but the concession by the ANC on the issue of power sharing helped to mollify the critics.

The choices as they were seen by the ANC at this point were set out in a document entitled 'Negotiations: A Strategic Perspective', which was adopted by the national working committee of the ANC in November 1992. Three options were given:

(a) resumption of the armed struggle and the perspective of revolutionary seizure of power . . . ;

(b) a protracted negotiations process, combined with mass action and international pressure until the balance of forces is shifted to such an extent that we secure a negotiated surrender from the regime;

(c) a swift negotiations process combined with mass action and international pressure which takes into account the need for national unity against counter-revolutionary forces, and, at the same time, uses phases in the transition to qualitatively change the balance of forces in order to secure thoroughgoing democratic transformation.[36]

The document recommended the choice of option (c), though it also warned against the organisation's being a captive to a given approach, concluding that a combination of factors, including the behaviour of the government, might require the organisation to reconsider. In the event, option (c) served the ANC well. Key to the success of the strategy was the concept of 'sunset clauses', first enunciated by Joe Slovo, under which the ANC justified power sharing for a limited period, as well as the honouring of the contracts of the existing civil service, a necessary gesture of reassurance to people whose cooperation the ANC would need in government.

The Record of Understanding prompted a realignment of political forces. However, it by no means either ended political violence or reduced its central role in politics. A further critical juncture occurred with the assassination of the SACP leader, Chris Hani, in April 1993. The spectre of anarchy in the wake of the assassination acted as a spur to the parties in the multi-party negotiating process to speed up the transition. At the beginning of July 1993, the Multi-Party

Negotiating Forum set 27 April 1994 as a deadline for the holding of the country's first non-racial elections. The decision coincided with an escalation in the level of political violence, with July 1993 the second most violent month of the transition, according to SAIRR figures (see Table 3.1). There was further political violence in 1994. Extreme right-wing intervention in Bophuthatswana in March unsuccessfully tried to prevent the homeland's incorporation into South Africa and hence its inclusion in the April 1994 elections. The IFP also demonstrated its capacity for disrupting the life of the country's commercial capital, Johannesburg, on 28 March 1994 before its eleventh hour decision to take part in the elections, while extreme right-wingers launched a bombing campaign before and during polling itself. These episodes are discussed in greater detail in the next two chapters.

To highlight the role of violence in the negotiations and the issue of violence as a subject of negotiations during South Africa's transition is not to discount the importance of constitutional issues in the transition or to underestimate the complexity of the choices that faced negotiators in this area. It is also the case that the process involved concessions by all the parties in relation to some issues. But there is also the danger in such an analysis of losing sight of the wood for the trees. The outcome of the transition was that the ANC achieved a position of such predominance as to be able to secure the passage during 1996 of a constitution that embodied its cherished aim of majority rule in a unitary state. None of the compromises entered into by the party on the constitutional provisions themselves put that outcome seriously at risk. However, it can be argued that the ANC's acceptance early on in the transition of a constitutional process of change, whereby the new dispensation required the approval of the old institutions, did involve the organisation in taking a calculated risk that it would be able to overcome efforts to weaken its position ahead of the holding of democratic elections. It was able to do so because of the international legitimacy it enjoyed. That made it impossible for the government unilaterally to lay down the terms for the ANC's participation in the process, by, in particular, imposing its own interpretation of political violence on the party.

On the contrary, the ANC's perspectives on the violence, both in its characterisation of the perpetrators and the victims and in its assumptions about the purpose of the violence tended to prevail in the outside world. It was, of course, accepted that acts of political violence were carried out by wide range of people with differing political motivations. However, violence is rarely judged without reference to the end for which it is employed. The actions of the ANC's supporters tended to be viewed in the light of the organisation's legitimate political demand for one person one vote. The strength of the ANC's position was underlined by the fact that its main political opponents, the National Party and the IFP, had little choice from the outset of the negotiations but to accept the legitimacy of that demand, yet even after their acceptance of the principle of one person one vote, their commitment to the democratisation was perceived as being in question. In general, the violent actions of the ANC's rivals tended to seen in the light of suspicions that their purpose was to thwart the holding of democratic elections. Partly because such suspicions were by no means entirely unjustified, they made it very difficult for the ANC's rivals to establish the legitimacy of any of their actions or to convince the outside world of their victimisation by ANC violence.

John Kane-Berman's book, *Political Violence in South Africa*, is worth examining in this context since it represents an attempt to place a large measure of the blame for the violence of the transition on the ANC. Firstly, he indirectly places a question mark over the ANC's commitment to democracy by strongly underlining its alliance with the SACP.[37] As explained in the last chapter, the end of the Cold War made it difficult to sustain the credibility of the threat that ANC rule might lead to the establishment of a Communist one-party state. Secondly, Kane-Berman argues that an end to apartheid would have come about, essentially for socio-economic reasons, without the assistance of either MK's armed struggle or the ANC's campaign to make the country ungovernable with the launch of people's war in 1985.[38] The case that Kane-Berman makes that socio-economic factors played an important role in propelling South Africa away from apartheid is an interesting and persuasive one. However, the implication that they would have been sufficient by themselves to have brought about the democratisation of the South African political system is difficult to reconcile with the assumptions most analysts made about the durability of white minority rule. To put the point in other language, the labelling of the democratisation of South Africa as a miracle stems, at least in part, from the perception of its being underdetermined, not overdetermined.

Indeed, the central role that political violence and the issue of political violence played in the transition suggests, contrary to the implication of Kane-Berman's argument, that the democratisation of South Africa cannot be explained without reference to the violence. This should not be interpreted as an intention to lend legitimacy to the violence by presenting it as an essential means to the end of democratisation. The argument is somewhat more complicated than that. The link between the violence and change was indirect. Further, the purpose of drawing attention to the role of the violence is analytical not judgmental. Thus, one part of the argument, which is discussed in the next chapter, is that the violence of the extreme right was counterproductive to the aims of its perpetrators and made an unwitting contribution to the ANC's triumph.

Notes on Chapter 3

1   John Kane-Berman, *Political Violence in South Africa*, South African Institute of Race Relations, Johannesburg 1993, p.29.

2   Timothy D.Sisk, *Democratization in South Africa: The Elusive Social Contract*, Princeton University Press, Princeton, New Jersey 1995, p.115 and p.122.

3   *Ibid.*, p.123.

4   Quoted in Carole Cooper, Colleen McCaul, Robin Hamilton, Isabelle Delvare, John Gary Moonsamy and Kristine Mueller, *Race Relations Survey 1989/90*, South African Institute of Race Relations, Johannesburg 1990, p.257.

5   Quoted in Sisk, *op. cit.*, p.79.

6   Cooper *et al.*, *Survey 1989/90*, p.158.

7   *Ibid.*, p.252.

8   At least as indicated by Mandela's 'enemies of change' speech to the ANC Congress in December 1997. See Chapter 8.

9   From 'Statement during the Rivonia Trial, by Nelson R.Mandela, 20 April 1964' quoted in Thomas Karis and Gail M.Gerhart (eds), *Challenge and Protest: Volume 3 of From Protest to Challenge*, Hoover Institution Press, Stanford 1977, p.777.

10 *Ibid.*, p.772.

11 *Ibid.*, p.778.

12 From '"Umkonto We Sizwe" (Spear of the Nation). Flyer "issued by command of Umkonto We Sizwe" and appearing on December 16, 1961' quoted in Karis and Gerhart (eds), *op. cit.*, p.717.

13 Joe Slovo, *The Unfinished Autobiography*, Ravan Press, Randburg 1995, p.152.

14 *Ibid.*, p.153.

15 *Ibid.*, p.151.

16 The text of 'Strategy and Tactics of the ANC (Document adopted by the Morogogo Conference of the ANC, meeting at Morogogo, Tanzania, 1969)' is available under the heading of ANC historical documents at the ANC Web site at http://www.anc.org.za.

17   Kane-Berman, *op. cit.*, p.1.

18   *Ibid.*, p.112.

19   See 'Statement to the Truth and Reconciliation Commission', August 1996, section 5.1., available at the ANC Web site at http://www.anc.org.za.

20   Kane-Berman, *op. cit.*, p.41.

21   See Allister Sparks, *Tomorrow is Another Country: The Inside Story of South Africa's Negotiated Revolution*, Struik Book Distributors, Sandton 1994, pp.21–36.

22   Quoted in Nelson Mandela, *Long Walk to Freedom: The Autobiography of Nelson Mandela*, MacDonald Purnell, Randburg 1994, p.511.

23   From the text of 'The Mandela Document: a document presented by Nelson Mandela to P.W.Botha in July 1989', available at the ANC Web site at http://www.anc.org.za..

24   *Ibid.*

25   From the text of 'Nelson Mandela's address to rally in Cape Town on his release from prison, 11 February 1990', available at the ANC Web site at http://www.anc.org.za.

26   Mandela, *op. cit.*, p.573.

27   *Ibid.*, p.578.

28   Quoted in 'Report, main decisions and *recommendations* of the Second National Consultative Conference of the African National Congress – Zambia, June 16–23, 1985', available under the heading of ANC historical documents at the ANC Web site at http://www.anc.org.za.

29   'Statement to the Truth and Reconciliation Commission', August 1996, section 6.2.5., available at the ANC Web site.

30   See, for example, Tom Lodge, 'Taking great pains to justify a "clean war"', *Mail and Guardian* (Johannesburg), 23–29 August 1996.

31   Stephen Ellis and Tsepo Sechaba, *Comrades against Apartheid*, James Currey, London 1992, p.200.

32   Text quoted in Carole Cooper, Robin Hamilton, Harry Mashabela, Shaun MacKay, Joe Kelly, Elizabeth Sidiropolous, Claire Gordon-Brown and John Gary Moonsamy, *Race Relations Survey 1991/92*, South African Institute of Race Relations, Johannesburg 1992, p.521.

33   Text of D.F.Malan quoted *ibid.*, pp.516–8.

34   Text of the National Peace Accord, *ibid.*, pp.522–56.

35   *South Africa: state of fear – security force complicity in torture and killings, 1990–1992*, Amnesty International, London 1992.

36   From the text of African National Congress, 'Negotiations: A Strategic Perspective (As adopted by the National Working Committee on 18 November 1992)' available at the ANC's Web site (see note 4).

37   e.g. Kane-Berman, *op. cit.*, p.67 and pp.83–8.

38   *Ibid.*, pp.63–4.

CHAPTER 4

The Passivity of the Extreme Right

In the Sherlock Holmes story, *Silver Blaze*, the following exchange takes place between the detective and Inspector Gregory:

"Is there any other point to which you wish to draw my attention?"
"To the curious incident of the dog in the night-time."
"The dog did nothing in the night-time."
"That was the curious incident," remarked Sherlock Holmes.[1]

The story is an appropriate metaphor for the behaviour of the extreme right during the South African transition. Contrary to widespread fears that it would be a major source of violence during the transition, the threat posed by the extreme right only materialised at the very end of the process and even then fell far short of demonstrating the capacity 'to disrupt the entire process of transformation',[2] as Johann van Rooyen had warned. Thus, in the period from July 1990 to June 1993, dubbed three years of destabilisation by the Human Rights Commission (HRC), the right wing was a source of 54 deaths out of a total of 8,580 fatalities as a result of political violence or 0.6 per cent of the total, on the HRC's figures.[3] The low level of extreme right-wing violence in South Africa is even more extraordinary when viewed in an international context. The early 1990s saw a resurgence of right-wing extremism in Europe, which developed out of a racist response to high levels of unemployment and the presence of immigrants and asylum seekers from the Third World.[4]

However – and this is where the analogy of the dog that did not bark in the night breaks down – it would be misleading to conclude from the low level of extreme right-wing violence that its impact on the transition was slight. Three episodes of extreme right-wing violence played a major role in the transition but not in the way that the perpetrators hoped. They were the assassination of the SACP leader, Chris Hani, in April 1993, the attack on the Multi-Party Negotiating Forum in June 1993, and the intervention in Bophuthatswana in March 1994. While the counter productive effect of these episodes may provide part of the explanation for the relative passivity of the extreme right, it leaves the problem of explaining why the most deadly acts of violence by the extreme right did not precede but followed these three episodes.

The puzzle of why South Africa's ultras did not offer greater resistance to the establishment of a government dominated by the ANC is related to another larger issue, the acquiescence of the white community as a whole in the transfer of power, contrary to virtually all indications of white opinion prior to 1990.[5] It has especial relevance to the common journalistic explanation of white acquiescence, which is that there was a transformation of the racial attitudes of whites during the 1990s under the spell of Mandela's commitment to reconciliation. However, declining racism does not present a credible explanation of the passivity of the extreme right, given the evidence of the virulence of that racism. That suggests either that a different argument is required to account for the quiescence of the extreme right, or the need for an altogether different explanation for the evolution in white political attitudes during the transition.

Before these questions are tackled, a brief history of the extreme right in South Africa is needed to explain why it was seen at the outset of South Africa's transition as such a potent threat to the process of reform. The zeal with which Hendrik Verwoerd, South Africa's Prime Minister between 1958 and 1966, pursued the policy of apartheid left little room on the far right of the political spectrum. It was only after his death that the government started to be criticised from the right. By the late 1960s, the policies of the South African government were becoming increasingly offensive to opinion in the West. The evolution of attitudes on race in the United States and in the former colonial powers such as Britain and France created the danger that South Africa would become isolated. In fact, that was already happening in the symbolically important field of sport. To avert the danger of further isolation, Verwoerd's successor, B.J.Vorster, modified his predecessor's rigid policies. The change of direction resulted in a minor split in the ruling National Party. The break came over the government's decision to allow a New Zealand rugby team containing Maoris to visit South Africa. The alternative would have been no tour at all as the New Zealand Rugby Union was no longer prepared to accept racial restrictions on its choice of players for tests against South Africa.

Those who continued to oppose the new policy were expelled from the National Party in 1969. They formed the *Herstigte Nasionale Party* (HNP – Refounded National Party). The party's candidates fared poorly in the 1970 general election. However, the failure of the HNP did not put an end to political conflict in the Afrikaner community. It was encapsulated by the use of terms, *verligtes* and *verkramptes*, to describe respectively progressives and traditionalists in and outside the ranks of the ruling party.[6] During the 1970s these divisions spawned a number of organisations, particularly among traditionalists alarmed at the gradual erosion of social segregation as a result of further adjustment of the government to external pressures. The most significant of the new organisations was the *Afrikaner Weerstandsbeweging* (AWB – Afrikaner resistance movement). According to the founders of the movement, it was formed by seven worried Afrikaners in 1973. Its leader was Eugene Terre Blanche. He was a former policeman whose duties had included acting as a bodyguard for Prime Minister B.J.Vorster. He had stood for the HNP in the 1970 general election after resigning from the police.

The AWB remained a secret organisation until 1979 when it achieved instant notoriety after members of the organisation tarred and feathered a distinguished Afrikaner nationalist historian, Professor F.A.van Jaarsveld. His offence in the eyes of the AWB was that he delivered a lecture in which he questioned the basis for treating as a holy day the Day of the Vow, which celebrated the victory of the voortrekkers over the Zulus at the battle of Blood River as a God-given deliverance. Terre Blanche and 13 of his followers faced a number of charges over the incident and were heavily fined. In 1980 the AWB published a political programme, outlining its commitment to the creation of a *Blankevolkstaat* (white people's state). At the same time, it adopted a three-legged swastika as its emblem. But while the AWB drew some of its inspiration from European fascism, Afrikaner nationalism remained the foundation of its appeal. For example, the suggested boundaries for the *Blankevolkstaat* were those of the nineteenth century Boer Republics that had fought to maintain their independence from incorporation in the British Empire. The organisation also stood for the strict maintenance of racial separation. In the past, such a commitment would hardly have distinguished the AWB from the National Party.

However, with the election of P.W.Botha as Prime Minister in 1978, the ruling party had embraced reform and had started to distance itself ideologically from apartheid as conceived by Verwoerd. While Botha's predecessor, B.J.Vorster, had presided over the erosion of segregation in a number of fields, he had justified the changes as compatible with apartheid ideology by using the rubric of multi-nationalism. Thus, permission had been given to 'international' hotels to admit guests of different races. Botha's abandonment of fundamental aspects of the ideology transformed the political prospects of the extreme right. The HNP achieved a breakthrough in the 1981 general election, securing 14.3 per cent of the national vote compared to 3 per cent in 1977. However, it failed to win a single seat under the first past the post electoral system. A smaller right-wing party picked up another 1.4 per cent of the vote.[7]

That was followed in 1982 by a further split in the National Party over the issue of constitutional reform, leading to the formation of the Conservative Party under the leadership of the former leader of the National Party in the Transvaal, Andries Treurnicht. The Conservative Party quickly became the dominant force on the extreme right of the political spectrum. The government presented its constitutional proposals as a step towards power sharing with the Coloured and Indian communities, who were to be represented in separate chambers of a tricameral parliament, though in fact they ensured continuing white control of the political system. However, a few people on the extreme right took the government at its word and saw the new constitution as an irreversible step justifying resort to violence. In 1983 two former members of the AWB were convicted under the Internal Security Act of planning bombing attacks on multi-racial hotels and, more significantly, the offices of the President's Council, the embodiment of 'power sharing' under the new constitution. In the same year Eugene Terre Blanche and a number of other AWB leaders were convicted of terrorism on the basis of the illegal possession of arms and received suspended sentences, while the government announced an inquiry by the Ministry of Law and Order into the activities of the AWB.

By this time the AWB was acquiring paramilitary trappings with a uniformed bodyguard, the *Blitzkommando*, accompanying the leader in his public appearances. This was the first of many paramilitary units to be established by the AWB. The *Blitzkommando* gave added menace to the increasingly virulent rhetoric Terre Blanche employed after the passage of the new constitution. Nonetheless, the threats of blood flowing in the streets remained couched in the future conditional tense. This was partly because it was still possible for the government to be defeated by constitutional means. Thus, the white electorate still had the power to throw the government out and to reverse the process of change. While Terre Blanche complained that the new constitution meant that the white nation had lost its sovereignty without a shot being fired, in fact, the principle of white self-determination remained largely intact. A further difficulty for the extreme right was that the government sought and secured the support of white voters for the new constitution in a referendum in November 1983. A third of voters opposed the new constitution, though by no means all of these were supporters of the extreme right.

At the same time, the success of both the Conservative Party and the HNP in by-elections in the mid 1980s lent practical weight to a constitutional approach. The Conservative Party won the Soutpansberg by-election in February 1984, while the HNP captured the seat of Sasolburg in October 1985 in a strongly racist campaign fought around the government's repeal of legislation prohibiting marriages across the colour line. The government tried to embarrass the Conservative Party over its close links with the AWB, but these ties were more a reflection of the faith of AWB members in the continuing potency of the ballot box than evidence of the revolutionary intent of the Conservative Party. Furthermore, with the upsurge in township political violence after 1984, it became possible for paramilitary posturing to be presented in a defensive light.

The growing strength of the AWB within the extreme right became evident in the course of 1986, fuelled by a white backlash over the possibility of negotiations between the government and the ANC as a result of a Commonwealth mission to South Africa. AWB members took over a public rally for the National Party in Pietersburg in May that was to have been addressed by the Minister of Foreign Affairs, while the police looked on indifferently. Concern over AWB influence in the security forces had already led to the imposition of a ban on members of the South African Police (SAP) or South African Defence Force (SADF) joining the AWB. At the end of May, an AWB rally at the Voortrekker Monument outside Pretoria to celebrate Republic Day attracted a crowd of 50,000, the largest gathering at the Monument since 1960. These signs of dissent prompted a change in direction by the government, which reimposed the state of emergency lifted earlier in the year and made it clear that there was no prospect of negotiations with the ANC. This was still the government's posture in May 1987 when elections to the white House of Assembly took place. However, the tough stance of the government did not prevent a large swing to the extreme right, with the Conservative Party and the HNP picking up almost 30 per cent of the vote. The election clearly established the dominant position of the Conservative Party within the extreme right. Among the Conservative Party's successful candidates were three members of the AWB. At the same time there was a sharp fall in the vote for the liberal Progressive Federal Party.

The electoral success of the extreme right was reflected in a further proliferation of extreme right pressure groups. The most radical of the new groups to emerge in 1987 was the *Blanke Bevrydingsbeweging* (BBB – white freedom movement). It stood for 'the removal of all non-whites from white South Africa'.[8] However, in the first instance the organisation threatened that its members would enforce residential segregation in areas where the government had turned a blind eye to infringements of the Group Areas Act, so-called 'grey' areas such as Mayfair in Johannesburg. A number of incidents of intimidation followed in Mayfair and elsewhere, resulting in the government's warning the BBB on more than one occasion that it would not be allowed to take the law into its own hands over enforcement of the Group Areas Act. However, in the event the incident that prompted the government to take action against the BBB did not even involve a member of the organisation.

In November 1988, Barend Strydom, a member of the AWB and a former policeman, opened fire on a lunch time crowd of Africans in central Pretoria. Seven people died as a result of the attack. While white vigilantes were suspected of responsibility for a number of other random killings of Africans in 1988, this was the single most serious instance of right-wing vigilante violence during the 1980s. Strydom claimed that he was the leader of the *Wit Wolwe* (White Wolves). There had been speculation in the press at the time about the *Wit Wolwe*, after a claim of responsibility was made in the group's name for a bombing attack on the headquarters of the South African Council of Churches at the end of August 1988. However, it is now known that the bombing of Khotso House was, in fact, a covert police operation. Indeed, the attack had received approval at the highest level, reflected in the fact that the Minister of Law and Order, Adriaan Vlok, appeared at a party to celebrate the deed at Vlakplaas, the headquarters of the police unit responsible. Vlok admitted his responsibility when he applied for amnesty to the Truth and Reconciliation Commission.[9] Strydom described his actions as the start of the *Derde Vryheidsoorlog* (third freedom war), a reference to the fact that Afrikaners commonly referred to the wars between Britain and the Boer Republics prior to the establishment of the Union of South Africa as the first and second freedom wars. In the aftermath of the incident the government banned the BBB.

The major political developments of 1988 were the restrictions placed on the functioning of 17 anti-apartheid organisations including the United Democratic Front (UDF) in February and the holding of local elections to 'white' municipalities in October 1988. The two were connected. While the first indicated that the government intended to rely on security measures to quell township unrest, it was also intended to convince right-wing voters of the toughness of the government's approach. The policy was a failure at both levels. Black opposition was too well entrenched for the banning of organisations to prevent re-organisation of the opposition under the new umbrella of the Mass Democratic Movement (MDM). The National Party suffered further setbacks in by-elections in March. As a consequence it was widely predicted that the government would be routed in the municipal elections. In the event, the Conservative Party's gains were more limited than the by-election results had suggested might be possible. They were very significant, nevertheless, with the Conservative Party winning control of a majority of the municipalities in the Transvaal. In many of cities and towns it won control of, such as Boksburg and Carletonville, the Conservative Party reimposed petty apartheid, denying blacks entry to facilities such as parks, halls and swimming pools. What happened next provided white voters in these towns with a salutary lesson in the country's changing power realities. Where apartheid was reimposed, black consumer boycotts followed, with devastating effects on local retailers.[10]

A general election of all three houses of the tricameral parliament took place in September 1989. By this time, F.W. de Klerk had succeeded P.W.Botha both as leader of the National Party and head of government. The National Party fought the election on the basis of a five year Plan of Action, the aim of which was the creation of a new South Africa through negotiations leading to a political dispensation in which there would be participation by all, with group rights providing a safeguard against domination.[11] This vague formula was accompanied by the promise that any new constitutional principles would be submitted to the (white) electorate before implementation. Furthermore, any changes would have to be approved by the tricameral parliament. The government lost ground to both the extreme right and to the liberal opposition in the election, but retained its overall majority in the white House of Assembly. However, significantly in a number of seats which the Conservative Party had hoped to capture, where Conservative municipal councils had reimposed apartheid, there was actually a swing against the extreme right.[12]

While the tone of the National Party's 1989 campaign differed from that of 1987, there was little hint of the radical change to come, culminating in the package of measures announced by President de Klerk on 2 February 1990. The unbanning of the ANC, PAC and SACP and the promise of Nelson Mandela's imminent release were a considerable shock to the extreme right, which was not mollified in the least by the simultaneous lifting of the ban on the BBB. The tone of the extreme right's response to De Klerk's dramatic initiative was set at a rally in Pretoria on 15 February, four days after Mandela's release, at which the two most prominent slogans on display were 'Hang Mandela' and 'Free Barend'. To many on the extreme right, the unbanning of the ANC and the release of Nelson Mandela appeared to represent the point of no return.

There seemed to be good reasons for taking the threat of extreme right-wing violence seriously. Firstly, the opponents of reform represented a substantial section of the white electorate with the support of close to half of the Afrikaner community. Secondly, there were a number of precedents for resort to violence by radical Afrikaner nationalists. In particular, South Africa's participation in support of Britain in the First World War had prompted a rebellion within the Afrikaner community. Rebel commandos took to the field led by three generals from the Anglo-Boer War at the turn of the century. They were rapidly defeated by government forces, but a total of 332 people died in the rebellion. There was also violent opposition from within the Afrikaner community to the country's participation in the Second World War. This took a variety of forms from street brawling to bombing. Most of the violence was carried out by members of the *Ossewabrandwag* (ox-wagon sentinel), which was formed as a result of Afrikaner nationalist enthusiasm engendered by the celebration of the centenary of the Great Trek in 1938. Thirdly, while de Klerk's bold actions had initially attracted white support, in part because they held out the prospect of an end to international economic sanctions against South Africa, disillusionment grew as it became clear that in the short term liberalisation of political activity had increased rather than reduced the level of disorder. The extent of the disillusionment was underscored by a by-election in June 1990 in Natal in which there was a massive swing among white voters to the Conservative Party.

In the event, the level of violence from the extreme right after the unbanning of the ANC did not match the virulence of its rhetoric. In

April 1990 a number of weapons were stolen from an Air Force arsenal in Pretoria. Piet 'Skiet' Rudolph of the small *Boerestaat* (Boer state) party claimed responsibility for the raid when he released a series of videos calling for the violent overthrow of the Government. This was followed by a spate of bombing attacks on National Party and Democratic Party offices attributed to the underground organisation Rudolph founded, *Orde Boerevolk* (Order of the Boer People). Other targets of extreme right-wing bombers during the year were the British embassy, trade union offices, the homes of Johannesburg city councillors, and newspaper offices. A variety of organisations were involved in white vigilante violence, including the *Orde van die Dood* (Order of Death), which lived up to its name through the random killing of blacks, and the inevitable *Wit Kommando* (White Commando). Rudolph was arrested in September and after calling on his followers to return the stolen weapons announced that he intended to apply for indemnity under the programme agreed between the government and the ANC to bring an end to the 'armed struggle'.

In addition to covert violence, the extreme right was involved in a number of ugly racial confrontations at a local level. The most serious of these took place in the mining town of Welkom in May. It was precipitated by an attempt of a local white vigilante organisation, *Blanke Veiligsheid* (BV – White Safety) to impose a 'white at night' curfew on the town by force. The confrontation spread to the mines themselves, leading at one mine to the deaths of two whites and injuries to 14 Africans. Following the repeal of the Separate Amenities Act in October, ending the legal basis for the segregation of public facilities, there were a large number of incidents of assaults on Africans attempting to use such facilities, particularly in small towns that had elected Conservative councils. According to the Human Rights Commission, the right-wing was responsible for 26 deaths between July and December 1990. However, that was out of a total of 1,811 deaths from political violence during that period.[13]

The relatively small scale of extreme right-wing violence in comparison with other sources of violence remained the pattern throughout the transition, as the figures quoted at the outset of this chapter underline. The main exception to this pattern was the spate of extreme right-wing bomb attacks on the eve of South Africa's first non-racial general election in April 1994, in which 21 people died. Even this did little to disturb the elections which otherwise generally passed off remarkably peacefully. But despite its small scale, fear of extreme right-wing violence persisted throughout the transition. This was partly because of the high profile of some of the incidents involving the extreme right. It was also partly because of continuing threats by leaders of the extreme right to plunge the country into a civil war. Despite their repetition, these threats retained their credibility because of the fragility of the political situation. A further and substantial reason for the perception of the extreme right as a threat to the transition was its links with other groups involved in violence.

The extreme right dubbed 2 February 1990 when President de Klerk announced the unbanning of the ANC and his intention to release Nelson Mandela 'Red Friday'. But even though De Klerk's initiative was seen as a watershed, it did not resolve the extreme right's dilemma over how it should act. In particular, his promise to consult the (white) electorate held out the possibility that the process De Klerk had set in train might yet be defeated through the ballot box. Consequently, a large section of extreme right-wing opinion continued to argue that the best strategy was to rely on constitutional means to defeat the government. Violence, except when it could be presented in a defensive light, was seen as an obstacle to this strategy because it alienated white voters. But not merely were there divisions within the extreme right over means, they were also divided over policy. An increasingly influential section of the extreme right argued that it was no longer realistic to advocate the restoration of apartheid and that the plans the extreme right formulated for the future had to take into account the shift that had taken place in the balance of political forces in the country.

This was an acknowledgement of an important aspect of the dynamic of the reform process. The South African government had faced a crisis of governability since 1976 when the brutal suppression of a protest by schoolchildren in Soweto had sparked off nation-wide unrest. Social and economic reforms followed as the government accepted that repressive measures alone were not sufficient to quell the unrest. However, the government found that the reforms it had introduced produced a shift in the balance of power in the society, which forced the government to make further concessions to the subordinate communities. Adding to the pressure on the government for reform was an accompanying demographic shift in the country's population. During the first 50 years of the country's existence, the white ratio of the population had remained at approximately a fifth of the total. By 1991, the white ratio had fallen to 14.1 per cent and was projected to fall to 11.4 per cent by the year 2000.[14] Another complicating factor in the extreme right's response was uncertainty over the government's intentions. At the time of Mandela's release, the government was still insisting that any future dispensation would have to incorporate the concept of group rights. As the ANC rejected the notion of group rights out of hand, the government's commitment to the concept seemed hard to reconcile with its hopes for a negotiated settlement.[15]

At the start of 1991, the position of the extreme right seemed relatively strong. It enjoyed widespread support among whites. At the same time, the launch of the Inkatha Freedom Party (IFP) in August 1990 presented a challenge to the ANC's domination of the townships. Further, the extreme right claimed persuasively that there was widespread support for its position among whites in the security forces, and especially in the police. By the end of the year, its position had weakened considerably. In February 1991 De Klerk had announced that racially discriminatory legislation would be repealed, maintaining the momentum of reform. In August the AWB announced its intention to confront President de Klerk when he addressed a meeting in Ventersdorp, a stronghold of extreme right-wing opinion. The AWB mobilised over 2,000 of its members for the confrontation. They were met by a large contingent of police. Three AWB members were killed and 58 people injured in the ensuing conflict between the police and AWB paramilitants. The readiness of Afrikaner policemen to open fire on the extreme right undermined a widespread assumption that the extreme right could count on, at the very least, the passivity of the security forces in any conflict with the state. Finally, in December, negotiations began among 19 political parties on a future political dispensation for the country. The Convention for a Democratic South Africa (CODESA) proceeded despite a boycott by the extreme right-wing parties. The extreme right argued that the talks were doomed to failure because of the absence of parties which, the extreme right claimed, enjoyed the support of a majority of whites.

The Conservative Party's capture of the Potchefstroom constituency from the National Party in a by-election in February 1992 appeared to provide a measure of support for that claim. In response President de Klerk was forced to call a referendum on the reform process among white voters, staking the whole future of the process on its outcome. While the ANC objected in principle to the notion of a white veto on the reform process, it did nothing to obstruct the referendum and indeed urged whites to vote 'yes' to the continuation of the reform process. The government in its campaign made great play of the threat of a resumption of international sanctions against South Africa in the event of a 'no' vote and of the link between the extreme right-wing parties and violent paramilitants. The 'yes' campaign took full advantage of the far greater resources at its disposal. For example, 'in full-page advertisements, the AWB was represented by a hooded thug with menacing pose and large calibre revolver and the headline: "Free with every CP vote, the AWB and all they stand for".'[16] These tactics proved successful. The government won the backing of 69 per cent of those who voted, a result further underpinned by a very high turn-out.

The outcome of the March 1992 referendum was a devastating blow to the extreme right. It had always attacked the legitimacy of the reform process on the grounds that it conflicted with white self-determination. White endorsement of the process undercut this position. The parties at CODESA in December 1991 had signed a Declaration of Intent establishing parameters for their negotiations. This included a commitment by all the parties to universal adult suffrage on a common roll of voters in an undivided South Africa. While the government continued to emphasise the importance of minority rights and of the principle of power sharing during the referendum campaign, the CODESA Declaration of Intent left little doubt that whites had endorsed a major shift in power to the previously voteless African majority. This presented the extreme right with the further dilemma as to whether it could safely remain outside of the negotiations on the country's future dispensation.

In the event, there was deadlock in the negotiations at CODESA in May 1992 and a breakdown in relations between the government and the ANC, partly prompted by continuing political violence in the townships and in Natal. In particular, there was deep suspicion within the ANC that the violence was directed towards the weakening of the ANC and enjoyed the support of elements both of the security forces and of the government. The ANC launched a campaign of mass action to put pressure on the government, but it threatened to spiral out of control. In September the government and the ANC stepped back from the brink, signing the Record of Understanding. This signalled the determination of the two sides to reach a political accommodation. It infuriated Chief Buthelezi of the IFP, since it clearly indicated that the government had abandoned the strategy of seeking to promote a leading role for Buthelezi and his party.

Even before the Record of Understanding, the prospect of the resumption of multi-party negotiations had precipitated division within the ranks of the extreme right over the issue of negotiations with the ANC. In August *Afrikaner Volksunie* (AVU – Afrikaner people's union) under Andries Beyers broke from the Conservative Party in order to be able to negotiate with the ANC, which it recognised as representing a majority of the African population. Such realism was a minority position, but an indication of the shift of opinion occurring within the extreme right. It was followed by a change in the approach of the principal organisation on the extreme right, the Conservative Party. Its leader, Andries Treurnicht, persuaded the party that it could not stand aside from negotiations on a new dispensation. As a first step the party participated in a conference to prepare the ground for multi-party negotiations. That paved the way for the party's participation in the Multi-Party Negotiating Forum that got under way in April 1993 at the World Trade Centre outside Johannesburg. At the same time, the breach that had occurred between the National Party government and the IFP as a result of the Record of Understanding created new possibilities for the extreme right. They were reflected in the establishment of the Concerned South Africans Group (COSAG) in October 1992. It included the IFP, the leaders of two of the country's independent homelands, President Lucas Mangope of Bophuthatswana and Brigadier Oupa Gqozo of Ciskei, the Conservative Party, and the AVU. Another indication of changing alignments was De Klerk's suspension or retirement in December of 23 senior officers of the South African Defence Force accused of involvement in efforts to sabotage negotiations.

Throughout this period of tumultuous political change, violence continued to be a significant component of extreme right-wing political activity. For example, there were a spate of bomb attacks attributed to the extreme right during the referendum campaign in 1992. However, the impact of extreme right-wing violence remained slight until Easter Saturday, 10 April 1993. On that day a Polish immigrant with extreme right-wing sympathies and connections, Janusz Walus, shot dead an immensely popular ANC leader and general secretary of the SACP, Chris Hani, at his home in Boksburg near Johannesburg. A neighbour of Hani witnessed the slaying and was able to give the police the number of the vehicle used by the assassin. Walus was quickly picked up by the police. His arrest was followed by that of a prominent member of the Conservative Party, Clive Derby-Lewis and his wife, Gaye. The speed of the police investigation owed much to the opportunistic nature of the murder. Walus was on a mission of surveillance when he took advantage of the fact that Hani's bodyguard had been sent home for Easter.

Hani was a much loved and admired figure among the voteless. He had a huge following among the militant youth in the townships because of his role in the armed wing of the ANC and SACP, *Umkhonto we Sizwe* (MK). In this role he had seen action as far back as the late

1960s, when the ANC had made common cause with Zimbabwean nationalists to fight the Smith regime in Rhodesia. By the time of the legalisation of the ANC in February 1990, Hani's exploits as a guerrilla spanning a twenty year period had become the stuff of legend. At the same time, Hani was a strong supporter of the ANC leadership's decision to seek a negotiated settlement with the National Party government and was seen as a crucial figure for selling a settlement in the townships.

Hani's assassination provoked a wave of anger that threatened to engulf the country in violence. The situation was presented in the media as a major crisis in the country's progress towards democracy. Typical of the coverage was the lead story in *The Guardian Weekly* by David Beresford, which described South Africa as 'poised for racial confrontation'.[17] A month later Beresford reassessed this judgement in an article entitled 'Shards of optimism grow out of crises'.[18] In fact, the crisis produced a very large shift in power towards the ANC. It underlined Mandela's indispensability to the country's future political stability. This was well described by Allister Sparks:

> As the crisis swelled, there was little that De Klerk could do to calm the nation; but Mandela could, for they were his people who were aggrieved. He went on national television at the height of the furore and issued a moving appeal to whites and blacks to close ranks and prevent their emotions from destroying their joint future.[19]

To militants who wanted Hani's death avenged, Mandela pointed out that the assassin was a recently arrived Eastern European immigrant and that the neighbour who came to the assistance of the Hani family an Afrikaner. Far from furthering the aims of the extreme right, the assassination of Hani ended a period of drift in the negotiating process which had threatened to weaken the ANC's position.

The spur given by the crisis to the negotiating process was reflected in the setting on 3 June of a provisional date (27 April 1994) for the country's first non-racial democratic elections. This was despite protests from COSAG. The setting of a date for elections effectively place a time limit on the negotiations on the other constitutional issues. As Adam, Slabbert and Moodley explain, 'once the Nationalists had agreed to Slovo's proposal of an election date *before* having settled most contentious issues, they had handed the initiative to their opponents and had to go along with their proposals'.[20] The prospect of the date's confirmation by the Multi-Party Negotiating Forum prompted a further high profile act of political violence by the extreme right. On 25 June, over three thousand members of the AWB, some in khaki, others in the black uniforms of the AWB's elite paramilitary unit, the *Ystergarde* (Iron Guard) invaded the World Trade Centre, venue for the Multi-Party Negotiating Forum. They used a yellow armoured vehicle to smash their way into the building through its plate-glass frontage. The protesters took over the negotiating chamber, hurling abuse at any delegates to the talks they encountered, but most especially African delegates regardless of their political affiliation. The police charged with guarding the talks did not intervene, justifying their inaction on the grounds that any attempt to have arrested protesters would have endangered lives, since the AWB paramilitants were heavily armed. After having disrupted the proceedings of the Multi-Party Negotiating Forum for the day, the protesters eventually withdrew.

The protesters achieved massive publicity. The pictures of their dramatic entry into the World Trade Centre were relayed round the world. However, in other respects, they achieved relatively little. They did not prevent the confirmation on 2 July of the election date by 19 of the 26 parties participating in the Multi-Party Negotiating Forum. Further, their actions strained relations within COSAG, due to the overtly racist behaviour of many of the AWB protesters. But a troubling aspect of the incident for the government and the ANC was the behaviour of the police, notwithstanding the case that could be made for the tactics they adopted. It reinforced the need for ways to be found to defuse the threat posed by the extreme right, especially in the light of its tactical alliance with the IFP and two of the independent homelands. The persistence of that alliance, despite strains, was underscored by the launch of the Freedom Alliance in October 1993, a repackaging of COSAG designed to enhance its popular appeal.

An important development in extreme right-wing politics preceded the dramatic events at the World Trade Centre. This was the formation in May 1993 of the *Afrikaner Volksfront* (AVF – Afrikaner people's front). Headed by four generals, the AVF provided an umbrella for a multitude of extreme right-wing organisations. The formation of the AVF was partly a response to the polarisation that occurred as a result of the unrest that followed Hani's assassination. It also reflected a crystallisation of the objectives of the extreme right into demands for the creation of a *volkstaat* or Afrikaner homeland. This approach chimed in well with the regionalist demands for self-determination of other members of the Freedom Alliance. These demands were backed up by the threat of a boycott of the country's first non-racial elections that would have been damaging to the legitimacy of the whole process.

Potent though the weapon of an election boycott was, it had two major disadvantages. Firstly, it alienated international opinion sympathetic to the case for federalism, which provided the most moderate gloss on the demands of the extreme right. Secondly, it ran counter to the strong desire of Africans in every region of the country to participate in the election. Indeed, the attempt of President Lucas Mangope to prevent the people in Bophuthatswana from taking part in the election brought about a revolution. After Mangope announced that Bophuthatswana would not be taking part in the election, civil servants in the independent homeland went on strike. When the police joined in the strike, conditions became increasingly chaotic. Mangope then appealed for assistance from his allies in the Freedom Alliance. Had the effort to help Mangope been entirely channelled through the generals of the AVF, the outcome might have been different. It was the intervention of the AWB that doomed the Mangope regime. A force of several hundred AWB paramilitants entered Bophuthatswana after they had been mobilised in response to appeals for assistance for the Mangope government broadcast over the radio station run by the extreme right, Radio Pretoria.

The racism of the AWB members proved their undoing. When AWB members opened fire at random on civilians in Mmabatho, the capital of Bophuthatswana, this proved too much for hitherto loyal members of the Bophuthatswanan Defence Forces. They mutinied, turning their guns on the paramilitants of the AWB. That prompted their rout. In the AWB's retreat from Bophuthatswana on 11 March 1994, two of its members were shot dead in cold blood by Bophuthatswanan policemen in full view of the world's media. The impact was immense. An influential section of the extreme right treated these events as proof of the disutility of violence as a means for furthering the cause of a *volkstaat*. Immediately after the confrontation in Bophuthatswana, General Constand Viljoen in defiance of the majority of the AVF submitted lists of party candidates to the Independent Electoral Commission enabling the extreme right to participate in the elections through the Freedom Front. His action quickly won the support of many of the leading figures on the extreme right.

The overthrow of Mangope put pressure on the other members of the Freedom Alliance. Brigadier Gqozo of Ciskei voluntarily gave up power after civil servants there went on strike. That left Buthelezi and the IFP. Their resistance to the election lasted longest. In fact, the IFP's agreement to participate only came in the week before polling began. The achievement of an inclusive election was not simply the product of the negative pressures on the parties attempting to disrupt the process, it was also the product of positive incentives to participate. Having secured all its principal objectives in the negotiations on the interim constitution, the ANC recognised how important inclusiveness would be to international perceptions of the legitimacy of the elections. It was consequently willing to explore any avenue to secure the participation of the other parties that did not threaten to prevent the achievement of majority rule in a unitary state after the transitional period it had already conceded to secure the National Party's acceptance of the transfer of power.

In the run-up to the election, a series of concessions were made to the other parties. In the case of the extreme right, the ANC and the National Party agreed to an accord with the Freedom Front in early April to ensure its full commitment to the election. The accord provided for the formation after the election of a *volkstaatsraad*, a statutory council consisting of 20 members. In addition, there was provision for an advisory body consisting of 25 elected representatives of local communities from areas where the general election showed there was support for the concept of a *volkstaat*. The two bodies were to report to the Constituent Assembly charged with drawing up the constitution on the feasibility of setting up a *volkstaat*, bearing in mind references in the interim constitution to the principle of self-determination within the context of a united South Africa. What this amounted to was the promise that if the extreme right was able to demonstrate widespread support within the white community, serious efforts would be made to accommodate its demands. However, this impressed neither the Conservative Party nor the AWB, both of which denounced the accord as worthless. They continued to urge a boycott of the election.[21]

The election campaign consequently was a battle for influence over the extreme right between the Freedom Front and the Conservative Party. The defection of nine Conservative M.P.s to the Freedom Front was an indication of its success in this contest. In the election itself, the Freedom Front polled 2.2 per cent of the national vote. It did substantially better in the elections to the nine regional parliaments, with 3.2 per cent of the total votes cast. Ironically, in view of the image of right-wing Afrikaners as farmers, it achieved its best result in the overwhelmingly urban province of Pretoria-Witwatersrand-Vereeniging, where it polled 6.2 per cent of the vote in the regional elections.[22] While the total number of votes cast for the Freedom Front in the national elections was less than half that of the 'no' vote in the 1992 referendum, the previous benchmark of support for the extreme right, its relatively small share of the vote was, of course, fundamentally a reflection of the fact that the overwhelming majority of the electorate was African. Thus, it has been estimated that in the regional elections, the party polled 41 per cent of the votes of white Afrikaners.[23]

A bomb placed near the ANC regional office in the city centre of Johannesburg on 24 April killed nine people and injured approximately a hundred people. The following day there were bomb attacks on a restaurant in Pretoria, which killed two people and injured 29, and on a taxi rank in Germiston, which killed ten people and injured 41. There were also other bomb attacks mainly directed at property, including two polling stations. However, none of the attacks had any discernible impact upon the process of polling. Reassurance to the public was provided by the early arrest of a number of AWB members in connection with the blasts. From a political perspective, the threat of extreme right-wing violence reinforced the dominance of peace as an election issue. The party that may have been damaged by that was the PAC, with its association with the slogan 'one settler one bullet' contributing to the party's dismal result.

Neither the constitutional nor the violent wing of the extreme right made much of an impression on South African politics after the 1994 elections. The demand for a *volkstaat* made little headway in the deliberations on a new constitution. In February 1996, the *volkstaatraad* presented a report to the Constituent Assembly proposing the creation of a tenth province. However, it did not specify what the boundaries of such an entity should be. In any event, its proposal was rejected by both the ANC and the National Party, with the latter favouring as an alternative the establishment of a commission on cultural affairs to protect the rights of Afrikaners.[24] The fundamental problem for the constitutional extreme right was that the size and nature of the territory that could realistically be demanded for an Afrikaner homeland had little appeal in practice to most Afrikaners, including even the supporters of the extreme right.

Extreme right-wing violence did not cease after the 1994 elections, but threats of civil war had lost their potency, along with their credibility. The most serious incidents of violence attributed to the extreme right were the assassination in November 1994 of a former leader of the main Dutch Reformed Church, Professor Johan Heyns, and two bomb attacks in Wellington in the Western Cape which killed four and injured 60, which were claimed in the name of *Boere Aanval Troepe* (Boer attack troops). The threat of further extreme right-wing violence was underlined by the interception by the police of weapons destined for the extreme right. The arms had been sent to South

Africa by American extreme right-wingers.[25] The international links of the South African extreme right were also highlighted in a series of three articles in the anti-fascist monthly published in Britain, *Searchlight* in 1996.[26] The articles give details of the recruitment of extreme right-wing mercenaries in Europe, sent down the line to South Africa ahead of the 1994 elections. The intention was that they would assist the AWB in seizing part of the western Transvaal to provide the base of a *volkstaat*. The plot foundered, though as a precaution the government declared a state of emergency in the area during the election period.

South Africa has often been compared to other deeply divided societies such as Northern Ireland and Israel. It is possible to make the comparison at a number of levels. In particular, there are a number of parallels between the violence of the extreme right in South Africa and Loyalist violence in Northern Ireland during the province's latest troubles between 1968 and 1994. In both situations, right-wing violence was a response, in the first instance, to reform initiated from within the dominant community as well as to the erosion of segregation between the communities. In both cases there were numerous instances of violence being directed in a totally indiscriminate manner against members of the subordinate community. Another similarity between the paramilitaries in the two cases was their links with elements in the security forces, especially in the lower ranks of those drawn from the dominant community. In both there were allegations of collusion between the security forces and right-wing paramilitaries that led to suspicion being cast on the role and attitude of government, though the most common charge against government was of failure to control rogue members or elements of the security forces.

But for all the similarities between the two cases, there was a very substantial difference between them. The scale of extreme right-wing violence during South Africa's transition never reached the level or intensity of Loyalist violence during Northern Ireland's troubles. There are a number of possible explanations that can be given for the difference. Firstly, the historical experience of vigilantism in the two societies was different. In Northern Ireland the threat of force in the form of the Ulster Volunteer Force helped to stave off the imposition of Irish home rule before the First World War, establishing a precedent for the successful use of violence by the dominant community. By contrast, the National Party rejected the use of such tactics by Afrikaners during the Second World War and its insistence on following a constitutional road to power was vindicated by its electoral victory in 1948. Secondly, the numerical preponderance of the subordinate community in South Africa meant that indiscriminate violence against members of the subordinate community appeared (and was in practice) more obviously self-defeating than in a situation where the subordinate community was a minority. Thirdly, the fact that agencies of the South African state were so active over the years in conducting covert warfare against the government's political adversaries provided a further reason for restraint by the white extreme right. Fourthly, although the process of reform was much more far reaching in the South African case, every step on the way was carried through by a government elected by whites. In Northern Ireland, the dominant community lost its veto on reform within the province when the British government imposed direct rule in March 1972. This provoked a sharp escalation in the level of Loyalist violence.

The primary agency for political change in South Africa was the realisation among whites that they had to come to terms with the shift in power that was taking place in the country as a result of demographic and economic change. Such pressure was not present to the same degree in Northern Ireland, though sufficient to provide the basis of a negotiated settlement in 1998. In South Africa, even the extreme right was influenced by the power realities. This was not unprecedented. A similar process of change had taken place in other African societies where a white minority had wielded power over an African majority. However, as the Algerian case in the early 1960s shows, the potentiality did exist for a catastrophic ending. A variety of factors contributed to the relative smoothness of the change in the South African case, including a favourable international climate for such change. Among the most important internal factors were the tactics employed by the ANC to defuse the threat from the extreme right, most particularly the encouragement the ANC gave to the pursuit of a constitutional option by the extreme right. This was a reflection of the fact that the ANC did not underestimate the potential threat from the extreme right during the transition.

Of the actions taken by the extreme right, the assassination of Chris Hani had arguably the greatest impact on the transition. In particular, it can be argued that the crisis created by the murder had an importance equal to that created by the Boipatong and Bisho massacres in determining the outcome of the transition. However, because it came after the Record of Understanding, its significance has tended to be overlooked. In his book, *Forty Lost Years*, Dan O'Meara gets the date of assassination wrong. He places it in April 1992, treating it as a contributory factor in the breakdown of the CODESA negotiations.[27]

Another experienced analyst of South African politics made a similar error in a lecture he gave in 1997 on the South African experience. Frederik van Zyl Slabbert correctly dated the Hani assassination, but then argued that it had contributed to the Record of Understanding, placing that agreement a year late in September 1993.[28] In fact, although the Record of Understanding and the other agreements reached by the National Party and the ANC at the end of 1992 presaged the outcome of 1994, it took the further crisis caused by the assassination of Chris Hani to ensure it by demonstrating that order depended on the leader of the ANC. In sharp contrast to Yitzhak Rabin's assassin, Walus helped to precipitate what he was trying to prevent.

Notes to Chapter 4

1   Sir Arthur Conan Doyle, *The Memoirs of Sherlock Holmes*, Penguin, Harmondsworth 1950, p.28.

2   Johann van Rooyen, *Hard Right: The New White Power in South Africa*, I.B.Tauris, London 1994, p.211.

3   *Supplement to Special Report SR-13: Three Years of Destabilisation*, Human Rights Commission, Johannesburg 1993.

4   See, for example, Peter H.Merkl and Leonard Weinberg (eds), *The Revival of Right-Wing Extremism in the Nineties*, Frank Cass, London 1997.

5   See, for example, the survey evidence examined by Jannie Gagiano, 'Ruling group cohesion' in Hermann Giliomee and Jannie Gagiano (eds), *The Elusive Search for Peace: South Africa, Israel and Northern Ireland*, Oxford University Press, Cape Town 1990, pp.191–208.

6   See J.H.P.Serfontein, *Die Verkrampte Aanslag*, Human & Rousseau, Kaapstad en Pretoria 1970.

7   Van Rooyen, *op. cit.*, pp.119–20.

8   Quoted in Carole Cooper, Jennifer Shindler, Colleen McCaul, Robin Hamilton, Mary Beale, Alison Clemans, Lou-Marie Kruger, Michael Markovitz, Jon-Marc Seimon, Pierre Brouard and Glen Shelton, *Race Relations Survey 1987/88*, South African Institute of Race Relations, Johannesburg 1988, p.718.

9   Jacques Pauw, *Into the Heart of Darkness: Confessions of Apartheid's Assassins*, Jonathan Ball Publishers, Johannesburg 1997, pp.75–6.

10 Van Rooyen, *op. cit.*, pp.178–9.

11 *Five-year Plan of Action of the National Party 1989–1994*, National Party, Cape Town 1989.

12 Van Rooyen, *op. cit.*, p.180.

13   *Back to the Laager: The Rise of White Rightwing Violence in South Africa*, Legal Education Action Project, Institute of Criminology, University of Cape Town, Cape Town 1991, p.12.

14   The figures are cited in *South Africa 1993*, South Africa Foundation, Johannesburg 1992, p.9.

15   See, for example, Nelson Mandela, *Long Walk to Freedom*, Macdonald Purnell, Randburg 1994, p.544–5.

16   Van Rooyen, *op. cit.*, p.154.

17   David Beresford, 'Hani killing stuns South Africa', *The Guardian Weekly* (London), 18 April 1993.

18   David Beresford, 'Shards of optimism grow out of crises', *The Guardian Weekly* (London), 16 May 1993.

19   Allister Sparks, *Tomorrow Is Another Country: The Inside Story of South Africa's Negotiated Revolution*, Struik, Sandton 1994, p.189.

20   Heribert Adam, Frederik van Zyl Slabbert and Kogila Moodley, *Comrades in Business: Post-Liberation Politics in South Africa*, Tafelberg, Cape Town 1997, p.54.

21   (21) Andrew Reynolds (ed.), *Election '94 South Africa: The campaigns, results and future prospects*, David Philip, Cape Town 1994, p.97.

22   (22) *Ibid.*, p.208.

23   *Ibid.*, p.104. The figure should be treated as a rough estimate. See Chapter 6.

24   Elizabeth Sidiropoulus, Anthea Jeffrey, Shaun MacKay, Herma Forgey, Cheryl Chipps and Terence Corrigan, *South Africa Survey 1996/97*, South African Institute of Race Relations, Johannesburg 1997, p.549.

25   *The Star* (Johannesburg), 22 November 1994.

26   *Searchlight* (London), No. 253 July 1996, No. 254 August 1996, No. 255 September 1996.

27   Dan O'Meara, *Forty Lost Years: The apartheid state and the politics of the National Party, 1948–1994*, Ravan Press, Randburg 1996, p.411.

28   Frederik van Zyl Slabbert's lecture, 'The South African experience', was delivered as part of a series of lectures on the theme of openings to peace organised by the Institute of Irish Studies, University of Liverpool. Each lecture was delivered to audiences in Liverpool, Dublin and Belfast. Slabbert gave his in October 1997.

CHAPTER 5

Buthelezi and the UNITA Option

The conflict between the ANC and the IFP can be divided into four phases: the period between 1985 and 1990 before the unbanning of the ANC, when the conflict involved the ANC's internal surrogates; the first stage of the transition from De Klerk's speech on 2 February to the Record of Understanding between De Klerk and Mandela on 26 September 1992; the second stage of the transition of cooperation between the ANC and the National Party and consequent alienation of the IFP from the government; and the period since Mandela's inauguration as President of South Africa of a gradual de-escalation of the conflict between the two parties. This chapter will consider each of these phases, while concentrating on the implications of the conflict for the transition itself.

At the outset, an explanation of the term, UNITA option, and its association with the IFP and its leader, Chief Mangosuthu Buthelezi, is necessary. The analogy became commonplace following the Record of Understanding. This agreement raised hopes of a constitutional settlement between the two major political forces in the country, the ANC and the National Party, but at the price of the alienation of the IFP, which denounced the agreement in the most strident terms. From this point on, the IFP became the core of opposition to the transition. It linked up under the loose banner of the Concerned South Africans Group (COSAG) with a number of other reactionary and extreme right-wing leaders and groups, including Chief Lucas Mangope of Bophuthatswana, Brigadier Oupa Gqozo of Ciskei, the Conservative Party and the *Afrikaner Volksunie* (AVU).

The Record of Understanding in South Africa coincided with the holding of multi-party elections in Angola on 29 and 30 September

1992. The two developments increased optimism about the future of southern Africa as a whole. However, these hopes were dashed in the case of Angola by the refusal of *Uniao Nacional para a Independencia de Total de Angola* (UNITA – National Union for the Total Independence of Angola) to accept the outcome of the elections after the party was defeated by the governing party, *Movimento Popular de Libertacao de Angola* (MPLA – Popular Movement for the Liberation of Angola) in the elections to the National Assembly and in which the party's candidate for President, Jonas Savimbi, was outpolled by the MPLA candidate, President Jose Eduardo dos Santos. The vote for President dos Santos fell just short of the 50 per cent of the vote that he required to secure election in the first round of voting. He polled 49.57 per cent of the vote to 40.07 per cent for Savimbi. The resumption of the civil war after UNITA's denunciation of the elections prevented the holding of a second round of voting. The MPLA won the legislative elections with 57.85 per cent of the vote and 129 seats to UNITA's 31.39 per cent and 70 seats.

After October 1992, South Africa became haunted by the example of the breakdown of Angola's transition to multi-party democracy. Even Mandela's inauguration as President of South Africa and the head of a new government of national unity, which included the IFP, did not completely exorcise the spectre. After the Angolan elections, journalistic comparisons of Angola and South Africa became common. They tended to centre on comparison between the personality of the leader of UNITA, Jonas Savimbi and that of the leader of the IFP, Chief Mangosuthu Buthelezi, though they have also compared the strategies of the two parties, with reference being made to the IFP's 'UNITA option' or to Buthelezi's 'Savimbi option'. Some examples will illustrate the thrust of the comparison. The journalist, Daniel Reed, referred to the 'Savimbi option' on the final page of his 1994 book, *Beloved Country: South Africa's Silent Wars*, in the context of the discussion of the possibility of secession by KwaZulu-Natal. He concluded that '[t]he Zulu civil war in Natal will continue to present the biggest single obstacle to peace in South Africa',[1] but doubted the IFP's military capacity to prevail against the South African security forces.

After the IFP's representatives walked out of the multi-party negotiations at the World Trade Centre in Kempton Park in July 1993, there were continued efforts by both government and the ANC to involve the IFP in the process through separate consultation. The rationale for these secret talks was explained by Billy Paddock in *Business Day* as follows: 'ANC and government negotiators are also mindful of the threat of Buthelezi taking the "Savimbi option", especially with his constant "warnings" of a civil war.'[2] Paddock's analysis was underlined by a report in *Business Day* a week later that quoted Buthelezi as saying: 'We are not prepared to accept responsibility for the civil war which we know will be the consequence of allowing a constituent assembly to write our constitution.'[3] The same piece reported Mandela as asserting that the mistake countries such as Angola and Mozambique had made after independence was fighting rather than negotiating with the opposition.

Concern that what had happened in Angola set a precedent for South Africa was expressed in a variety of contexts. When President de Klerk was interviewed by journalists in October 1993, he was asked: 'How do you prevent a Savimbi-type situation after an election?'.[4] Three weeks before the South African elections, the editor of *The Star*'s Africa Service, Gerald L'Ange argued that 'events in South Africa are taking this country perilously close to the Angolan scenario and away from the Namibian one'.[5] An article in *Business Day* in November 1993 by Paulette Bethlehem on the seemingly innocuous subject of providing voters with the necessary information to cast their ballots was headed: 'Voter education must ward off ghost of Angola'.[6] Rob Amato's 1994 instant book on the interim constitution also mentioned ' "Renamo" or "Savimbi" options', but he dismissed them as 'romantic war "options" from the north' without 'much real attraction to South Africans'.[7]

After the IFP's eleventh-hour decision to participate in the elections, John Carlin of *The Independent* wrote the following:

> If any dangers still lurk, they will surface after the elections. All polls indicate that Inkatha will be defeated by the ANC in Natal, and that the majority of Zulus will not vote for Inkatha. In such circumstances Chief Buthelezi might cry foul in the manner of Jonas Savimbi in Angola.[8]

In the event, the IFP won a narrow majority of the votes in KwaZulu-Natal, though Buthelezi did cry foul before the results were announced, laying the ground for a possible rejection of the outcome if it proved unsatisfactory from his perspective.[9] In an article discussing concerns over the manipulation of the outcome, Denis Beckett wrote the following in *The Star*:

> Better for us all to keep Inkatha sweet and on board and a nation elated, than send them off in dudgeon like Savimbi to lead us to trauma like Angola. The only thing is: I would appreciate knowing what cooking went into the brew.[10]

It is clear from these examples that the comparison with Savimbi cast Buthelezi in a negative light. Admittedly, negative comparison of two leaders was not new. Gerhard Mare headed the conclusion of his 1992 book, *Ethnicity and Politics in South Africa*, 'Jamba at Nkandla?'.(12) In it Mare discusses the implications of IFP control over the administration of the KwaZulu homeland and concludes:

> This undemocratic control over one of the structures of apartheid has allowed Inkatha access to national negotiations. It could also allow Inkatha to reject or ignore any regional or national majority vote against it. This raises the spectre of a Jamba, the bush headquarters of Unita in Angola, at Nkandla, the Zululand forest headquarters for Bambatha in his last stand against centralised white power at the turn of the century.[11]

Mare's analysis, in contrast to the journalistic examples quoted above, dates from before October 1992. The book was first published in South Africa in 1992 and cites speeches by Buthelezi up to January 1992. A much earlier instance of the comparison is quoted by Kane-Berman. This was from a broadcast on ANC-in-exile's Radio Freedom in November 1986, which declared:

> It is clear that Gatsha [Buthelezi] is being groomed by the West and the racist regime to become a Savimbi in a future free South Africa. The onus is on the people of South Africa to neutralise the Gatsha snake, which is poisoning the people of South Africa. It needs to be hit on the head.[12]

However, while there were superficial similarities between the comparisons made between Buthelezi and Savimbi in the different periods, there was a huge difference in political context. The point of departure of comparisons in the 1980s was their militantly anti-Communist and pro-Western outlook and this provided the basis for the drawing of favourable as well as negative parallels between the two leaders and their parties. After 1992, they were primarily compared as ethno-nationalists whose political ambitions and secessionist inclinations were seen a threat to the continued existence of South Africa and Angola, a perspective that inspired far fewer positive comparisons. These issues are explored further below, but at this point some background on each case is needed to bring out the resonances of the analogy between the two conflicts and to account for its influence on the second stage of the South African transition.

Mangosuthu Buthelezi was born on 27 August 1928 in Mahlabatini, Natal, heir to the chieftainship of the Buthelezi clan. After a childhood in a traditional household, he entered Fort Hare University in the Eastern Cape in 1948, where he joined the ANC Youth League. After expulsion from Fort Hare for participating in a student political protest, he completed his education at the University of Natal before returning to Mahlabatini to take up his position as Chief. In 1970 the KwaZulu Territorial Authority was set up and Buthelezi became its Chief Executive Officer. When KwaZulu became a fully fledged homeland in 1977 (a self-governing territory within the Republic of South Africa, in accordance with the Bantu Homelands Constitution Act of 1971), he became its Chief Minister.

Inkatha was founded in March 1975. An organisation of the same name had existed in the 1920s and there had been other attempts to revive the movement without success. Its emergence was described as follows by the South African Institute of Race Relations annual survey for 1975:

> In mid-1975 information was released about a body called Inkatha YakwaZulu, described as a "national cultural liberation movement", of which Chief Buthelezi was president. The aim was stated to be to promote "African democracy", considered to be more suited to the Zulu way of life than was Western-type democracy. Membership of Inkatha would be open to all Zulus. There would be one political party only. Paid-up party members would not be precluded from expressing disagreement with courses of action discussed at meetings, decisions being made on the basis of consensus. Members would, however, have to refrain from making public criticism of the movement, its actions, or activities of members in connection with the affairs of the organisation.[13]

However, a different picture of the organisation, now described as Inkatha Yenkululeko Yesizwe, is given in the 1977 survey. Its membership was described as 'open to all Africans over 18 years of age' and the organisation characterised (in the view of its leadership) as 'a non-violent liberation movement, committed to African solidarity but recognising the need for justice for people of all racial groups, and the necessity for both black and white participation in the future of S.A.'.[14] The same survey reported that pressure had been put on Buthelezi to restrict membership to Zulus. It reported Buthelezi's public response as being 'that while the National Party did not exclude English-speaking South Africans and Jews, in the same way Inkatha could not exclude other Africans'.[15]

One factor in the organisation's ambiguity on the issue of ethnicity was its relationship with the banned ANC. In the early years, Inkatha played up the idea that it represented a reincarnation of the banned organisation and even the notion that the organisation had been set up with the sanction of the ANC. It adopted symbols associated with the ANC, including its colours. Buthelezi constantly referred to the fact that he had been a member of the ANC Youth League. He appears to have hoped that a meeting between the two organisations in London in late 1979 would pave the way to the ANC's public recognition of Inkatha's legitimacy.[16] But even after the deterioration of its relations with the ANC in exile, Inkatha continued to stress the link, drawing a distinction between the ANC's founding fathers and what it derisively referred to as the external mission of the ANC. A second factor was that Buthelezi's ambitions extended beyond simply being seen as the leader of what was an ethnic minority within South Africa, even if, as Buthelezi constantly emphasised, it was the largest group in the country.

A third factor was the realisation that stress on the political importance of ethnicity did not go down well with potential political allies in the struggle against apartheid. This was particularly the case abroad, as the following extract from an early speech of Buthelezi in Holland in September 1975 illustrates:

I realise that some people might think that when I talk of freedom and liberation, I am thinking of the Zulu as distinct from my other African brothers and sisters in South Africa. This is far from being the case. There is no Zulu freedom that is distinct from the black man's freedom in South Africa. Black opposition has no ethnic boundaries. We have one common destiny as black people. We have indeed a common destiny even with our white countrymen who have rejected this idea for several generations.[17]

As the organisation's profile developed, it became increasingly careful to couch its policies in universalist terms. This was particularly important in the context of Buthelezi's efforts to woo opinion in the West, which included a meeting with President Carter in 1977. Thus, Inkatha continued to stress its adherence to the goal of one person one vote in a unitary state. When the Buthelezi Commission, which had been set up at the initiative of the Inkatha Central Committee, reported in March 1982, Inkatha portrayed its willingness to treat the Commission's consociational proposals as a basis for negotiations with the government as an indication of its readiness to pursue all peaceful avenues for political advance, rather than a change in its attitude towards majoritarianism as a principle.

However, in practice, in the course of the 1980s, Inkatha became increasingly conservative in its political orientation. The shift aided rather than hindered Buthelezi in the West, given the dominance of conservative opinion in Britain and the United States. Buthelezi's strong opposition to economic sanctions and his anti-Communism enhanced his popularity on the right, reflected in a triumphal visit to the United States in 1986. At the same time, he continued to present himself and Inkatha as leading opponents of apartheid. In particular, Buthelezi vigorously opposed the tricameral constitution implemented in 1984. However, he was outflanked in his opposition to the new constitution by the emergence of the United Democratic Front (UDF), which was formed in August 1983.

With a far better claim to constitute the internal wing of the ANC, the UDF presented a serious challenge to Inkatha's prospects of establishing itself as the leading anti-apartheid political force within South Africa. An early indication that political competition between Inkatha and the UDF might lead to violence occurred in October 1983 when in response to student protests, an Inkatha youth brigade launched an attack on the University of Zululand. Five people were killed and over a hundred injured in the episode. After the forma-tion of the Congress of South African Trade Unions (COSATU) in November 1985, Inkatha formed a rival trade union organisation in May 1986, the United Workers Union of South Africa (UWUSA). This gave a further dimension to the rivalry between Inkatha and forces increasingly clearly aligned to the ANC. By the late 1980s, political violence associated with this rivalry had reached the proportions of a civil war in the Natal Midlands. The annual figures for deaths in the Natal violence between 1985 and 1995 given by Anthea Jeffrey in her detailed study of the conflict are set out in Table 5.1.

As the figures underline, the unbanning of the ANC and other political organisations and the freeing of Nelson Mandela in 1990 led to an escalation in the level of violence in the province. Further, the province was not the only arena of conflict between the ANC and the Inkatha. The conflict spread to the industrial heartland of the country, Pretoria-Witwatersrand-Vereeniging, in July 1990, coinciding with Inkatha's decision to launch itself as a nation-wide political party under the name, Inkatha Freedom Party (IFP). The fighting first erupted in the Vaal Triangle, then quickly spread to the East Rand townships of Kathlehong, Thokoza and Vosloorus, where there had long been tensions between hostel dwellers, many of them Zulu-speaking migrants from Natal, and other township residents. Close to two million people lived in these townships. Between 1990 and 1994, approximately 3,000 people died in political violence in this area.[18]

Fissures between migrant workers who lived in single-sex hostels and constituted the poorest and most marginal element in the labour force and the permanently settled urban population had become

Table 5.1

Number of people killed in violence in KwaZulu-Natal, 1985–1995

Year	Total
1985	117
1986	101
1987	451
1988	912
1989	1279
1990	1811
1991	1684
1992	1427
1993	1489
1994	1464
1995	684

Source: Anthea Jeffrey, *The Natal Story: 16 Years of Conflict*, South African Institute of Race Relations, Johannesburg 1997, pp.1–2.

apparent in the unrest in the townships in 1976–77. They became a source of conflict once again with the onset of unrest in the townships in September 1984. In the mid 1980s Inkatha injected itself into this conflict by championing those who opposed the use of militant tactics such as stayaways to oppose the government. In particular, it offered protection to those accused of collaboration with the government, such as those elected in the widely boycotted elections to municipal authorities in November 1983. The abolition of influx control in 1986 improved the position of migrant workers and facilitated the development of family life within the hostels. However, a social divide still remained between the hostels and the rest of the township, a divide that the perception of many of the hostels as the preserve of a particular ethnic group tended to reinforce. These divisions played a part in the political competition between the ANC and IFP, facilitating the development of ANC-aligned self-defence units (SDUs) and IFP-aligned self-protection units (SPUs).

The conflict between the ANC and the IFP in Natal can also be related to social divisions, with the ANC's strength lying in the urban areas among unionised labour and the IFP's stronghold being the KwaZulu homeland, the administration of which it controlled. Another dimension to the conflict commonly identified was a generational battle between militant youth and elders upholding traditional tribal authority. The battleground between the parties

where most of the violence was concentrated lay 'along the border of
the KwaZulu homeland on the margins of the industrialised centres
along the Pietermaritzburg-Durban corridor', areas that were 'home
to mass informal settlements'.[19] Morris and Hindson have described
how Inkatha gained a foothold in these settlements as follows:

> From 1985 onwards, Inkatha increasingly turned to recruiting shack dwell-
> ers as it lost ground within the formal townships of Natal. Since shack
> dwellers have no legal rights to the land, de facto control is established
> through their capacity to defend a piece of ground. In these circumstances,
> shack dwellers turn readily to local squatter leaders and warlords with
> whom they trade obedience and levies, tribute and other payments for
> residential security. These warlords have turned to Inkatha and the
> KwaZulu authorities to uphold their de facto rights to land and to
> consolidate their control in the shantytowns.[20]

However, none of these generalisations about the social sources of
support for the parties fit perfectly with actual political affiliations,
which reflect many more factors, including issues specific to particular
localities. Taylor and Shaw identify apartheid as the root cause of the
violence. Their argument is that the mass informal settlements created by apartheid constituted breeding grounds for conflict because
of their desperate poverty.[21]

But while the explanation of the social context in which the violence
occurred aids understanding of it and sometimes these conditions
may be a source of violence that is independent of the rivalry between
the parties, so that the dividing line between political and other forms
of violence becomes difficult if not impossible to draw, political rivalry
between the parties still provides by far the most convincing explanation of the violence. Thus, in relation to the rise in violence before
the IFP's decision to participate in the 1994 elections and the fall
immediately thereafter, Johnston concludes justifiably:

> [I]t is difficult to see the coincidence between rising and falling death
> tolls and first a crescendo and then a (temporary) settlement of political
> conflict as anything but an indication that the political conflict thesis
> should be taken more seriously than Shaw and Taylor claim.[22]

In January 1991, Buthelezi and Mandela met in Durban and signed a
joint declaration on behalf of their parties calling on their members
and supporters to cease using violence against each other. However,
this agreement failed to stem the violence and in April 1991 the ANC
sent the government an ultimatum threatening to suspend negotiations unless it took steps to deal with the violence. Buthelezi described

the ultimatum as a recipe for civil war. He was particularly perturbed by ANC allegations that township violence was being orchestrated to elevate the importance of the IFP politically. The credibility of these allegations received a boost in July 1991, with revelations of government financing of the IFP. A further effort to stem bloodshed was made by the leaders of the main political parties in September 1991 with the signing of the National Peace Accord. It established local and regional peace committees to mediate in areas of conflict. In addition a standing commission of inquiry into political violence was established. It became known as the Goldstone Commission after Justice Richard Goldstone who was appointed its chairman in October.

The issue of security-force complicity in the violence between the ANC and the IFP was a source of controversy throughout the transition. It was encapsulated in the concept of the existence of a 'third force' fomenting the violence. While this conveyed the idea of a sinister hidden hand behind the violence, it also appeared to suggest that the elements in the security forces engaged in this activity were pursuing an agenda of their own, independent of, if not contrary to the policies of the government. However, third force activities clearly had their origin in official policy, in particular P.W.Botha's total strategy to counter a total onslaught. Jacques Pauw describes the objective behind the establishment of the third force as follows:

> The idea of a 'third force' was a brilliant stroke: to use Inkatha as a bulwark against the United Democratic Front and ANC by building up the organisation as a counter-revolutionary force. Its impis would be organised into death squads by training, arming and supporting them. This would allow the architects of this evil plan to foment 'black-on-black' violence, yet shrug their shoulders and tell the world that blacks were not capable of ruling. The idea of forming a 'third force' goes back to the mid-1980s when the struggle against apartheid reached unprecedented levels. The state adopted equally drastic measures to counter these threats, which included the use of terrorism and guerrilla warfare.[23]

In support of his account Pauw quotes directly from minutes of a meeting of the State Security Council in May 1986 at which the formation of the third force was discussed. The name, third force, was proposed so that its activities did not tarnish the Defence Force or the police.

In the first stage of the transition, the financing, training and arming of Inkatha continued with the evident approval of high-ranking officers in the security forces. In particular, large quantities of weapons were channelled to IFP-aligned hostels in the East Rand and elsewhere in the PWV region. While this could be rationalised as providing hostel dwellers with the means to defend themselves, Pauw paints a much more proactive picture of what happened:

> First, Zulu-speaking outsiders would be bussed into the hostels. Second, a bloodbath would take place inside the hostels as the outsiders battled for supremacy with established residents, many of whom would flee. Third, the hostels having been secured as Inkatha strongholds, the impis would set off on nightly rampages against the communities round them, indiscriminately killing and looting. Large areas around the hostels would become desolate no-go areas.[24]

In December 1991 substantive negotiations on a constitution for a democratic political system began with the inauguration of the Convention for a Democratic South Africa (CODESA), involving the government, the ANC, the IFP, and 16 other groups. In May 1992 deadlock was reached in the negotiations over the issue of power sharing. That was followed in June by the Boipatong massacre carried out by IFP-aligned hostel dwellers. In response, the ANC suspended its participation in the negotiations. After a further massacre in September 1992 in Bisho, the capital of Ciskei, arising out of the ANC's mass action campaign, the pressures on both the government and the ANC drove the two sides to seek agreement. The result was the Record of Understanding between the government and the ANC.

Two key elements of the agreement signalled a radical change in the government's attitude towards the conflict between the ANC and the IFP. The government agreed to the fencing off of hostels and to the prohibition on the carrying of dangerous weapons in public places. Chief Buthelezi responded by insisting that hostel dwellers would tear down any fences erected round the hostels and that he would not seek the permission of anyone to carry 'a Zulu cultural weapon'.[25] In practice, neither of these elements of the Record of Understanding was enforced. However, much more importantly the government took steps to rein in the security forces and to retire elements of the security forces still implicated in third force activities. Such activities did not in fact cease but they no longer enjoyed the government's tacit support. Allegations of the persistence of third force activities were mainly made in relation to elements of the security forces over which the central government had no direct control, such as the KwaZulu Police (KZP). A task force of the Transitional Executive Council (TEC) reported in March 1994 that 'hit-squad activity in Natal, particularly in areas under the jurisdiction of the KZP, was rife'.[26]

Furthermore, the Record of Understanding was decisive in bringing about a political realignment. The IFP recognised that its tacit alliance with the government was at an end and through the Concerned South African Group (COSAG) made common cause with the extreme right and homeland leaders left high and dry by the abandonment of apartheid. In December 1992 the IFP-dominated KwaZulu Legislative Assembly adopted a constitution for the state of KwaZulu-Natal. It envisaged KwaZulu-Natal as 'a sovereign member of the Federal Republic of South Africa'[27] with its own citizenship. This represented a considerable departure from Inkatha's previous commitment to a unitary state, but was perfectly explicable, given its opposition to a deal between the government and the ANC and the political perspective of its new allies on the extreme right.

The IFP's efforts to block a bilateral deal between the government and the ANC were reflected in its negotiating tactics during the course of 1993. In June the Multi-Party Negotiating Forum provisionally set 27 April 1994 as the date for South Africa's first non-racial elections. The confirmation of the date prior to agreement on an interim constitution prompted a walk-out by the IFP and the Conservative Party as well as an unsuccessful legal challenge to the decision by the IFP on the grounds that it violated the principle of sufficient consensus agreed upon among the parties. In September the forum reached agreement on the establishment of the TEC to oversee the government of the country in the run-up to the elections. In October, COSAG was relaunched as the Freedom Alliance, which emphasised the need for a constitution entrenching the right of self-determination. Despite the opposition of the Freedom Alliance, negotiations continued leading to the adoption of an interim constitution on 18 November and the installation of the TEC on 7 December.

These developments took place against the background of continuing political violence and continuing efforts by both the government and the ANC to draw the boycotting parties into the process. These efforts continued even after the official proclamation of the election in February 1994. Later that month the tricameral parliament was reconvened to enact changes to the interim constitution embodying further concessions to the various elements of the Freedom Alliance. These included strengthening the powers of the nine provinces to determine their own legislative and executive structures, a change in the name of the province of Natal to KwaZulu-Natal and a provision that voters would be able to cast separate ballots for the National Assembly and their provincial legislature. The deadline for the registration of parties for the elections was extended. There was one deadline for the registration of parties and a further deadline for the submission of the lists of party candidates. But if these concessions seemed to reflect desperation on the part of the government and the ANC in the face of the threat of civil war posed by the Freedom Alliance, pressures were also mounting on the Freedom Alliance, as became clear during March.

By this time, the military ruler of Ciskei, Oupa Gqozo, had agreed to participate in the elections. At the beginning of the month Mandela persuaded Buthelezi to register the IFP provisionally by agreeing to submit their differences over the constitution to international mediation. That prompted Constand Viljoen, one of the leaders of the extreme right-wing *Afrikaner Volksfront*, to register for the elections as the *Vryheidsfront* (Freedom Front). However, in the light of the hostile reaction on the extreme right to his action, it seemed likely that he would allow the registration to lapse at the second deadline. Then the government of Bophuthatswana collapsed under the impact of widespread protests against its decision to boycott the elections. The debacle of the extreme right's intervention in Bophuthatswana prompted Viljoen to confirm the registration of the Freedom Front minutes before the deadline. The TEC's take-over of Bophuthatswana was followed by that of Ciskei when its government resigned after a strike by civil servants fearful for their pensions under the continuation of the homeland administration.

That left Buthelezi isolated, as he had failed to confirm the IFP's participation in the elections and its provisional registration had lapsed. Tensions rose dramatically. The seriousness of the threat posed by Buthelezi's warning that he would fight a 'liberation war'[28] if the elections took place without him was underlined by a report of the Goldstone Commission confirming the existence of a third force within the security forces linked to political violence and involved in the supply of arms to the IFP. According to the Human Rights Commission, 266 people died in political violence in Natal in March, the highest monthly total in three years of monitoring of the violence. Fifty-three people also died in disturbances arising out of an anti-election march on 28 March in the centre of the country's commercial capital, Johannesburg. Among the dead were eight demonstrators who were killed outside the ANC headquarters at Shell House by ANC security officers. The circumstances of their deaths have remained a source of controversy in post-transition South Africa. On 31 March President de Klerk imposed a state of emergency in KwaZulu-Natal.

A series of crisis meetings involving Mandela, De Klerk, Buthelezi and King Goodwill Zwelithini took place in early April. Zwelithini's participation reflected the fact that the IFP had increasingly made an issue of the status of the Zulu king under the new constitution. At the same time, Zwelithini's involvement was a moderating influence on the IFP, since he had made clear his disapproval of the strategy of violent disruption of the elections. On 12 April Henry Kissinger and Lord Carrington appeared on the scene to assist in international mediation, only to depart just as quickly when the parties failed to agree on the terms of reference of the mediators. A week later on 19 April and just a week before voting began, the IFP agreed to take part in the elections after further talks with the government and the ANC. The constitution was amended yet again to guarantee the position of the Zulu monarchy. In the elections, the IFP did much better than most observers had expected polling 10.54 per cent of the national vote and securing an overall majority in the regional parliament of KwaZulu-Natal. That gave the IFP three ministers in the Government of National Unity and the regional premiership of KwaZulu-Natal. Buthelezi became Minister of Home Affairs.

The formation of South Africa's Government of National Unity did not end conflict between the ANC and the IFP. In particular, political violence arising out of their rivalry has continued in KwaZulu-Natal, though at a lower level than in the run-up to the elections. A further decline occurred after local elections in the province in 1996 which lifted the threat that the IFP might press for secession. The outcome of those elections forced the IFP to come to terms with the strength of the ANC's support in the urban areas within KwaZulu-Natal, while also forcing the ANC to recognise that the IFP was the leading party in the province by reason of its overwhelming support in the rural areas. In Gauteng, as the PWV region was renamed after the 1994 elections, the violence between the parties ended in the face of the ANC's decisive victory in the region. Another factor that acted as a restraint on the IFP after the 1994 elections was a political rift between Buthelezi and the Zulu king, Goodwill Zwelithini.

Before assessing the IFP's strategy during the transition in the light of the history of the conflict sketched above and the notion of the UNITA option, a brief account is necessary of Savimbi's career since it helps to illuminate the assumptions that underlined the comparison. Jonas Savimbi was born on 3 August 1934 at Munhango, a small town on the Benguela railway situated in eastern Angola. At the time of the nationalist revolt against Portuguese rule in Angola in 1961, he was a student in Switzerland. He joined what at the time appeared to be the principal nationalist movement under Holden Roberto, *Uniao das Populacoes de Angola* (UPA – Union of the Angolan Peoples), the forerunner of *Frente Nacional de Libertacao de Angola* (FNLA – National Front for the Liberation of Angola). Savimbi resigned from the UPA in 1964. He went to China where with a small group of other Angolan exiles he trained in guerrilla warfare.

UNITA was founded in 1966 with a Maoist ideological orientation. In the same year UNITA launched attacks against Portuguese troops in the far east of the country bordering Zaire. By 1968 UNITA had established a base area within Angola. However, in comparison with its two rival nationalist organisations, the MPLA and the FNLA, UNITA carried out relatively few attacks against Portuguese forces. In fact, from an early date UNITA seems to have been more concerned to combat the influence of its African nationalist rivals than to defeat Portuguese colonialism. This was reflected in contacts and collaboration between the Portuguese authorities in Angola and UNITA which dated back to 1971.[29]

The April 1974 revolution in Portugal brought the war against Portuguese rule in Angola, such as it was, to an abrupt halt. The rival African nationalist organisations directed their efforts to securing their position in the negotiations on Angola's independence, as did the settler community. The country divided along regional lines. FNLA influence was strongest in the north on the border with Zaire; MPLA influence was centred on the capital, Luanda; while UNITA established a strong hold over the southern highlands. Each of the organisations sought external allies to bolster its position. That dashed settler hopes of exploiting the divisions to their political advantage and in the course of 1975 there was a mass exodus of settlers from the country. A contributory factor to their departure was the outbreak of civil war among the rival nationalist organisations in April 1975. The war was exacerbated by foreign intervention even prior to the Angola's independence on 11 November 1975, with Zairean troops directly assisting the FNLA; Cuban the MPLA; and South African UNITA.

South African support for UNITA swung opinion in the rest of Africa behind the MPLA, which emerged the victor in this phase of the civil war in Angola. An attempted coup d'etat in Luanda in May 1977 underlined the fragility of the MPLA government, however. Further, the government never gained control of the whole of the country. In particular, UNITA continued to wage a guerrilla war against the government from its stronghold in the southern highlands. UNITA's activities were given added impetus at the end of the 1970s by South Africa's adoption of a policy of destabilisation in the southern African region. In Angola's case this involved support for UNITA. In the 1980s South African arms supplies were followed by troop invasions, encouraged by the sympathetic view taken of such South African enterprise by the Reagan Administration. Its disposition was reflected in the lionising of Savimbi in January 1986 when he visited Washington in the wake of Reagan's approval of American covert aid to UNITA.

The increased external support for UNITA was reflected in a civil war in Angola of growing intensity through the 1980s. Stalemate in this war was broken by external developments, particularly a shift in Soviet policy under Gorbachev and a change in South African policy as a result of the high cost of its military intervention in Angola. In the first instance, this paved the way to an agreement over Namibia. Under the December 1988 New York Accords South Africa agreed to independence for Namibia and Cuba to withdraw its forces from Angola. The collapse of Communism in Eastern Europe added to the pressures on the MPLA government to alter its ideological orientation, with the result that in 1990 the MPLA abandoned Marxism-Leninism in favour of democratic socialism. After active Portuguese mediation, the MPLA and UNITA reached agreement in May 1991 to end the civil war. Under the Bicesse Accords, the MPLA and UNITA agreed to a cease-fire, the holding of multi-party elections before November 1992, and to the demobilisation of their military forces.

Elections were duly held in September 1992. The results showing a turn-out of 91 per cent and giving victory to the MPLA were announced on 17 October. They were denounced by UNITA which alleged widespread fraud. However, UNITA's claims were not supported by the 800 international observers of the poll. In early November UNITA was violently expelled from the capital, Luanda. That set the seal on the resumption of the civil war. A number of factors contributed to this outcome, but two were especially important. Firstly, the demobilisation of the respective armies of the MPLA and UNITA, which was supposed to occur in terms of the Bicesse Accords, had hardly begun by the time of the elections. That was partly a reflection of the inadequacy of the United Nations Angolan Verification Mission (UNAVEM), which was created to oversee the process, but had not been given the resources needed for the task. Further, neither the MPLA nor UNITA had looked beyond the holding of the elections. Thus, there was no provision for power sharing after the elections or, indeed, any other provision to lessen the blow of defeat for the losers in the poll. The pleas of international mediators on this score were rejected. In particular, ahead of polling

Savimbi refused even to consider the possibility that he and UNITA might be defeated in the elections. However, when President dos Santos named a transitional government in December 1992 to run the country until the run-off of the Presidential election, he allocated six posts to UNITA. This was conditional on UNITA's abiding by the Bicesse Accords and by then the civil war had resumed.

The ferocity of the renewed civil war was encapsulated by a UN estimate in mid-1993 that 1,000 people were dying each day as a result of the war. In the fighting itself, UNITA achieved a string of victories over the MPLA forces, but this was partly counterbalanced by UNITA's increasing international isolation. In May 1993 the United States recognised the MPLA government. The decision was explained in *Keesing's Record of World Events* as follows:

> The policy change followed pressures from leaders of the South African African National Congress (ANC) who had emphasized to US delegations at the funerals of two ANC leaders in April the disturbing precedent which UNITA's rejection of the September 1992 elections was likely to set for future elections in both South Africa and Mozambique.[30]

In September 1993 the UN Security Council imposed a mandatory oil and arms embargo on UNITA.

These pressures brought concessions from UNITA and prompted further talks between the two sides in Lusaka from mid-November 1993. However, by April 1994 the talks deadlocked over the issue of the allocation of government posts to UNITA. The deadlock in the negotiations was broken in the second half of 1994 following a change in the military balance of forces. A string of government military victories, culminating in the capture of the city of Huambo in early November, weakened UNITA's position on the ground substantially. Savimbi himself was reportedly seriously injured during the government offensive. When an agreement was finally signed between the government and UNITA in Lusaka on 20 November, he did not appear at the ceremony. The Lusaka protocol provided for a cease-fire, power sharing, the integration of UNITA forces into Angola's armed forces, the completion of the 1992 elections, and supervision of the implementation of the accord by a joint commission of the Angolan parties and representatives of the international community. However, the implementation of the agreement proved problematic and still had not been completed by 1998.

A number of points of similarity can be identified in the two cases. Both Buthelezi and Savimbi started out as members of older established nationalist movements, which they left, creating their own parties which they continue to lead. Both are dominant figures within their parties, with a very low tolerance for any form of dissent. However, despite their hold over their parties, it has commonly been argued in Angola and South Africa that they personally have presented a larger obstacle to accommodation and reconciliation than their respective political parties. Both faced accusations that they were more concerned to combat nationalist rivals than to bring about an end to minority or colonial rule and of collaboration to this end.

Both they and their parties have shown a great deal of ideological flexibility. Thus, Savimbi made a rapid transition from Maoist to anti-Communist after the Portuguese revolution. Buthelezi has shown a similar readiness to alter his colours to suit the needs of the moment. In the 1980s he cultivated the Israelis and pro-Israeli American politicians by exploiting the ANC's vulnerability over its affinity with the PLO. However, that did not prevent the IFP from forming an alliance with the white extreme right in the 1990s, despite its strong neo-Nazi component. In full-page advertisements for the IFP in South African papers during the course of 1993, it was apparent that the party was trying out various themes. In particular, to begin with, the party played down the notion that it was in any sense an ethnic party. For example, a senior figure in the party, Ben Ngubane claimed that there was 'almost complete consensus across the political spectrum on a united, non-racial, non-sexist and non-ethnic South Africa' and he went on to argue: 'Inkatha is the party most likely to end up having the most ethnically representative support base of any party'.[31] The IFP's poor showing in the polls during 1993 suggests that this approach failed to win support for the party. Mobilisation on ethnic issues proved far more effective. As Tom Lodge records in his account of the election in the *Southern African Review of Books*, there was 'a distinct leap in Inkatha's popular standing when it began to rally its supporters around the issue of the Zulu King's political status'.[32]

The peak of the international influence of the two leaders was reached in 1986, when they appeared to be attractive anti-Communist alternatives to the American right in the era of the Reagan Doctrine. The collapse of Communism in Eastern Europe in 1989 weakened, though did not eradicate, this appeal. But as both men came to be seen increasingly as obstacles to a transition to liberal democracy in southern Africa, their reputation suffered accordingly. Even so, both domestically and internationally, some of their supporters or allies continued to attach importance to their anti-Communist credentials. It was a theme that the IFP continued to use in its advertising up to polling day. The most striking example was an advertisement showing President de Klerk alongside flagpoles with the old South African flag being lowered and the hammer and sickle being raised in its place, with the mocking slogan: 'He's made the change' and 'If you wish to resist, the IFP is your only guarantee'.[33] In speeches by IFP leaders mention of the ANC was usually accompanied by reference to its alliance with the SACP.

In both parties ethnic mobilisation and the threat of secession helped to fill the vacuum left by the reduced effectiveness of anti-Communism as a means of engendering support. The declining salience of anti-Communism internationally coincided with the lifting of the international community's anathema against secession, reflected in the recognition granted to Slovenia and Croatia. Consequently, the hostility of the international community is no longer as strong a barrier to the adoption of a stance in favour of secession. Neither UNITA nor the IFP started out as secessionist movements, but the changing international political climate tempted them to contemplate that option. However, the threat of secession is best viewed as a bargaining tactic to secure concessions from the central government rather than necessarily their ultimate goal. The two elections, the Angolan election of September 1992 and the South African election of 1994, were very revealing of the nature of the support base for the two parties. Thus, in the case of Angola, John Marcum's 1978 characterisation of UNITA seems to have been amply borne out:

> It maintained a strong ethnoregional appeal among Ovimbundu, Chokwe, Lwena, and Ovambo; shared (if less intensively) FNLA hostility toward mestico leadership; and continued to rely on an Afrocentric populism that was at the same time aggregative and demogogic.[34]

James Hamill explaining the party's surprising failure to oust the MPLA after its unimpressive record in power attributed it to the following factors:

> an appalling human rights record, both towards dissenters within its own ranks and towards the civilian population generally; the overbearing personality cult of Savimbi; and, finally, the overt Ovimbundu chauvinism and blatant racism against mixed-race Angolans.[35]

At the same time, UNITA's strength among the Ovimbundu, who constitute 40 per cent of the population of Angola, made it apparent that the country would be difficult if not impossible to govern without the support of UNITA. The outcome of the South African election strongly underlined the ethno-regional appeal of the IFP, with the detailed district by district figures demonstrating that the IFP's strength lay largely in the rural areas of KwaZulu-Natal.[36] Thus, it is striking how poorly the IFP fared among Zulu-speakers (and indeed all other voters) outside KwaZulu-Natal. Also of note was the derisory vote received by all the other homeland based parties, undercutting the argument that IFP support can be explained simply by the disposal of patronage through its control of the KwaZulu administration. But however the pattern of support for the IFP is explained, it is clear that the IFP occupies a much weaker position in South Africa than does UNITA in Angola.

In an article entitled 'Ethnicity is not Enough: Reflections on Protracted Secessionism in the Third World', James Mayall and Mark Simpson argue that ethnic divisions are likely to lead to protracted secessionism only where a number of other conditions exist.[37] The most important of their conditions is different treatment of the ethnic groups under colonial rule, reinforced by policies pursued by the post-colonial government. Their argument is derived from an examination of the cases of Eritrea and southern Sudan. But it might also be applied to the division between coast and highland in Angola and between Natal and the rest of South Africa. In the former case, the division can be seen as a reflection of the different impact of colonial rule in the two areas; in the latter, as a legacy of Theophilus Shepstone's policy of indirect rule in Zululand during the nineteenth century. The consequence of that policy was that traditionalism retained a far greater measure of legitimacy in Natal, the poorest and least economically developed of the four provinces of the old South Africa. The election results in the two countries provide an obvious starting point for such a structural analysis.

In the run-up to the 1994 elections, South Africa was haunted by the IFP's pursuit of the UNITA option. One element in the perception of the South African transition as a miracle lay in the sudden receding of this threat just one week before polling commenced. However, with the benefit of hindsight it is apparent that the new direction taken by Buthelezi and the IFP after the Record of Understanding was a sign of weakness rather than strength. In the 1980s Buthelezi had presented himself as an apostle of moderation in the eyes of white South Africans through his opposition to economic sanctions and to the armed struggle. At the same time, he was careful not to allow himself to be coopted and remained consistent in his insistence on inclusive negotiations. However, Inkatha was compromised by the covert assistance it received from the state in its conflict with other anti-apartheid forces in the 1980s. In the context of P.W.Botha's total strategy, Inkatha was seen as an asset in the war against ANC surrogates. After February 1990, the IFP figured in the National Party's hopes of building a multi-racial coalition that could defeat the ANC in one person one vote elections.

That illusion was shattered by the crisis in the South African transition in the winter of 1992. In fact, the impact of the conflict generated by ANC-IFP rivalry became a potent factor in forcing the government to make concessions to the ANC. Firstly, the violence projected an image of instability that threatened investment and hence economic growth, particularly because the location of one of the main arenas of conflict, the townships of the East Rand, lay at the heart of South Africa's manufacturing industry. Secondly the violence also threatened to reverse the progress the government had made towards the normalisation of South Africa's relations with the outside world as the result of the liberalisation of the political system in 1990. Thirdly, the scale of the violence was such as to generate fears that it could make the country ungovernable, creating the spectre of social breakdown and political fragmentation. All of these factors helped to make agreement with the ANC a palatable alternative for the government. Indeed, so clear were the threats, if no deal was done, as to generate during the course of the transition a massive shift in white attitudes towards the prospect of an ANC-led government. Ironically by challenging the ANC so forcefully, Buthelezi and the IFP actually contributed to its triumph.

Notes to Chapter 5

1   Daniel Reed, *Beloved Country: South Africa's Silent Wars*, BBC Books, London 1994, p.196.

2   Billy Paddock, 'Secret talks keep Inkatha in negotiating process', *Business Day* (Johannesburg), 13 August 1993.

3   *Business Day*, 20 August 1993.

4   *Business Day*, 21 October 1993.

5   Gerald D'Ange, 'Africa's mistakes can point us in the right direction', *The Star* (Johannesburg), 5 April 1994.

6   Paulette Bethelehem, 'Voter education must ward off ghost of Angola', *Business Day*, 30 November 1993.

7   Rob Amato, *Understanding the New Constitution*, Struik, Cape Town 1994, p.58.

8   John Carlin, 'Buthelezi poised for U-turn: Fears of terror campaign recede as Inkatha prepares to take part in Natal poll', *The Independent* (London), 19 April 1994.

9   See, for example, Lloyd Coutts, 'Buthelezi reserves judgement on poll', *Business Day*, 4 May 1994.

10   Denis Beckett, 'Drawing a line at deception', *The Star*, 20 May 1994.

11   Gerhard Mare, *Ethnicity and Politics in South Africa*, Zed Books, London 1993, pp.112–113.

12   John Kane-Berman, *Political Violence in South Africa*, South African Institute of Race Relations, Johannesburg 1993, p.55.

13   Muriel Horrell and Tony Hodgson, *A Survey of Race Relations in South Africa: 1975*, South African Institute of Race Relations, Johannesburg 1976, p.131.

14   Loraine Gordon, Suzanne Blignaut, Sean Moroney, and Carole Cooper, *A Survey of Race Relations in South Africa: 1977*, South African Institute of Race Relations, Johannesburg 1978, p.36.

15   *Ibid.*, p.37.

16   See the account given in Gerhard Mare and Georgina Hamilton, *An Appetite for Power: Buthelezi's Inkatha and the Politics of 'Loyal Resistance'*, Ravan Press, Johannesburg 1987, pp.142–145.

17   Quoted in Ben Temkin, *Gatsha Buthelezi: Zulu Statesman*, Purnell, Cape Town 1976, pp.323–324.

18   Judith Hudson, 'Riding the Tiger: Urban Warfare on the East Rand' in William Gutteridge and J.E.Spence (eds), *Violence in Southern Africa*, Frank Cass, London 1997, p.109.

19   Rupert Taylor and Mark Shaw, 'The Natal Conflict' in John D.Brewer (ed.), *Restructuring South Africa*, Macmillan, Basingstoke 1994, p.39.

20   Mike Morris and Doug Hindson, 'The Disintegration of Apartheid: From Violence to Reconstruction' in Glenn Moss and Ingrid Obery (eds), *From 'Red Friday' to CODESA: South African Review 6*, Ravan Press, Johannesburg 1992, p.162.

21   Taylor and Shaw (as cited in note 19), pp.39–45.

22   Alexander Johnston, 'Politics and Violence in KwaZulu-Natal' in Gutteridge and Spence (eds), *op. cit.*, p.87.

23   Jacques Pauw, *Into the Heart of Darkness: Confessions of Apartheid's Assassins*, Jonathan Ball Publishers, Johannesburg 1997, p.127.

24   *Ibid.*, p.124.

25   Anthea Jeffrey, *The Natal Story: 16 Years of Conflict*, South African Institute of Race Relations, Johannesburg 1997, p.372.

26   *Ibid.*, p.721.

27   Amato, *op. cit.*, p.61.

28   Quoted in *Keesing's Record of World Events*, Longman, London: News Digest for March 1994, p.39894.

29   A full account is given in William Minter (ed.), *Operation Timber: Pages from the Savimbi Dossier*, Africa World Press, Trenton N.J. 1988.

30   *Keesing's Record of World Events*, Longman, London: News Digest for May 1993, p.39447.

31   *Business Day*, 24 March 1993.

32   Tom Lodge, 'SA '94: Election of a Special Kind', *Southern African Review of Books*, March/April 1994, p.4.

33   Carried for example in the *Sunday Times* (Johannesburg), 24 April 1994.

34   John A.Marcum, *The Angolan Revolution: Volume II – Exile Politics and Guerrilla Warfare (1962–1976)*, The MIT Press, Cambridge, Mass. 1978, p.276.

35   James Hamill, 'Angola's road from under the rubble', *The World Today*, January 1994, p.9.

36   See *Republic of South Africa 1994 General Election: National Results by Province/District*, Election Administration Directorate, Independent Electoral Commission, Johannesburg 26 May 1994. See also the map based on these figures in *Sunday Times*, 3 July 1994.

37   James Mayall and Mark Simpson, 'Ethnicity is not Enough: Reflections on Protracted Secessionism in the Third World', *International Journal of Comparative Sociology*, Vol. 33 (1–2), 1992, pp.5–25.

CHAPTER 6

The Heart of the Miracle: the 1994 elections

The transition that President de Klerk initiated on 2 February 1990 culminated in Nelson Mandela's inauguration as President of South Africa on 10 May 1994. While the centrepiece of the day was the swearing in of the President and his Deputies, the crowd's loudest cheers were reserved for a spectacular display by the air force that followed President Mandela's first speech. Those who cheered well understood the significance of this demonstration of loyalty to the new order by forces that had played a key role in upholding white minority rule. The scene is described well by Mandela himself:

> A few moments later we all lifted our eyes in awe as a spectacular array of South African jets, helicopters and troop carriers roared in perfect formation over the Union Buildings. It was not only a display of pinpoint precision and military force, but a demonstration of the military's loyalty to democracy, to a new government that had been freely and fairly elected. Only moments before, the highest generals of the South African Defence Force and police, their chests bedecked with ribbons and medals from days gone by, saluted me and pledged their loyalty. I was not unmindful of the fact that not so many years before they would not have saluted but arrested me. Finally, a chevron of Impala jets left a smoke trail of the black, red, green, blue and gold of the new South African flag.[1]

At the start of the year, such an orderly transfer of power had seemed almost inconceivable given the obstacles that lay in the path of the Transitional Executive Council (TEC) as it attempted to create the conditions for the holding of free and fair elections by the end of April. The achievement of the holding of elections with the participation of all the major strands of opinion in the country from the far left to the extreme right and encompassing all races and ethnic groups and the acceptance by the parties of the results were seen by many inside the country as a miracle. But if that term is applied more expansively to the whole period of the transition from 2 February 1990 to 10 May 1994, then the elections from 26 to 29 April may best be described as the heart of the miracle.

The euphoria that swept South Africa during those days in 1994 stands in very marked contrast to the negative judgement on the elections of some of the country's political scientists. For example, in the most substantial academic study of the elections, *Launching Democracy in South Africa: The First Open Election, April 1994* edited by R.W.Johnson and Lawrence Schlemmer, Professor David Welsh is quoted as follows:

> For 'reasons of state' South Africans have been required to subscribe to the latest national myth, namely that the elections were 'substantially free and fair'. They were nothing of the kind and hardly any of the sanctimonious foreign observers who fell about themselves to declare it so would for one moment have accepted the validity of an election subject to such flaws in their own country.[2]

In part, such criticism of the international monitoring of the elections stemmed from a misunderstanding of the relative narrowness of the remit of the monitors. In part, it reflected resentment of the assumptions foreign observers of the elections made about the South African situation. For their part the critics tended to mix up two very different sets of issues; firstly, the integrity of the voting process itself, including whether all those who had the right to vote had the opportunity to do so and whether the counting of votes was conducted properly, and secondly, whether the electors were able to exercise their choice free from intimidation and coercion and with sufficient knowledge of the alternatives available to them so that their votes could be said to have represented a genuine expression of their preferences. The first set of issues may best be described as technical, while no less important for that. The second goes to the heart of what kind of society South Africa was in the first half of 1994 when these elections took place.

The technical problems are considered first in the context of a description of the conduct of the elections and an analysis of their outcome. Responsibility for the organisation of the elections in terms of the agreements reached by the parties in 1993 was vested in the Independent Electoral Commission (IEC). However, while the parties had agreed in principle to the creation of the IEC in September

1993, its actual establishment had to await the finalisation of the drafting of the interim constitution, under which the elections were to
take place, and the accompanying passage of the Electoral Act 1993.
Consequently the IEC only came into existence in January 1994 with
a remit to administer, organise and conduct the elections within four
months and finally to reach a judgement within ten days of polling at
the end of April on whether the elections had been free and fair.
Established at the same time was the Independent Media Commission
(IMC), which was given the task of ensuring equitable treatment by
broadcasters of the parties during the election.

Under the Electoral Act 1993, any person 18 years or older who
was citizen of South Africa or a permanent resident and who was in
possession of one of a number of specified documents was entitled to
vote. But because so many people did not possess any of the usual
documents, provision was made for the issue of a temporary voter's
card (TVC) to help those without one of the other valid documents
to establish their entitlement to vote. The IEC estimated the number
of people without such a valid identification document at two million. There was widespread criticism of the issue of TVCs, with allegations both of lax control resulting in teenagers under the age of 18
being able to vote and of shortage of application forms and other
administrative failures denying eligible voters the TVCs they needed
to exercise their vote. The time available for the organisation of polling meant that establishing a register of eligible voters was out of the
question. It was up to the voter as to where he or she cast his or her
vote. It was possible to vote for the National Assembly at any polling
station in the country, but an elector could only vote for the provincial
assembly of the specific province in which his or her vote was cast.

Without a register of voters, the IEC could only make rough
estimates of the number of ballot papers that might be needed at a
particular polling station. The IEC estimated the total number of
eligible voters at 22.7 million, of whom it calculated 73 per cent were
African, 15 per white, 9 per cent Coloured and 3 per cent Indian.[3]
The IEC's figure for the African proportion of the electorate differs
slightly from the figure given by *The Independent on Sunday* of 75.6 per
cent, as well as from Robert Mattes's estimate that African voters
constituted roughly 69 per cent of the electorate.[4] All of these figures
have been thrown into further doubt by the publication in 1997 of
the preliminary finding of the 1996 census giving a total figure for
South Africa's population of 37.9 million.[5] This was millions fewer
than the expected total. In particular, it can be compared to the
Development Bank of Southern Africa's estimate of South Africa's

population in 1996 of 44.6 million,[6] which itself was based on projections from the 1991 census.

The claim of the 1996 census to accuracy rests on the fact that unlike the 1991 census, which used aerial photography and like information to calculate estimates of the African population, it entailed a full enumeration by household of the African population. However, the preliminary finding of the 1996 census on the total population of the country has itself come under criticism on the grounds that it is inconsistent with information on the size of the population that can be gleaned from other sources, such as, for example, school enrolments. The thrust of much of the criticism is that the new figure is an underestimate of the population. It remains to be seen whether it will prove possible to establish reliable figures for the current population and whether it will be possible by projecting these backwards either to validate or to require a modification of the IEC's estimate of the numbers of eligible voters for the 1994 elections. Given that there was a very high turn-out of electors on the IEC's estimate of the total number of eligible voters, there is relatively little scope for a large reduction in that figure without there being a strong implication that the phenomenon of under age voting had a significant impact on the elections.

The IEC's difficulties in running the elections were compounded by the series of changes that were introduced by the TEC to secure the participation of parties in the Freedom Alliance. The original deadline for the registration of parties was extended. A further concession was that there would be two ballots instead of one, giving the elector the option of casting his or her vote for one party at the national level and another at the provincial level. The single ballot had been widely criticised but the effect of the change was a doubling of what was required of the IEC in terms of the distribution and counting of ballot papers. An even greater challenge was presented to the IEC by the IFP's very late entry into the elections. The ballot papers had already been printed for both the national elections and the nine sets of provincial elections. To accommodate the IFP a sticker had to be added to every ballot paper.

Polling in South Africa's first democratic elections was scheduled to take place over three days, between 26 and 28 April 1994. The first day of polling, 26 April, had been designated for special voters, including the old, patients in hospitals, the disabled, prisoners and members of the security forces . Those without a special dispensation to vote on the first day could vote on either of the two days designated as general days of voting, 27 and 28 April. The weaknesses of the IEC's organisation were apparent from the first day. Many stations failed to open or opened very late in the day because of a lack of voting materials. At some polling stations voters waited in vain for eight hours for polling to begin, only to be told to return the following day. Even where polling took place, the slowness of the process led to the formation of long queues of voters waiting patiently to vote. The abiding image of the first day of voting was of the determination of the old and disabled to make their mark come what may, an immensely powerful metaphor for the fact that the majority of these electors had had to wait a lifetime to cast their vote in a democratic election.

On 27 April, queues of voters began to form outside many polling stations well before their designated opening time of 7 a.m. The slowness of the process meant that most voters faced a wait measured in hours before they could vote. The readiness with which this was accepted by voters of all races became a further metaphor for the elections, as if the very act of standing together politely in a line had drawn all of the poison out of the country's racial antagonisms. In a number of provinces there were serious problems in the distribution of election materials, particularly Pretoria-Witwatersrand-Vereeniging (PWV), KwaZulu-Natal, Eastern Cape and Northern Transvaal. Worst affected were the former homelands. The IEC was forced to request emergency assistance from the military in the form of helicopters and vehicles to distribute election material to remote areas where the system of distribution of the material had broken down. Because of these problems, 29 April was declared as an extra day of voting in the affected areas.

Voting was by the party list system of proportional representation. It was a closed party list system with the voters afforded no opportunity to express a preference for any particular candidate within the party of their choice. Voters received two ballots, one to elect members of the National Assembly and one to elect members of one of nine provincial legislatures. The National Assembly consisted of 400 members, with 200 seats filled from the party lists for each province, according to the allocation of seats to each province given in Table 6.1. The other 200 seats were filled on a national basis from national party lists. Provincial legislatures varied in size according to population, but with a minimum of 30 seats in each legislature. The number of seats for each province is given in Table 6.1. In addition, each provincial legislature elected 10 members proportionately according to party strength to the Senate, an indirectly elected second chamber. The National Assembly and the Senate sitting together constituted the Constituent Assembly empowered to draw up the country's final constitution subject to principles laid down in the interim constitution.

Table 6.1

Region	Assembly seats	Provincial legislature
Western Cape	21	42
Northern Cape	4	30
Eastern Cape	28	56
KwaZulu-Natal	40	81
Orange Free State	15	30
PWV	43	86
North West	15	30
Eastern Transvaal	14	30
Northern Transvaal	20	40

Source: Murray Faure and Jan-Erik Lane, *South Africa: Designing New Political Institutions*, Sage, London 1996, p.93

The inefficiency with which ballot papers were distributed damaged the IEC's reputation for competence but not its reputation for honesty, though there was considerable concern that the IEC's failings had been exploited by some parties to perpetrate fraud and at the IEC's capacity to waste money. In particular, the IFP and the ANC accused each other of cheating. It was commonly if cynically assumed that the irregularities tended to cancel each other out. The long counting of votes then began, with partial results being released in dribs and drabs. The slowness of the count did further damage to the IEC's reputation. Lack of experience in handling elections was not confined to the IEC, however. The media also showed an extraordinary inability to analyse the results as they came in, perhaps because of a reluctance to make the obvious connections between race and voting behaviour. As it happened, results from the Western Cape were among the first to come in. Little attempt was made to explain that the province was unrepresentative of the racial composition of the country (see Table 6.4) and thus not a good indicator of the likely outcome of the elections.

The first step in the counting process was the reconciliation of ballots, which was checking that the number of ballots in the boxes from particular polling stations matched the number of ballots that the polling station's presiding officer had issued. This was meant to precede the allocation of ballots by party. Because of the chaotic conditions that had prevailed at a number of polling stations, this proved a more difficult process than had been anticipated and ultimately led to a ruling by the chairman of the IEC, Judge J.C. Kriegler that it was not essential. By midday on 2 May, three days after the close of polls, little over a third of the results had been declared. At this point, the IEC discovered that there had been interference with the computer system it was using to collate results. The effect was that small percentages were being added to the votes recorded for some small parties on each incoming tally. To sort out the problem, the IEC suspended the release of results for 24 hours. However, by this time, the outcome of the elections was not in doubt. That evening President de Klerk conceded victory to the ANC, while the ANC staged its own victory party in the Carlton Hotel in central Johannesburg, providing the cue for celebrations of its supporters across the country.

The full results of the election were finally announced by the IEC on 6 May. Besides providing a national tally and a tally of the votes for each of the nine provincial legislatures, the IEC provided a breakdown of the voting for the National Assembly by each of the nine regions. The IEC also estimated the turn-out of voters in the elections to each of the provincial legislatures (see Table 6.2). However, at first detailed results of the elections by district were not released. The failure to do so was strongly criticised by a number of the bodies monitoring the elections, though when they were eventually published on 26 May they attracted relatively little interest. The IEC published its final report on the elections in October 1994. This justified the decisions that the IEC had made in response to complaints by the parties, particularly the Democratic Party and the National Party, of widespread fraud. Concern that everyone entitled to vote should be able to do so had led to the issue of three and a half million TVCs, one and a half million of them between 25 and 29 April. The IEC report accepted that 'abuses of the system for issuing of TVCs occurred on a substantial scale'.[7]

Johannesburg's main newspaper, *The Star*, reacted to the results by proclaiming 'It's a dream outcome!' in banner headlines, with the explanation in a sub-heading: 'ANC, NP, IFP can all draw satisfaction from final result'.[8] The possibility of such an outcome had been foreseen by *The Weekly Mail and Guardian* just ahead of the announcement of the outcome. Its lead story on the count was headed: 'The votes horse-trade: Behind closed doors, deals to stem the bloodshed'.[9] Concern that the results had been massaged to ensure their acceptance by the major parties continued to be expressed after the announcement by the IEC of the outcome.[10] The IEC itself acknowledged failings in the electoral process, but denied that there

Table 6.2

Total valid vote in each region for the National Assembly and for provincial legislatures and the IEC's estimate of percentage turn-out in the elections to the provincial legislatures.

Region	National	Provincial	Turn-out
Western Cape	2 126 013	2 137 742	92
Northern Cape	404 579	439 149	92
Eastern Cape	2 857 709	2 908 506	92
KwaZulu Natal	3 750 606	3 664 324	80
Orange Free State	1 368 251	1 354 266	83
P W V	4 208 301	4 198 250	86
North West	1 588 255	1 572 142	89
Eastern Transvaal	1 309 993	1 326 068	85
Northern Transvaal	1 919 790	1 909 793	84

Source: Independent Electoral Commission, Johannesburg.

had been manipulation of the voting tallies and characterised the election as 'substantially free and fair'.[11] Nonetheless, the suspicion of a deal among the parties lingered for good reason: the scale of reported irregularities and the extent of sheer incompetence in the running of the election were such that the voting and the counting of the votes would hardly have borne scrutiny if the process had been denounced by any of the major political parties.

One undisputed result was that only three parties had emerged from the election in a position to claim to belong in that category. These were the African National Congress (ANC), the National Party (NP), and the Inkatha Freedom Party (IFP). Three other parties had been thought of before the election as serious contenders for a place in government; the Freedom Front of General Constand Viljoen on the extreme right; the Democratic Party (DP), representing the liberal tradition long associated with the veteran M.P., Helen Suzman; and the Pan Africanist Congress of Azania (PAC), the radical Africanist party. Each failed to win even half of the five per cent of the vote needed to lay claim to representation in the Government of National Unity. However, each won seats in the National Assembly, as did the African Christian Democratic Party (ACDP). Details of the perform-ance of the seven parties gaining seats in the National Assembly are given in Table 6.3, along with the number of seats these parties won in the Senate. The other 12 parties contesting the election to the

National Assembly failed to secure the 0.25 per cent of the vote needed to win a seat in the National Assembly.

Table 6.3

Votes, seats, percentage share of poll of parties gaining representation in the National Assembly and allocation of seats in Senate as a result of outcome of provincial elections

Party	Votes	Seats	Percentage	Senate seats
ANC	12 237 655	252	62.65	60
NP	3 983 690	82	20.39	17
IFP	2 058 294	43	10.54	5
FF	424 555	9	2.17	5
DP	338 426	7	1.73	3
PAC	243 478	5	1.25	0
ACDP	88 104	2	0.45	0

Abbreviations of parties: ANC = African National Congress; NP = National Party; IFP = Inkatha Freedom Party; FF = Freedom Front; DP = Democratic Party; PAC = Pan Africanist Congress of Azania; ACDP = African Christian Democratic Party.

Source: Independent Electoral Commission, Johannesburg.

Interest in the possible outcome of an election held on the basis of a universal adult suffrage began as soon as President de Klerk initiated the liberalisation of the South African political system on 2 February 1990, as the holding of democratic elections was seen as an inevitable element in any negotiated political settlement. It was reflected in the commissioning and publication of a number of opinion polls throughout the transition. Their lack of consistency and, in particular, the failure of most of them to reflect the IFP's hold on the rural areas of KwaZulu-Natal, cast doubt on their reliability. Nonetheless, they had a considerable influence on the approach of the major parties towards the negotiations. Mattes argues that the timing of the South African elections more than four years after the liberalisation of the political system was in part due to the government's desire to prolong the process based on the belief derived from polling done on its behalf by the Human Sciences Research Council that prolonging the transition process was in its electoral interest.[12]

He suggests this calculation was a factor in the breakdown of negotiations in May 1992 and he cites evidence from later in that year that ministers, such as the Minister of Foreign Affairs, Pik Botha, believed that the National Party could put together a coalition capable of defeating the ANC in a one-person-one-vote election.[13] There was a radical change in the government's standing following Hani's assassination Mattes records how the government resorted to one expedient after another as it saw its poll ratings falling and he argues this played an important role in its negotiating posture during the final stages of the transition.

> In the final analysis, the most important NP concessions came not as a result of the ANC's mobilisation of popular power, but rather as a result of the NP's own inability to attract new supporters and its inability to hold those it had, especially during its decline in the polls. It was this dynamic that sent real shockwaves and tremors through the government and led to a series of concessions designed to bring about elections as quickly as possible and to obtain enough positions in the new government, before the party entirely imploded.[14]

Opinion polls in the month before polling pointed to a high measure of racial polarisation among voters.[15] It was also evident that Coloureds and Asians were becoming anxious about their position under African majority rule and were opting in increasing numbers for what had been traditionally white political parties. These polls also provided evidence of the likely turn-out of different groups. Under South African electoral law polling in the days immediately before voting was banned. Consequently, the polls were unable to trace what was happening in the case of the substantial number of voters still undecided before the final stages of the election campaign. Exit polling, which might have provided a valuable check against fraud, was also prohibited.

Crude confirmation for the thesis of the polarisation of the electorate between African and non-African voters is suggested by comparing the total vote for parties principally appealing to African voters and that for white-led parties with a breakdown of the electorate between Africans and non-Africans (see Table 6.4). If the figures provided by *The Independent on Sunday* on racial composition of the electorate are used, an even closer fit is suggested. Of course this establishes very little since such a result would also be obtained if there was substantial voting across these lines of division, but in equal numbers each way so that one cancelled the other out. Further, it does not take into account the possibility of differential turn-out between Africans and non-Africans. However, in this context Reynolds estimates on the basis of comparison of voting patterns and survey results that there was little difference in the turn-out on racial lines. His figures suggest that white, Indian and African turn-out differed from the national turn-out of 86 per cent by less than one per cent but that Coloured turn-out was four per cent above that for the country as a whole.[16]

Table 6.4

Comparison of share of poll of 'African' and 'non-African' parties with racial breakdown of the electorate, excluding parties failing to gain representation in the National Assembly

Africans as per cent of electorate	73
'African' parties as per cent of the vote	75
'non-Africans' as per cent of electorate	27
'non-African' parties as per cent of vote	24

'African' parties = ANC, IFP, PAC, and ACDP.

'non-African' parties = NP, FF, and DP.

Sources: Calculated from figures from Independent Electoral Commission, Johannesburg.

To obtain a clearer picture, an examination of the details of the voting by region is necessary (see Table 6.5). In parenthesis, it is worth noting that the figures show slight differences in the voting for the National Assembly and for the provincial legislatures. In particular, in the case of the National Party, in each region it received a smaller share of the vote in the elections to the provincial legislatures than in the election to the National Assembly. Conversely, with the exception of Northern Transvaal, the Freedom Front did better in the elections for the provincial legislatures. Among the 'African' parties, the ANC did better in elections to the National Assembly, except in KwaZulu Natal, while the admittedly very small ACDP received a higher percentage of the vote in every region in the elections to the provincial legislatures.

A racial breakdown of the electorate in each region is given in Table 6.6. In seven of the nine regions, Africans constituted an absolute majority of the electorate. In six of these the ANC won an absolute majority of both votes and seats in the provincial legislature. The exception was KwaZulu-Natal in which the IFP narrowly won an absolute majority of votes and seats. In two regions, the Western Cape and the Northern Cape, Coloureds constituted an absolute majority of voters. In the Western Cape, the National Party won an absolute majority of the votes and seats in the provincial legislature. In the Northern Cape, the ANC won exactly half of the seats in the provincial legislature, as did the three white-led parties between them. In the

Table 6.5

Parties' percentage share of vote by region for both the National Assembly and for the provincial legislatures:

		WC	NC	EC	KZN	OFS	PWV	NW	ET	NT
ANC	N:	33.60	49.81	84.39	31.61	77.42	59.10	83.46	81.87	92.73
	P:	33.01	49.74	84.35	32.23	76.65	57.60	83.33	80.69	92.14
NP	N:	56.24	41.94	10.60	15.76	14.53	27.58	10.10	10.27	3.64
	P:	53.25	40.48	9.83	11.21	12.59	23.88	8.84	9.00	3.29
IFP	N:	0.65	0.47	0.24	48.59	0.62	4.13	0.45	1.59	0.15
	P:	0.35	0.42	0.17	50.32	0.51	3.66	0.38	1.52	0.12
FF	N:	1.97	4.32	0.65	0.46	3.68	3.68	3.10	3.51	1.51
	P:	2.06	5.97	0.80	0.51	6.03	6.17	4.63	5.66	1.21
DP	N:	4.18	1.29	1.24	1.61	0.54	3.00	0.37	0.42	0.18
	P:	6.64	1.87	2.05	2.15	0.57	5.32	0.50	0.56	0.21
PAC	N:	1.00	0.97	1.99	0.62	1.70	1.25	1.53	1.36	1.51
	P:	1.06	0.93	2.04	0.73	1.81	1.47	1.73	1.63	1.21
ACDP	N:	0.97	0.32	0.38	0.46	0.46	0.48	0.25	0.34	0.26
	P:	1.20	0.40	0.51	0.57	0.67	0.61	0.35	0.48	0.78

N = National Assembly; P = Provincial Legislature.

Abbreviations for the regions: WC = Western Cape; NC = Northern Cape; EC = Eastern Cape; KZN = KwaZulu-Natal; OFS = Orange Free State; PWV = Pretoria Witwatersrand Vereeniging; NW = North West; ET = Eastern Transvaal; NT = Northern Transvaal.

Source: Independent Electoral Commission, Johannesburg.

Western Cape, white voters outnumbered African. The reverse was the case in the Northern Cape.

By comparing the percentage of votes for 'African' parties with the proportion of Africans in the electorate and the percentage of votes for 'non-African' parties with the proportion of 'non-Africans' in the electorate in each region, it is evident that the different pattern of voting in the regions largely simply mirrors the differences in their racial composition. As the percentages in Table 6.7 show, there was a reasonably close fit between the vote for 'African' parties and the proportion of Africans in the electorate in seven of the nine regions. The exceptions were the two provinces with a substantial Coloured electorate, a substantial minority of whom voted for the ANC. In the case of 'non-African' parties, there is only a reasonably close fit in two regions, though here the effect of the rounding off of low percentages in the figures for the racial breakdown of the population is a

Table 6.6

Racial breakdown of electorate (in per cent) and region's share of total national electorate (in per cent)

	African	White	Coloured	Asian	TOTAL
WC	19	25	55	1	10.6
NC	31	18	51	0.2	1.9
EC	84	8.2	7.5	0.3	14.0
KZN	76	10	1.6	13	20.2
OFS	82	15	3	0	7.2
PWV	69	26	4	1	21.4
NW	85	12	3	0.3	7.6
ET	83	16	1	0.5	7.0
NT	96	4	0.2	0.1	10.1

Source: Independent Electoral Commission, Johannesburg.

distorting factor. However, the figures do provide a sufficient basis for putting forward two propositions, that across the country as a whole, fewer than one in ten Africans voted for a 'non-African' party, and that fewer than one in four non-Africans voted for an 'African' party.

Using survey material, but without explaining how exactly the calculations were made, Reynolds estimated that the ANC won 2–3 per cent of the white vote and the National Party 3–4 per cent of the

Table 6.7

Percentage share of 'African' parties of African votes and percentage share of 'non-African' parties of 'non-African' votes by region (in votes cast for the National Assembly)

Region	'African' parties	'non-African' parties
Western Cape	191	76
Northern Cape	166	69
Eastern Cape	104	80
KwaZulu-Natal	107	97
Orange Free State	98	104
P W V	94	111
North West	101	89
Eastern Transvaal	103	81
Northern Transvaal	99	124

Sources: Calculated from previous tables.

African vote.[17] It is unclear which surveys were used for the purpose of Reynolds's calculations, but in the light of the poor record of some of the regional surveys, only limited reliance can be placed on the results, though it does provide strong confirmation of the polarisation of African and white voters. That was also confirmed by a post-election survey commissioned by the Institute for Democracy in South Africa (IDASA). Its fit with voting patterns in the April elections is sufficiently good to be treated as providing a reasonable indication of the division of support for the main political parties on racial lines (see Table 6.8).

Table 6.8

Distribution of Party Identification

Party	Total	African	White	Coloured	Indian
ANC	57.6	75.2	0.7	28.4	21.9
NP	15.0	1.6	48.3	53.1	48.9
IFP	5.3	6.4	3.8	0.2	–
FF	2.2	–	13.8	–	–
DP	1.3	–	7.3	1.4	–
PAC	1.4	1.8	–	0.9	–
ACDP	0.4	–	1.7	1.7	–
Other	1.4	0.6	4.2	0.4	7.9
None	12.0	11.1	15.1	11.7	19.5
Confidential	3.5	3.3	5.3	2.2	1.8

Source: Robert Mattes, *The Election book: Judgement and choice in South Africa's 1994 Election*, Institute for Democracy in South Africa, Cape Town 1995, p.132.

Within the African electorate, the main cleavage was between the ANC and the IFP. It was predominantly a regional cleavage. The vote for the IFP in KwaZulu-Natal constituted 88.5 per cent of its total national vote. Outside of KwaZulu-Natal, the IFP's share of the vote for the National Assembly was just under 1.5 per cent. While KwaZulu-Natal is a stronghold of Zulu-speakers, approximately a third of Zulu-speakers live outside the region. In particular, in their analysis of the party's electoral prospects, Mark Gervisser and Chris Louw estimated that there were a million Zulu voters in the PWV region.[18] This was the IFP's strongest region after KwaZulu-Natal, accounting for a further 8.4 per cent of the party's vote nationally. Taking the regional turn-out of voters into consideration, the IFP vote of a little under 175,000 was equal to about a fifth of the number of Zulu voters in the

PWV. This was much lower than might have been expected in view of the violent conflict in the region between Zulu hostel dwellers and other township residents. What it indicates is that the IFP had little appeal to the majority of Zulu-speakers who did not live in the hostels. An important difference between the hostel dwellers and other township residents was that the hostel-dwellers retained their links with the rural areas of KwaZulu-Natal from which they had come as migrant workers. Outside the PWV, the IFP fared even worse. The obvious conclusion would seem to be that the IFP is more of a regional than an ethnic party, notwithstanding the emphasis given by the party itself to ethnic mobilisation.

By contrast, the IFP's performance in KwaZulu Natal far exceeded the expectations of political analysts and pollsters.[19] A variety of explanations have been put forward to account for it. One explanation was that it was a vote for peace in the recognition that unless the IFP got something out of its late decision to participate in the election, it was likely to revert to a policy of destabilisation. The very high level of violence in the region before the party changed its mind on the question of participation gave voters an uncomfortable indication of what could be expected if the IFP did not like the outcome of the poll. Given the importance attached by voters to peace as an issue in the elections and to the elections as a means of bringing out peace, this is a plausible line of argument, though it carries the danger of understating the authenticity of support for the IFP especially in its homeland stronghold. However, it does link up with an explanation for the very poor showing of the PAC, which received 1.25 per cent of the total national vote. This was that the PAC was severely damaged by its association in the public mind with the slogan 'one settler one bullet', which in the context of the balance of forces in South Africa appeared tantamount to a call for civil war.

Another explanation put forward for the IFP's success in KwaZulu-Natal was that support for the party had been underestimated as a result of the urban bias of opinion polls. Further, the polls reflected the IFP's campaign against the elections, a campaign which was unpopular among its own supporters, and not its eleventh hour decision to take part. KwaZulu-Natal generated more complaints about irregularities than any other region of the country. That they played a role in the party's success, especially in the light of the party's control of the machinery of government in the homeland of KwaZulu, cannot be excluded as a possibility. The poor organisation of polling in the region, itself partly due to the lateness of the IFP's decision to take part, meant that many opportunities for fraud presented themselves. The issue of how the parties dealt with allegations of irregularities is discussed further below. A clearer picture of the basis of the IFP's electoral success emerged from the IEC's publication of the results of the election by district. They bring out the extent to which the IFP dominated the rural areas of the province. For example, in the district of Mahblabathini the party received 127,418 votes out of a total of 128,881 valid votes cast (i.e. 99 per cent of the vote).

While there were regional fluctuations in the level of support for parties other than the IFP that were not simply a function of the racial composition of the electorates in the different regions, none of the other parties gaining representation in the National Assembly could be described as a regionally based party. While the Freedom Front wished to demonstrate strength in particular areas to buttress its claim to the creation of an Afrikaner *volkstaat*, the outcome of the elections failed to help its case. While the stereotype of right-wing Afrikaners was that they were men of the soil in the Afrikaner heartlands, the truth was rather different. Over 90 per cent of the white electorate was to be found in the urban areas. By contrast, a majority of Africans still lived in the rural areas.[20] That was reflected in the results of the elections. Thus, in places traditionally associated with conservative Afrikaners, such as the Northern and Eastern Transvaal, the ANC emerged as overwhelmingly the dominant party (see Table 6.5). By contrast, the Freedom Front achieved its best result in the elections for the provincial legislature of the one almost entirely urban region in the country, the PWV, the core of which is Johannesburg.

The liberal Democratic Party also achieved its best result in the provincial elections for the PWV (see Table 6.5). The Democratic Party's poor showing across the country reflected its inability to generate support outside the ranks of affluent English-speaking white South Africans. In the light of the party's long record of opposition to apartheid as the Progressive Party and then the Progressive Federal Party before becoming the Democratic Party, its failure to break out of the suburbs at first sight seems most surprising. Its supporters were inclined to blame the outcome on the difficulty it encountered in campaigning in the townships because of intimidation by supporters of the ANC. IDASA's post-election survey suggests that another factor was important to the party's lack of success outside the suburbs. Respondents were asked to place the political parties and themselves along a left-right spectrum. African voters placed themselves on the left of the spectrum, slightly further to the left of both the PAC and the ANC. The IFP occupied a position just slightly to the right of centre, while African voters placed both the Democratic Party and the National Party on the right of the spectrum. Coloured voters placed themselves to the right of both the PAC and ANC while placing the National Party and the Democratic Party to the right of their position. But while the Coloured respondents placed themselves at a point in the spectrum that was roughly equidistant from the ANC and the National Party, they actually put the Democratic Party to the right of the National Party. The image of the Democratic Party as a right-wing party owed much to the late infusion into the party of libertarian ideology, particularly through the influence of its energetic Transvaal leader, Tony Leon. This influence was reflected in the party's campaign slogans of 'more freedom – less government' and 'federalism, free enterprise, and freedom'.

By and large, the two largest parties, the ANC and the National Party campaigned on national issues. The main exception to this was the National Party's campaign in the Western Cape, which focused on the threat posed to Coloureds by the movement of Africans into the region and on the likelihood that an ANC government would give preferential treatment to Africans over Coloureds. The ANC denied any intention to treat Africans more favourably than Coloureds while defending its commitment to affirmative action for those who had been disadvantaged by apartheid. Nationally, the National Party campaigned on the theme that the ANC's policies would ruin the economy, pointing to examples of socialist failure in the rest of Africa. For its part, the ANC promoted its plans for the country's reconstruction under the slogan 'jobs, peace, and freedom', promising to repair the devastation brought about by apartheid.

The appeal of national themes to the electorate was reflected in the fact that in the voting for the provincial legislatures, only one party that had not won a seat in the National Assembly managed to gain representation at the provincial level. This was the Minority Front, an Asian-based party which won a single seat in the KwaZulu-Natal legislature with 1.34 per cent of the vote. The votes for some other small parties were also concentrated in particular regions, especially in the case of parties linked to former homeland rulers, but the size of their vote was so minute that they fell far short of winning a seat anywhere. The negligible support for conservative homeland parties provided a striking testimony to the failure of apartheid to engender any regional loyalties to its servants.

The shambolic organisation of the elections by the IEC meant that at the counting stage, there were huge numbers of ballots in dispute among the parties, particularly from the former homelands where breaches of procedures had been commonplace. It was in relation to the parties' dealings with the IEC over disputed ballots that the suspicions of a negotiated outcome to the elections arose. Room for negotiation was created by the fact that the ANC was more concerned that the result should be accepted by the parties than it was to maximise the scale of its victory. In particular, in accepting the IFP's victory in KwaZulu-Natal, the national leadership of the ANC over-ruled the provincial leadership in KwaZulu-Natal who had cried foul. A factor in the ANC's readiness to accept the huge majorities piled up by the IFP in the homeland of KwaZulu was a recognition that the very high turn-out of ANC voters in the Transkei was also open to question.

At one point during the long counting of votes it seemed possible that the ANC was going to win a two-thirds majority in the Constituent Assembly. There was a negative reaction in the financial markets to the speculation. Calm was restored when the announcement of the full results by the IEC showed that the ANC had fallen short of get-ting a two-thirds majority in the Constituent Assembly by 15 seats (see Table 6.3). Mandela's attitude towards the issue is given in his autobiography:

> Some in the ANC were disappointed that we did not cross the two-thirds threshold, but I was not one of them. In fact I was relieved; had we won two-thirds of the vote and been able to write a constitution unfettered by input from others, people would argue that we had created an ANC constitution, not a South African constitution. I wanted a true govern-ment of national unity.[22]

What was important to the National Party, apart from its victory in the Western Cape, which was not in doubt, was that it should cross the 20 per cent threshold enabling the party to secure one of the two Deputy Presidents for its leader. This it did. The disqualification of large numbers of ballots from the homelands would have benefited both the Democratic Party and the Freedom Front, but only very slightly in view of the low level of their vote, so muting their objec-tions. Further, all the parties recognised that many of the irregulari-ties were a product of incompetence and inefficiency rather than fraud. That was also the view of most of the foreign observers of the elections. For example, the Commonwealth Observer Group made the following assessment of the elections:

> In the final analysis, the elections represented a free and clear expression of the will of the South African people. The outcome was the result of a

credible democratic process which was substantially fair. We do not believe that abuses were widespread or had a determinative impact on the overall result.[23]

What the debate over the failings of the IEC's conduct of polling and the counting of votes did not address was the argument that the outcome was a reflection of party control of territory in the run-up to polling which had the effect of depriving many voters of a real choice. Proponents of this argument highlighted the difficulties that parties other than the ANC had in campaigning in most African townships, the exclusion of the ANC from much of rural KwaZulu-Natal by the IFP and the problems the ANC encountered in gaining access to farm-workers to put its case because of the hostility of farm-owners to the party. The implication that follows from this, given the perceived importance of the townships as an electoral battleground, is that the ANC's victory in the elections was achieved at least in part by intimidation. This argument is worth considering in some depth, not because it provides a persuasive basis for questioning the outcome of the elections, but because it helps to illuminate important issues, such as why there was polarisation between white and African voters.

One obvious weakness of the argument was that it underestimated the steps that were taken by the IEC in accordance with international practice to ensure that the voting process itself was free of intimidation. Thus, an integral part of voter education explaining the mechanics of voting to electors also drove home the message that their ballot was secret. Confidence in the secrecy of the ballot was reinforced by the arrangements at polling stations for the casting of votes, including the use of voting booths. A further weakness is that the polling itself took place in conditions of quite extraordinary tranquillity. The point is very well made in the report of the Commonwealth Observer Group:

> What was remarkable, too, about the voting days was the exceptional peace that prevailed throughout the country, which for several years and up to the last week before polling had been ravaged by political violence. Some of our group had come to South Africa with trepidation because of the images of violence and brutality relayed internationally. The initial briefing we received, especially in KwaZulu/Natal, only seemed to confirm the worst fears of some observers. But the IFP decision to participate in the elections lifted the pall of fear and uncertainty over security on voting days. Even the senseless carnage which briefly burst upon the elections in a spate of bombings in the PWV, allegedly by the extreme right, only served to stiffen the resolve of all to vote. In the event, those three days were the

most peaceful that South Africans could remember in a long time. There was virtually no reported incidence of violence because of political rivalry. After the voting ended, IEC Chairman Mr Justice Kriegler asserted that there was not a single death attributable to the elections during the voting period. There was also hardly any report of large-scale intimidation of any kind. The Bharagwanath Hospital in Soweto, reportedly the largest in the Southern Hemisphere, recorded one of the quietest periods ever experienced in the emergency departments of the hospital.[24]

Clearly, such conditions would not have prevailed if it had not been an inclusive election with the participation of the IFP and even of the extreme white right in the form of the Freedom Front.

Nevertheless, Welsh's comment quoted earlier in this chapter that 'hardly any of the sanctimonious foreign observers . . .would for one moment have accepted the validity of an elections subject to such flaws in their own country' is not entirely unjustified (even if unfair as a description of how they approached their task as monitors). What it helps to highlight is that the conditions for campaigning in the South African elections did not match those in established or politically stable liberal democracies. That is obviously the case. However, the complaints of lack of political access across community divides is a familiar one in deeply divided societies, including societies, such as Northern Ireland, that have had long experience in the holding of elections in such circumstances. Extreme inequality between communities and conflicting identities are commonly associated with deeply divided societies and are often cited as reasons for describing South Africa as a deeply divided society. However, in fact, neither is a defining characteristic of a deeply divided society. Much more fundamental to the nature of a deeply divided society is that communities within the society differ in their attitude not simply to particular government policies but to the very legitimacy of existing political institutions. Where communities are polarised in their attitudes towards the legitimacy of existing political institutions, they also tend to be polarised in their attitudes towards the security forces of the state, viewed as instruments of coercion used to uphold the authority of the status quo.

Conflict between the communities in such a society may remain latent for decades, particularly where a dominant community is able to impose its political will on subordinate communities. But in such circumstances, relations between the communities still tend to be shaped fundamentally by the relationship of force between them. Thus, even in times of tranquillity, members of the dominant community remain vigilant for signs of rebellion in the subordinate communities on the assumption that the obedience of the subordinate communities rests on acquiescence maintained by coercion rather than freely given consent. Fundamental change in such societies inevitably affects the force field between the communities. When De Klerk liberalised the South African political system, he hoped that he would be able to establish the rules within which the competition for votes would take place when democratic elections were held. However, the liberalisation of the system was not sufficient by itself to confer legitimacy on De Klerk and his government either within the country or internationally. The result was a violent contest for political control during the transition, in which the parties justified their actions as reactions to the illegitimate strategies being pursued by other political actors.

Robert Mattes argues that it is wrong to conclude from the polarisation of voting along racial lines in the 1994 elections that the elections were, in a phrase used by a number of analysts, 'a racial census'.

> Just because racially or ethnically defined groups of people voted largely for one party does not necessarily mean that race or ethnicity was a primary concern of any individual voter. Racial or ethnic classification . . . do not tell us *why* people voted the way they did. . . ...[A] high correlation between race or ethnicity and the vote need not necessarily be the result of non-rational or primordial factors.[25]

Mattes explores a number of explanations of the racial polarisation of voting in the 1994 elections, using material gathered in IDASA's post-election survey. His findings include:

- while most voters do possess ethnic or racial identities, and do attach importance to these identities, these voters do not appear to behave politically in vastly different ways from those voters who do not have such identities or who do not attach much importance to them;
- racial or ethnic concerns were not widely cited as primary reasons for party and candidate support; and
- the vast majority of voters saw the political parties they supported as open and representative of all South Africans (and apparently seemed to approve of that fact).[26]

At the same time, it is also clear from the survey that class (measured by income) was a much weaker indicator of voting patterns than race, notwithstanding the overlap between race and class as a legacy of apartheid. In short, IDASA's survey leaves the puzzle of the polarisation of white and African voters unsolved.

However, a clue is provided in the analysis of the issues of the campaign. Respondents were asked to identify the most important problems facing the new government. Violence headed the list for respondents of all races and of all parties except the ANC, whose supporters placed the issue narrowly second to that of jobs. Unfortunately, the survey does not probe this issue further. However, it seems likely that there were very different understandings among the different communities and the supporters of different parties as to where the primary responsibility for the problem lay. As the chapters on the role of violence during the transition have underlined, South Africa during the transition was a force field. Consequently, perhaps the simplest explanation of the way people voted is to be found in their different responses to this reality. It is partially captured in another common description of the election, one less pejorative than the notion of a racial census, that of a 'liberation election'.[27] This quite obviously had different meanings for the members of different communities.

Fear of violence was a potent factor during the election campaign itself. A small indication of that was the panic buying of groceries and other essentials ahead of polling. However, the fact that all political groupings, with only very minor exceptions, had come to accept the legitimacy of the elections ensured that the polling itself took place in conditions of peace. Indeed, the focus on the elections seems to have created a much wider truce in the society in which all manner of antagonisms were in suspension for the period of voting, an atmosphere that contributed to the palpable sense that what the country was experiencing was indeed little short of a miracle. In the next chapter the controversial issue of the contribution of the international community to this outcome is examined.

Notes to Chapter 6

1   Nelson Mandela, *Long Walk to Freedom: The Autobiography of Nelson Mandela*, MacDonald Purnell, Randburg 1994, p.614.

2   R.W.Johnson and Lawrence Schlemmer (eds), *Launching Democracy in South Africa: The First Open Election, April 1994*, Yale University Press, London and New Haven 1996, p.323.

3   Andrew Reynolds, 'The Results' in Andrew Reynolds (ed.), *Elections '94 South Africa: The campaigns, results and future prospects*, James Currey, London 1994, p.187.

4 Robert Mattes, *The Election Book: Judgement and Choice in South Africa's 1994 Election*, Institute for Democracy in South Africa, Cape Town 1995, p.19.

5 Figure issued by Central Statistical Services, Pretoria, in 1997.

6 *SA 97/98: South Africa at a Glance*, Editors Inc, Craighall 1997, p.18.

7 Johnson and Schlemmer (eds), *op. cit.*, p.325.

8 *The Weekend Star* (Johannesburg), 7–8 May, 1994.

9 *The Weekly Mail and Guardian* (Johannesburg), 6–12 May 1994.

10 See, for example, Denis Beckett, 'Drawing a line at deception', *The Star*, 20 May 1994.

11 *The Weekend Star*, 7–8 May, 1994.

12 Robert Mattes, 'The Road to Democracy: From 2 February to 27 April 1994' in Reynolds (ed.), *op. cit.*, p.4.

13 *Ibid.*, p.14 and footnote 54 on p.21.

14 *Ibid.*, p.18.

15 See, for example, the reports on The Star-MMR poll in *The Star*, 31 March 1994.

16 Derived from data in Andrew Reynolds, 'The Results' in Reynolds (ed.), *op. cit.*, pp.187–211.

17 *Ibid.*, p.190 and p.193.

18 *The Weekly Mail and Guardian*, 22–28 April 1994.

19 See, for example, John Battersby, 'Call for Zulu Kingdom Raises Ante in South Africa', *The Christian Science Monitor* (World Edition), 18–24 February 1994.

20 Anton Harber and Barbara Ludman (eds), *A-Z of South African Politics*, Penguin, Johannesburg 1994, p.285.

21 Mattes (1995), *op. cit.*, pp.55–6.

22 Mandela, *op cit.*, p.611.

23 *The End of Apartheid: The Report of the Commonwealth Observer Group to the South African Elections 26–29 April 1994*, Commonwealth Secretariat, London 1994, p.71

24 *Ibid.*, p.48.

25 Mattes (1995), *op. cit.*, pp.10–1.

26 *Ibid.*, p.5.

27 *The End of Apartheid, op. cit.*, p.67.

CHAPTER 7

South Africa and World Politics

One of the ways in which supporters of the process that led to South Africa's negotiated political settlement sought to legitimise the transition was to emphasise its South African-ness. During the1994 elections most parties tested, to a greater or lesser degree, the potential of appeals to a South African patriotism that cut across the racial identifications which had become so strongly entrenched under apartheid, by couching their appeals to voters in inclusive terms. However, it is worth noting in this context that in IDASA's post-election survey, only 13.6 per cent of the sample replied to questions on what community they belonged to by identifying themselves as South Africans, though a further 7.2 per cent combined the term South African with some other racial, ethnic or linguistic label.[1] Appeal to a common South African nationalism was also reflected in the insistence of the parties that the settlement which they had reached through the negotiations in the Multi-Party Negotiating Forum had been arrived at by South Africans between South Africans for South Africans without external interference. It will be argued in this chapter that a consequence of this attitude has been an underplaying of the role played by the international community in the outcome of the process. In particular, it will be argued that the interpretation that the international community placed on events was a factor in helping to ensure the ANC's triumph and a transition to African majority rule rather than to a consociational system of entrenched power sharing and minority vetoes.

South Africa's conflict with the international community did not begin with the political impasse of the 1980s, when Jack Spence described the country in a memorable phrase as 'the most popular corpse in history'.[2] In fact, it even preceded the election of the

National Party government in 1948 on a platform of apartheid. In November 1946 the United Nations rejected South Africa's request to incorporate South West Africa and the General Assembly passed a resolution recommending that the territory, which had been a mandate of the League of Nations, should become a UN trusteeship territory, while the issue of South Africa's treatment of the Indian minority came before the General Assembly in January 1947 as a result of representations by the government of India.[3]

In a book published in the early 1960s, Colin De B.Webb argued that South Africa's conflict with the international community had its origins in the changes to the international political system brought about by the Second World War.

> The decisive theatre of war . . . was not Europe, but the Far East. For it was there, with the Japanese attack on South-East Asia, that the first of the death-blows was struck at that world of European political ascendancy in which the South African system had had its appropriate place.[4]

While South African racial policies ran counter to the *direction* of policies being pursued in the rest of the world during the 1950s, resemblances between South African practices and segregationist policies to be found in European colonies and in the southern states of the United States helped to mute criticism within the West of the Union of South Africa.

The Sharpeville massacre on 21 March 1960 was a turning point in the country's relations with the outside world. It sharpened external perceptions of apartheid's lack of internal legitimacy. In the same year the UN General Assembly adopted a *Declaration on the Granting of Independence to Colonial Countries and Peoples*,[5] which in its interpretation of the principle of self-determination served to underline apartheid's lack of international legitimacy. This was even more forcefully underscored in the 1970 *Declaration of Principles of International Law concerning Friendly Relations and Co-operation among States in accordance with the Charter of the United Nations*. This emphasised the rights of peoples deprived of the right of self-determination 'to seek and receive support',[6] giving legitimacy to liberation movements fighting colonial or minority rule in southern Africa. A sharp line was drawn between these cases and states 'conducting themselves in compliance with the principle of equal rights and self-determination and thus possessed of a government representing the whole people belonging to the territory without distinction as to race, creed or colour'.[7]

By this time, there was not merely an international consensus as to the illegitimacy of apartheid, but it was also clear what would be required of South Africa to comply with international norms and that was a system embodying the principle of one-person-one-vote in a unitary state. That did not rule out a federal system with power devolved to different regions of the country, provided that was the choice of the people of South Africa. What arrangements would or would not be seen to comply with the prevailing interpretation of the principle of self-determination became an important area of contention. While the South African government's posture was frequently one of angry defiance of world opinion, it was by no means the case that the government sought isolation or was comfortable with its status as a pariah. Thus, even at the height of the implementation of apartheid during the 1960s, steps such as the granting of self-government to the Transkei were designed to persuade critics that apartheid entailed self-determination of the different nations of South Africa. The Muldergate scandal in 1978 arose out of efforts by the Department of Information to buy a better image for South Africa in the West. The 'sham consociationalism'[8] of the tricameral constitution of the mid-1980s was also an attempt to accommodate international norms by establishing a system with apparent resemblances to practices to be found in countries long considered to be 'in compliance with the principle of equal rights and self-determination'.

The international community used a variety of methods in seeking to persuade the South African government to change its policies. Deon Geldenhuys has labelled the different means used under four headings; intervention, isolation, conditional engagement, and mediation.[9] However, before considering the evolution of each of these, it is important to stress that South Africa's relations with the rest of the world were by no means only determined by the conflict between apartheid and international norms. Pressure on South Africa to change course naturally tended to be at its strongest during periods of internal upheaval within the country. Thus, South Africa came under pressure in the years immediately following the Sharpeville massacre. The pressure abated from the mid-1960s when it became clear that the government had succeeded in crushing internal dissent. At the start of the Nixon Presidency in the United States, a review of American policy towards southern Africa was conducted by the National Security Council under Kissinger. The study was completed in August 1969 and subsequently leaked to the media. It concluded: 'For the foreseeable future South Africa will be able to maintain internal stability and effectively counter insurgent activity.'[10]

The study recommended a change in American policy from a posture of one of limited association with the white states of southern Africa to the objective of a broader association with both black and white states. The change was a reflection of the countervailing influence of American strategic interests, a recognition of the role that South Africa could play in combating Soviet influence in the region, an objective that fitted into increased reliance being placed by the United States on regional powers in the context of the Nixon doctrine. The upheavals in southern Africa in the mid-1970s undermined the assumptions of the Kissinger study. With Jimmy Carter's election as President came a very different approach to foreign policy. Carter tried to rebuild a domestic consensus on foreign policy after the country's defeat in Vietnam by emphasising America's commitment to human rights. This normative approach entailed a posture of strong opposition to apartheid. However, concern over the extension of Soviet influence in Africa prompted arguments within the administration over its priorities, with the deterioration in relations between the United States and the Soviet Union from the late 1970s bringing about a reassertion of the importance of the strategic factor. With Reagan's election there was a return to option 2 of the Kissinger study under the new label of 'constructive engagement'.

However, South Africa's resort to a policy of destabilisation of neighbouring states in the context of the total strategy rapidly eroded support in the United States Congress for constructive engagement. It was comprehensively undermined by unrest in South Africa's townships from September 1984. The consequence was the passage of legislation in 1986, the Comprehensive Anti-Apartheid Act, imposing sanctions against South Africa that overrode President Reagan's veto. Reagan's successor, George Bush, responded to the mood in Congress by making it clear that he would not veto additional sanctions legislation if the South African government failed to take steps in the direction of the country's democratisation.[11] That was one of the factors that weighed with De Klerk when he announced the liberalisation of the South African political system in February 1990. By the time of Bill Clinton's election in November 1992, the South African government had already given up hope of defeating the ANC in democratic elections.

The divisions in the United States over policy towards South Africa were present to a greater or lesser degree in other Western countries. Governments and parties of the left generally supported a policy of sanctions against South Africa, while governments and parties of the right tended to be more sympathetic to the argument that change was best promoted by bridge-building and positive rather than negative inducements to whites to change their attitudes. While strategic factors played a part in the attitude of European governments towards South Africa, commercial considerations loomed much larger than they did in the case of the United States as a reason for resisting demands for the imposition of economic sanctions. But for all the differences among Western societies, two trends were apparent by the mid-1980s. Firstly, the strength of anti-apartheid opinion was such that consumers were imposing sanctions on South Africa independently of legislation to outlaw the importation of South African goods, reducing the significance of the ideological disposition of the party in power and secondly, the broad direction of Western policy was towards an intensification of sanctions.

In general, debate in the West over policy towards South Africa gravitated between the options of isolation and conditional engagement, to use Geldenhuys's terminology. For different reasons little consideration was given to Geldenhuys's other options of intervention and mediation. By intervention Geldenhuys had in mind coercive foreign interference to change the South African political system, whether directly by military action on the part of the state or states concerned, or indirectly through support to the 'armed struggle' against apartheid being waged by organisations such as the ANC. In practice, no state attempted to confront white minority rule directly through military action. African states, through support for the Organisation of African Unity's Liberation Committee or, at great cost to themselves in the case of states in southern Africa, through permitting the ANC to operate from their territory, made a modest contribution to the ANC's efforts to challenge the South African government by violent means. The main source of material support for the ANC's 'armed struggle' lay outside Africa in the Soviet bloc.

Soviet support for the ANC was a factor in the hostility of conservative opinion in the West to the ANC's campaign of violence against the South African government. However, the basis of Western opposition to the use of violence against apartheid lay deeper. It rested on the fact that Western societies tended to identify whites in South Africa as themselves a fragment of the West itself. On the one hand, this fuelled demands within Western societies that South Africa should be made to conform to current Western norms rejecting racial discrimination. On the other hand, their 'cultural proximity' to South Africa, to use Robert Jackson's phrase,[12] ruled out both direct military intervention by the West or support for anything other than non-violent methods in the struggle against apartheid. Unusually, in the

South African case, the West's attitude towards the legitimacy of the regime and its policies and its attitude towards the legitimacy of anti-system violence against that regime diverged. More usually, one is a function of the other. For example, Western rejection of the legitimacy of the regime installed by Soviet intervention in Afghanistan in 1979 was followed by Western military assistance to Islamic fundamentalist groups fighting to overthrow it.

Western opposition to the use of violent means in the struggle against apartheid was reflected in the characterisation of the ANC by conservative parties in the West as a terrorist organisation. Further, because conservatives tended to dominate discourse within the West on the subject of terrorism, it was a characterisation that was supported in the literature on terrorism and even in such official publications as the annual report of the American State Department's Ambassador-at-large for Counterterrorism, *Patterns of Global Terrorism*.[13] At the same time, there was recognition within the West of the violent methods being used by the South African government in defence of apartheid. Thus, during the 1988 Presidential campaign in the United States, the Democratic candidate, Michael Dukakis, argued that South Africa should be added to the list of the countries the State Department designated as 'terrorist states' because of their sponsorship of international terrorism. When the Commonwealth committee of foreign ministers on southern Africa commissioned a report on the subject of South Africa's policy of destabilisation of neighbouring states in the 1980s, it was published under the title, *Apartheid Terrorism*.[14]

Part of the appeal of sanctions to Western opinion was as an alternative means to bringing about change in South Africa that was non-violent. By contrast, the ANC and its supporters viewed sanctions as an important additional source of pressure on the South African government, while by and large white opinion within South Africa tended to be hostile to sanctions. Of course, sanctions took many forms, from the exclusion of South Africa from international sporting competition and cultural and academic boycotts to trade embargoes and bans on loans. The variety of different sanctions made it possible for there to be a multiplicity of views on the question of sanctions, so that within white South Africa there was an acknowledgement both of the legitimacy of the initial steps taken to oppose apartheid in sport and of their effectiveness. In the prelude to the referendum among whites on reform in March 1992, the threat of a renewal of sporting sanctions in the event of a 'no' vote was used very effectively by the 'yes' campaign. For example, one of the advertisements urging whites to vote 'yes' showed an overgrown cricket pitch as the consequence of a 'no' vote. What gave this message added salience was that the referendum campaign coincided with the holding of the cricket world cup in which a South African team was taking part for the first time.

This example illustrates how complex a task it is to analyse the role that isolation played in the South African transition. In this instance, the threat of the country's renewed isolation does appear to have influenced white opinion to accept change. However, if in the first place anti-apartheid campaigners had not accepted South Africa's readmission to international sport ahead of democratic elections, such an opportunity would not have arisen. In particular, it is arguable that if the ANC had taken a different attitude, the readmission might not have happened. As it was, the ANC chose the symbolic arena of sport to make concessions to white opinion through easing the re-entry of South African teams into international competition.

At the same time, De Klerk's thorough-going liberalisation of the South African political system in February 1990 was intended to win over world opinion so as to clear the way for the lifting of Western economic sanctions. Even more obviously, the government's repeal of the remaining pillars of legislative apartheid was explicitly directed at meeting the specific conditions for the ending of sanctions laid down in the American Comprehensive Anti-Apartheid Act. It is hardly surprising in these circumstances that a wide consensus has arisen among American commentators and politicians that the Comprehensive Anti-Apartheid Act represents a striking example of the political effectiveness of economic sanctions. However, the matter is not quite as simple as it appears. De Klerk's calculation that he would be rewarded for the liberalisation of the polity by the lifting of sanctions was based on the expectation that such a reversal could be achieved and that rested on the assumption that he could rely on influential political figures, such as the British Conservative leader, Margaret Thatcher, to press the case against sanctions. (Of course this is not suggest that Margaret Thatcher deserves special credit for the ending of apartheid, merely that the chain of causality may contain ironies.)

Once historians get access to the papers of this period, a fuller picture may emerge of how far the government was influenced in its course of action by assurances on the lifting of sanctions. It will be interesting to see whether the prospect of an ending of sanctions or a fear of the further tightening of sanctions, if it failed to act, loomed larger in the government's thinking. In any event, De Klerk's calculation that liberalisation would led to a substantial easing of sanctions was correct and the ANC's rearguard diplomatic efforts to persuade Western governments to continue economic sanctions until the completion of negotiations on a democratic settlement were largely unsuccessful. What is important to note in this context of the argument of this book is that sanctions cannot provide the answer to the ANC's emergence from the period of the transition in a position of political dominance, since in this area at least the ANC's leverage proved relatively weak. Indeed, it a matter of debate how successful the ANC would have been if it had attempted to keep sporting sanctions. The picture may well have been mixed with different consequences in different sports. Further, if sanctions did not play a crucial role in the outcome of the transition, it is also arguable that the end of the Cold War was a much more significant factor in the initiation of the transition, though the connection between the two factors needs to be noted in this context. The point here is that the end of bipolarity undermined Pretoria's case that it was a valuable bulwark against the spread of Communism and thus not an appropriate target for Western sanctions.

Geldenhuys's third category of conditional engagement was an important element in the European Community's policy towards South Africa in the period leading up to the transition and during the transition itself. In September 1985 the European Community agreed to a small package of sanctions against South Africa, including a ban on oil sales to the Republic and the ending of military cooperation with member states. The very limited nature of the package reflected disagreement among member states on the policy of sanctions. At the same time, member states agreed to the adoption of a strategy of giving assistance to those working for change in South Africa by non-violent methods. To this end, the European Community launched a special programme to assist the victims of apartheid. The Special Programme, which was run by the European Commission, channelled aid to South Africa through non-governmental organisations in five sectors: education and training; health; rural and agricultural development; community development; and good governance and democratisation. Under the last category aid was given to organisations monitoring the observance of human rights. The political impact of such measures and other forms of conditional engagement, such as the 1977 Sullivan principles providing a code of conduct for American multinational companies operating in South Africa, was indirect, though in its contribution to the empowerment of the subordinate communities of some assistance to the struggle against apartheid.

The fourth of Geldenhuys's categories, mediation, only arose towards the end of the apartheid era as a feasible mode of external engagement in South Africa and perhaps partly for that reason has tended to be neglected in accounts of the influence of external factors on South Africa. A striking exception to this is Chris Landsberg's chapter, 'Directing from the Stalls? The international community and the South African negotiation forum' in *The Small Miracle*, the account of South Africa's negotiated settlement edited by Friedman and Atkinson.[15] It will be argued below that external mediation had a profound impact on the outcome of South Africa's transition. Mediation presupposes that the parties to a conflict have reached the point of being ready to enter into negotiations with the other side. That assumption only became possible in the South African case in the mid-1980s. The first major effort at external mediation arose without prior consultation with the parties. As in the case of the European Community's positive measures, it arose out of disagreement over the policy of sanctions and, in particular, the opposition to sanctions of the British Prime Minister, Margaret Thatcher.

At the Commonwealth Heads of Government meeting in Nassau, the Bahamas, in October 1985 there was agreement on the adoption of sanctions against South Africa, but not on the scope of the package, thanks to Thatcher's strong resistance to a comprehensive package of measures, particularly in the economic field. As a compromise, it was agreed that a mission of eminent persons should be established to explore the possibility of dialogue between the South African parties, before consideration was given to the adoption of more restrictive measures against South Africa. The Commonwealth Accord on Southern Africa adopted at Nassau gave as the rationale for the strategy of combining mediation and sanctions 'impressing upon the authorities in Pretoria the compelling urgency of dismantling apartheid and erecting the structures of democracy in South Africa'. It argued that such a process demanded dialogue with 'the true representatives of the majority black population' and described the task of the Eminent Persons Group (EPG), as it became known, as being 'to encourage through all practicable ways the evolution of that necessary process of political dialogue'. It acknowledged the unilateral nature of this initiative:

We are not unmindful of the difficulties such an effort will encounter, including the possibility of initial rejection by the South African authorities, but we believe it to be our duty to leave nothing undone that might contribute to peaceful change in South Africa and avoid the dreadful prospect of violent conflict that looms over South Africa, threatening people of all races in the country, and the peace and stability of the entire Southern Africa region.[16]

Following consultations among a number of the heads of government, the seven names of the EPG were announced in November 1985. The co-chairmen of the group were the former Australian Prime Minister, Malcolm Fraser, and a former military ruler of Nigeria, General Olusegun Obasanjo. Other members of the group included a former British Conservative Chancellor of the Exchequer, the Anglican Primate of Canada, a former Tanzanian foreign minister, a former Indian defence minister, and a Barbadian who at the time was the President of the World Council of Churches.

The parameters of the EPG's mission had been effectively established by the five steps called for in the Commonwealth Accord on Southern Africa. They were that as a matter of urgency the authorities in Pretoria should:

(a) Declare that the system of apartheid will be dismantled and specific and meaningful action taken in fulfilment of that intent.
(b) Terminate the existing state of emergency.
(c) Release immediately and unconditionally Nelson Mandela and all others imprisoned and detained for their opposition to apartheid.
(d) Establish political freedom and specifically lift the existing ban on the African National Congress and other political parties.
(e) Initiate, in the context of a suspension of violence on all sides, a process of dialogue across lines of colour, politics and religion, with a view to establishing a non-racial and representative government.[17]

Despite their unpalatable implications in the context of its existing policies, the South African government decided, at least initially, to cooperate with the mission of the EPG, mindful both that its refusal would have prompted the automatic intensification of sanctions by most of the Commonwealth and that there was a possibility the ANC would respond negatively to the requirement of a suspension of violence, allowing blame for the political impasse to be shifted away from the government.

Three members of the EPG conducted a preliminary visit to South Africa and neighbouring states in February 1986 in the course of which they met representatives of the South African government, the main political parties, the United Democratic Front, the governments of neighbouring states and the ANC in exile. A visit of the full group to South Africa followed in March, with its engagements including a meeting with Nelson Mandela in Pollsmoor prison. A second visit of the group to South Africa and Zambia took place in May. This visit was cut short on 19 May when the South African Air Force launched a series of bombing attacks on the neighbouring states of Botswana, Zambia and Zimbabwe. By this time the EPG's mission had led to a white backlash in South Africa. That was reflected in the disruption of public meetings organised by the National Party by the extreme right-wing *Afrikaner Weerstandsbeweging* (AWB).

South Africa's military action was widely recognised as being directed at ending a mediation process the continuation of which the government no longer saw as in its interest. That was underlined by the South African foreign minister's reply to a letter from the EPG. Pik Botha's letter of 29 May to the mission's co-chairmen challenged the EPG's assumptions about the basis for negotiations. In particular, it made it clear that the South African government sought a termination of violence, not simply its suspension by its adversaries, while the government regarded its own measures for the maintenance of law and order as outside the scope of steps needed to create an environment free of violence and intimidation. The letter also declared that the government was only prepared to negotiate about a new constitutional dispensation that would provide for power sharing.[18]

The report of the EPG's mission to South Africa was published in June. It formed the basis of the decisions taken by a special summit of the Commonwealth on the issue of South Africa in August 1986. Its powerful indictment of the South African government provided the basis for all members of the Commonwealth, except Britain, agreeing to the intensification of sanctions. A particularly significant aspect of the EPG's report was its approach to the question of violence in South Africa, especially in the light of the politically diverse membership of the group. Its starting point was that apartheid was an inherently violent system, while it laid most of the responsibility for current political violence in the country at the door of the government, including so-called 'black on black' violence which it argued was partly encouraged and fomented by the government.[19] This assessment went hand in hand with the report's judgement of the relative political legitimacy of the parties:

The open identification with the ANC through banners and songs, in funerals and in churches throughout the country, despite the risks involved, supports the widely-held belief that if an election were held today on the basis of universal franchise the ANC would win it.[20]

President de Klerk's dramatic initiative of February 1990 appeared to leave little scope or need for external mediation. Further, in contrast to the cases of Zimbabwe and Namibia, there appeared to be little legal justification for the involvement of the international community through the United Nations. Ironically, one of the first calls for UN involvement in relation to the upsurge in political violence that followed the liberalisation of the South African political system was made by the South African foreign minister, Pik Botha, who suggested that the UN should put pressure on Mandela and Buthelezi to end the strife in the townships. Given the relationship between the government and Buthelezi at this time, it was a somewhat disingenuous suggestion. Further, Botha was seeking to embarrass the ANC. His objective was not to promote UN monitoring of the violence.

In April 1991, the ANC sent the government an ultimatum over the violence, threatening to suspend all negotiations unless the government took a number of steps to deal with the violence, including the dismantling of certain counter-insurgency units within the security forces and the outlawing of the carrying of traditional weapons. The ANC's stance on the issue of political violence was strengthened in July 1991 by revelations that the government had been financing the IFP. Progress towards the resolution of the issue of violence was made in September 1991 when the government, the ANC and the IFP signed the National Peace Accord. This led to the appointment of Judge Richard Goldstone at the head of a standing Commission of Inquiry Regarding the Prevention of Public Violence and Intimidation and to the setting up of a National Peace Committee supported by regional and local committees. However, these measures failed to stem the tide of violence, leading to concerted pressure during 1992 for greater international involvement in efforts to end the violence.

At the end of March 1992 the report of a fact-finding mission from the International Commission of Jurists (ICJ) was published. It was based on two visits to South Africa by a team of five lawyers, the first in September 1991 and the second in March 1992. The report was strongly critical of the IFP leader, Chief Mangosuthu Buthelezi, whom it described as bearing 'a heavy responsibility for the escalation of the violence'.[21] It called for international monitoring of the violence. It wanted the creation of a team of approximately a hundred monitors observing the behaviour of both the security forces and political organisations. The ICJ's proposal was taken up inside South Africa. When Nelson Mandela visited Alexandra following an upsurge of violence between the residents and hostel dwellers in the township after the white referendum, he called for the establishment of an independent international monitoring team as 'the only way we can stop the violence'.[22] His demand was supported by an Emergency Summit on Violence which was convened by church leaders on 22 April. Representatives of 19 organisations, including the ANC, the IFP and the PAC, attended the meeting. It unanimously called for the establishment of an international body to monitor the violence, though the IFP subsequently distanced itself from the meeting's decisions.

The Organisation of African Unity (OAU) backed the idea and officially requested that the issue be debated by the UN Security Council. The Danish foreign minister, Uffe Ellemann-Jensen, also supported international monitoring after visiting South Africa and raised the issue at a meeting of European Community foreign ministers. However, at the urging of the British government, a decision on the issue was deferred. The British position was that no proposal for international monitoring should be made without a request for such assistance from the South African government. Its position changed after the Boipatong massacre. International concern over the direction of events in South Africa grew in May 1992 with the breakdown of negotiations in CODESA and fresh revelations of security force involvement in the violence. In June Amnesty International issued a highly critical report on South Africa sub-titled *State of Fear – Security Force Complicity in Torture and Political Killings, 1990–1992*.[23] That was followed by the Boipatong massacre and the shooting of unarmed demonstrators during De Klerk's ill-judged visit to the squatter camp.

Eye-witness accounts of the Boipatong massacre alleging security force complicity in the killings by the hostel-dwellers received wide coverage internationally.[24] The attempts of the government to deflect the blame on to the ANC by highlighting the climate of tension created by its mass action campaign simply suggested a motive for the massacre. After Boipatong the ANC suspended its bilateral negotiations with the government and demanded an international inquiry into the violence. A sharp fall in the value of the financial rand underlined the reaction of foreign investors to the crisis. The government's response was to appoint a number of foreign experts to assist the Goldstone Commission, but that failed to stem speculation in the South African press of further international intervention as offering the best prospect for securing a resumption of negotiations.

On 24 June, the Chairman of the US Senate Foreign Relations Committee, Paul Simon, was quoted as suggesting that Pretoria should seek UN help, while the Australian foreign minister, Senator Gareth Evans, confirmed that soundings had taken place on the sending of a Commonwealth observer mission.[25] In an editorial *The Star* argued that 'the Government should take a new and less blinkered look at some of the proposals for international monitoring that are emanating from this country's friends abroad'.[26] A week later the *Cape Times* gave its opinion that 'the prospect of international mediation offers hope that the crisis of Boipatong can be resolved before lasting damage is done to the chances of a negotiated settlement'.[27] On 2 July *The Argus* gave banner headlines to a report that President Bush had sent messages to De Klerk and Mandela offering help 'to rescue SA's peace talks'.[28] In an editorial welcoming this development entitled 'Baker the Broker?', *The Argus* argued that 'some form of international brokering may be the only way to get the negotiating process going again'.[29] The Johannesburg *Sunday Times* reported 'Western diplomats' as being of the view that De Klerk's 'failure to address the ANC's demands on violence would make it difficult for negotiators within the ANC to convince their constituency to return to talks'.[30]

These pressures culminated in a debate in the UN Security Council on the crisis in South Africa on 15 and 16 July, during which the Security Council was addressed by Pik Botha, Nelson Mandela, Chief Buthelezi, Ken Andrew (for the Democratic Party), two homeland leaders and a representative of the Indian House of Delegates. Unusually for UN deliberations, the debate received extensive media coverage in South Africa. At the end of the debate the Security Council adopted Resolution 765 of 1992 which *inter alia* expressed concern at the breakdown of negotiations, condemned the escalation of violence, making particular reference to the events in Boipatong, called for effective implementation of the National Peace Accord, and underlined the importance of all parties cooperating in the resumption of negotiations. In effect, the resolution balanced criticism of the failure of the South African authorities to deal effectively with the issue of violence and pressure on the ANC to return to the negotiations. But the most important element of the resolution was the invitation to the UN Secretary-General:

> to appoint, as a matter of urgency, a Special Representative of the Secretary-General in order to recommend . . . measures which would assist in bringing an effective end to the violence and in creating conditions for

negotiations leading towards a peaceful transition to a democratic, non-racial and united South Africa.[31]

Following the passage of the resolution, the Secretary-General, Boutros Boutros-Ghali, appointed the former US Secretary of State, Cyrus Vance, as his special representative. Assisted by a small team from the Secretariat, Vance visited South Africa between 21 and 31 July. In the course of his visit he held discussions with a wide range of parties and interest groups. Vance found general support for the principle of UN monitoring of the violence, except from the extreme right, which saw UN involvement as an infringement of South Africa's sovereignty. But there was also scepticism as to whether UN monitoring would make any difference to the situation. For example, the columnist, Ken Owen, argued that the root of the crisis lay in De Klerk's and Mandela's diminished authority and saw the range and variety of interventions by lesser players as simply a demonstration of the weakness of the two leaders. He concluded that the country had been delivered into the 'capricious hands . . . of the anarchists of street theatre, and the militarists who watch the rising disorder with lip-smacking anticipation'.[32] Owen's column accurately reflected the fears of increased civil conflict fuelled by the looming confrontation between the government and the ANC over the next phase of the latter's campaign of rolling mass action.

In particular, Vance encountered intense concern that the general strike the ANC had called for 3 and 4 August might lead to a spiral of violence. As the UN Secretary-General noted in his report to the Security Council of 7 August,

> it was necessary, even during the mission, to ensure that the mass actions scheduled for 3 August did not erupt into uncontrollable violence despite the wishes of all parties concerned. . . It was therefore necessary for my Special Representative and me to take certain exceptional interim measures aimed at preventing, if possible, such a catastrophic possibility.[33]

Boutros Boutros-Ghali wrote to De Klerk, Mandela and Buthelezi to express these concerns. Mandela suggested that the UN send observers to witness the ANC's demonstrations. After Vance discussed the matter with De Klerk, the South African President indicated that he had no objection to the dispatch of UN observers to South Africa for this purpose and as a consequence a team of 10 UN monitors was able to observe the campaign of mass action as it reached its climax in the week of 3 August.

In the course of the week 48 people died in political violence, but there was no general breakdown of order and the major demonstrations of the week passed off relatively peacefully. The political correspondent of *The Argus*, Frans Esterhuyse, concluded that the outcome of the week's mass action campaign was a 'triumph for the peace-makers' and 'among the heroes who saved the day' he included 'United Nations observers whose presence clearly encouraged restraint'.[34] It was a common view. In two episodes, in particular, the UN observers were credited with averting bloodshed; a confrontation between ANC marchers and the Ciskei's security forces on the road to the homeland's capital, Bisho, and a showdown between ANC demonstrators and supporters of the extreme right-wing AWB in Krugersdorp. Their success led to South African newspapers' welcoming reports that Vance had proposed an enlarged UN presence. For example, *The Argus* commented: 'Given the manifestly positive role played by 10 UN observers during the week of mass action, further help can hardly be unwelcome, especially since it is abundantly clear that past efforts by the government have failed.'[35]

It was even suggested that Vance would make the ideal mediator in the constitutional negotiations between the government and the ANC. In the event the Secretary-General put forward a more modest proposal to the Security Council as a result of the Vance mission. His report recommended that the UN should 'make available some 30 observers to serve in South Africa, in close association with the National Peace Secretariat, in order to further the purposes of the Accord'.[36] Boutros-Ghali suggested that the UN observers should be supplemented by the addition of observers from other appropriate external sources, including the Commonwealth, the OAU and the European Community. On 17 August the Security Council unanimously adopted a resolution approving the sending of extra UN observers to South Africa, leaving the precise number to be determined by the Secretary-General.

However, the intensification of international monitoring of the violence did not prove a panacea. Further serious episodes of violence occurred, including a massacre of ANC demonstrators by members of the Ciskei Defence Forces in Bisho on 7 September 1992. But the presence of monitors did affect the interpretation of the violence and in the case of the Bisho massacre added to the pressures on the government to reach an accommodation with the ANC. On 26 September President de Klerk and Nelson Mandela signed the Record of Understanding, ending the suspension of formal negotiations between the two sides. With negotiations back on track with the Record of Understanding, the high profile of visible international involvement in the transition declined, so laying the basis for subsequent claims that the negotiated settlement was a product of the efforts of South Africans. This underestimates the role played by the international community in two very important respects.

Firstly, in helping to establish the terms under which the negotiations took place, the international community indirectly influenced their outcome. Those terms included the international community's understanding of the causes of political violence in South Africa and its view of the relative political legitimacy of the forces contending for political power. While it might be argued that the opinions of the international community on both these issues were vindicated by the outcome of the 1994 elections and the revelations that have been made about political violence during the transition to the Truth and Reconciliation Commission, this underplays the susceptibility of political violence to different interpretations. Thus, it is worth pointing out that the two reports on the violence in 1992 which exerted such a powerful influence on international opinion and the case for monitoring, the ICJ report and the Amnesty International report, both came under fierce attack from Anthea Jeffrey in a publication for the South African Institute of International Relations.[37] Further, Jeffrey was by no means alone in South Africa in 1992 in questioning the ANC's contention that violence was being fomented by a Third Force in the security forces. The well-known and respected analyst, Lawrence Schlemmer, threw doubt both on the existence and significance of the role of a Third Force in the violence in an article on the violence for *South Africa International*.[38] In general, analysts of the violence in the South African media were more inclined to lay the blame among all the factions of South African opinion than was international opinion. What of course remains difficult to estimate is how far the outcome of the negotiations and of the subsequent elections would have been affected if the government had been in a stronger position to act on an interpretation of the violence that disregarded international opinion.

Secondly, while the international community did not play a direct or overt role in the constitutional negotiations in the Multi-Party Negotiating Forum which convened in April 1993, the opinions of foreign governments did exert an influence on the outcome of the process. Chris Landsberg argues persuasively that foreign influence was not restricted simply to facilitating the success of the negotiations, but that 'attempts to shape the nature of the settlement were also evident'.[39] What is most striking is how little support the South

African government was able to muster for a consociational settlement, with provisions for the entrenchment of power sharing and minority vetoes. Further, it found little encouragement for its attempts to legitimise proposals for such arrangements through reference to practices in some long established European liberal democracies. The position of the Bush administration in the midst of the crisis following the Boipatong massacre was particularly striking. Giving evidence before the Africa sub-committee of the House of Representatives, the Assistant Secretary of State for African Affairs, Herman Cohen, stated the following:

> All sides must recognise the right of the majority to govern, while assuring that all South Africans have a stake in their government. . . [But no side could insist on] overly complex arrangements intended to guarantee a share of power to particular groups which will frustrate effective governance. Minorities have the right to safeguards; they cannot expect a veto.[40]

European diplomats played their part by, on the one hand, insisting that federalism should not be seen as a device lending itself to the maintenance of apartheid, while, on the other hand, correcting the South African government's portrayal of proposals for the entrenchment of power sharing as based on Swiss structures as a clear misunderstanding of the Swiss model. Landsberg concludes:

> Cohen's 1992 intervention on minority vetoes, as well as European tutorials for government ministers on the Swiss constitutional system, do seem to have had an impact: while no direct causal link has been established, government insistence on such devices as a revolving presidency and guaranteed veto powers for minority parties did wane as the negotiations continued. A growing perception that it would not have the world community on its side if it chose to make these demands non-negotiable presumably helped persuade it to modify its strategy.[41]

In the final phase of the transition, after the installation of the Transitional Executive Council in December 1993, the main concern of foreign governments was that the elections in April 1994 should be as inclusive as possible. Their efforts were directed towards achieving an accommodation between the ANC and the IFP that would persuade the latter to participate in the elections. Landsberg suggests that the idea of international mediation as a way of settling differences between the ANC and the IFP may have been put forward at a meeting between the former Algerian foreign minister, Lakdar Brahimi, who had been appointed as the Special Representative of the UN

Secretary-General, and Chief Buthelezi.[42] International mediation was offered to Buthelezi by Mandela at the beginning of March 1994, but only finally taken up in the second week of April. The team of seven mediators headed by the former American Secretary of State, Henry Kissinger, and the former British Foreign Secretary, Lord Carrington, arrived in South Africa on 12 April. In the event, their services were not required as the ANC and the IFP could not agree on terms of reference for the mediators. However, this effort did not prove entirely fruitless. A Kenyan academic appointed as an adviser to the team, Washington Okumu, stayed on in South Africa after the departure of Carrington and Kissinger and was credited with influencing Buthelezi's eleventh hour decision to participate in the elections.

Mandela's South Africa bears the imprint of the influence of the international community on the transition in a myriad of different ways. It is reflected most obviously in the change in the country's status from that of a pariah to a paragon, to use the terms employed by Geldenhuys among others.[43] This should perhaps be seen as less a tribute to the qualities of the Government of National Unity that emerged from the elections in 1994, though Mandela was recognised as a true political giant, than as self-congratulation on the part of the international community in helping to bring about such a complete transformation of the South African political system in accordance with international norms. Consciousness of the role that international factors played in its political triumph weighs heavily with the ANC. The sense that it owes a debt of gratitude to the international community is reflected both in the projection of the South African transition as a model for the resolution of conflict in other war-torn societies and in the emphasis placed on human rights in the conduct of foreign policy. At the same time, while the ANC's acknowledges a general debt of gratitude to the international community as a whole, its leaders feel a very special obligation to governments and countries that supported the movement during the long years in exile. These include states, such as Cuba and Libya, which are currently at odds with the international community, in relation both to their international conduct and in respect of their internal political arrangements.

South Africa's obligations to old allies have taken some strange forms such as involvement in Libya's dispute with the United States and Britain over the Gadafy regime's refusal to hand over two of its intelligence agents for trial in connection with the bombing of Pan Am Flight 103 over Lockerbie in Scotland. While the American and British use of the Security Council rather than relying on the legal remedies provided by the Montreal Convention for the Suppression of Unlawful Acts against the Safety of Civil Aviation is open to criticism, it is unclear what South African national interest is served by Mandela's concerning himself with the issue. Just as strange from the perspective of the pursuit of South Africa's national interest has been the government's and the ANC's involvement with the peace process in Northern Ireland. In particular, in maintaining a close relationship with Sinn Fein, the political wing of the Provisional Irish Republican Army (IRA), which is supported by a minority of Northern Ireland's Catholics, the ANC has run the risk of damaging South Africa's relations with Britain and the Republic of Ireland, two members of the European Union, collectively South Africa's most important trading partner. Admittedly, it can be argued that South Africa's engagement has made a positive contribution to the peace process, but events might easily have turned out quite differently with South Africa's being unable to influence their course. In effect, the ANC has treated the objective of a united Ireland as the goal of an anti-colonial struggle analogous to their own against minority rule and deserving of the ANC's solidarity without consideration of any benefits.

These two examples show the resistance that exists, partly as a result of the nature of South Africa's miraculous transition, to becoming, in Jack Spence's telling phrase, 'just another country'.[44] The strong influence of norms on the conduct of South African foreign policy is also illustrated by the debate that took place in the first two years of Mandela's Presidency over the question of the recognition of the People's Republic of China. What might have seemed a routine transfer of recognition in the light of the fact that the People's Republic of China is a veto power in the Security Council and the importance of UN peace-keeping operations to the security of southern Africa as a region became a highly contested issue. Opponents of the transfer of recognition from the Republic of China (Taiwan) were able to make great play of mainland China's relatively low profile during the struggle against apartheid and its poor human rights record compared to the Republic of China. They pointed to Taiwan's progress towards liberal democracy, drawing parallels with South Africa's own transition. They also emphasised the justice of the recognition of both states, with the implication that Mandela might be able to use his great moral authority to force other states to rethink their approach to the question of recognition and bring about a change in international practice that enabled South Africa to avoid the necessity of choosing one or the other. However, the long delay in South Africa's recognition of the People's Republic of China was also a testimony to the capacity of Taiwan to influence the South African political system through cheque book diplomacy.

Another way that international norms have imprinted themselves on Mandela's South Africa is shown in its sensitivity to criticism from outside the country. Most telling in this respect has been the reaction to a television programme entitled, 'Apartheid did not die', by the left-wing journalist, John Pilger. It was broadcast on South African television, but preceded by a disclaimer and followed by a panel discussion.[45] The thrust of Pilger's argument was that the Mandela government had failed to live up to the ideals that the ANC had proclaimed during the course of its liberation struggle, in particular, in its failure to promote and achieve greater equality. While Pilger's case is principally of relevance in the context of an examination of the country's domestic policies, its impact was partly a reflection of the fact that it was seen as a challenge to the international legitimacy of the new dispensation and for that reason requiring rebuttal and not merely dismissal, the much commoner reaction to criticism of the government. It is striking that in spite of the ANC's political domination, it is the contention that little has changed which has tended to have the greatest resonance outside South Africa and to produce the most anguished reaction within the country from ANC supporters.

The perception or suspicion that the explanation for white quiescence in the new dispensation is that whites have found the means to hang on to old privileges underpins a degree of scepticism on the far left of the political spectrum in the West about the South African miracle. It has even proved capable, if very faintly, of raising the spectre of the reimposition of consumer sanctions. For example, following strong criticism of working conditions on wine farms in the Western Cape and the failure of the boom in the export of South African wine since 1994 to be reflected in an improvement of conditions, the British retail chain, Marks and Spencer, demanded an investigation and threatened to take South African wines off their list.[46] Such pressure has by no means been entirely unwelcome to those seeking a more rapid transformation of South African society.[47] In the case of sport, this led to the extraordinary spectacle of the National Sports Council (briefly) requesting that other countries should apply sanctions against South African rugby in the context of its dispute with the President of the South African Rugby Football Union (SARFU), Louis Luyt, before the matter was resolved by Luyt's resignation.[48]

It is striking that post-independence Zimbabwe and Namibia have been much less concerned with international opinion since the holding of their democratic elections than South Africa has been, even though the international community played a more direct role in the transition to majority rule in those countries than in South Africa. It is partly a reflection of the fact that South Africa is a much larger society with a much higher international profile, but it also reflects the internalisation of international norms by those struggling against apartheid. That gives international norms far greater influence in political debates in Mandela's South Africa than is evident in the domestic politics of Zimbabwe or Namibia.

Notes to Chapter 7

1   Robert Mattes, *The Election Book: Judgement and Choice in South Africa's 1994 Election*, Institute for Democracy in South Africa, Cape Town 1995, p.41.

2   J.E.Spence, 'The Most Popular Corpse in History', *Optima*, Vol. 34, No. 1, March 1986.

3   James Barber and John Barratt, *South Africa's foreign policy: The search for status and security 1945–1988*, Cambridge University Press, Cambridge 1990, pp.23–5.

4   Colin De B.Webb, 'The Foreign Policy of the Union of South Africa' in J.E.Black and K.W.Thompson (eds), *Foreign Policies in a World of Change*, Harper and Row, New York 1963, p.426.

5   General Assembly Resolution 1514 (XV), 14 December1960.

6   General Assembly Resolution 2625 (XXV), 24 October 1970.

7   *Ibid.*

8   See Theodor Hanf, Heribert Weiland and Gerda Vierdag, *South Africa: The Prospects for Peaceful Change*, Rex Collings, London 1981, pp.408–17.

9   Deon Geldenhuys, 'International involvement in South Africa's political transformation' in Walter Carlsnaes and Marie Muller (eds), *Change and South African External Relations*, International Thomson Publishing, Johannesburg 1997, pp.37–9.

10   Quoted in Barry Cohen and Mohamed A.El-Khawas, *The Kissinger Study of Southern Africa*, Spokesman Books, Nottingham 1975, p.81.

11   See, for example, the comments by Stephen Ellis in *Africa Confidential*, 22 September 1989 and 20 October 1989, quoted in John Daniel, 'A Response to Guelke: The Cold War Factor in South Africa's Transition', *Journal of Contemporary African Studies*, Vol. 14, No. 1, January 1996, pp.102–3.

12 Robert Jackson, 'Negative Sovereignty in Sub-Saharan Africa', *Review of International Studies*, Vol. 12 No. 4, October 1986, p.260

13 See, for example, the listing for the ANC in 'Worldwide Overview of Organizations That Engage in Terrorism' in *Patterns of Global Terrorism: 1988*, Department of State Publication 9705, Washington D.C. 1989, p.82.

14 Phyllis Johnson and David Martin, *Apartheid Terrorism: The Destabilization Report*, The Commonwealth Secretariat in association with James Currey, London 1989.

15 Chris Landsberg, 'Directing from the Stalls? The international community and the South African negotiation forum' in Steven Friedman and Doreen Atkinson (eds), *The Small Miracle: South Africa's negotiated settlement*, Ravan Press, Johannesburg 1994, pp.276–300.

16 The Commonwealth Group of Eminent Persons, *Mission to South Africa: The Commonwealth Report*, Penguin Books for the Commonwealth Secretariat, Harmondsworth 1986, p.143.

17 *Ibid.*, p.142.

18 Botha's letter is reproduced in Stephen Chan, 'British and Commonwealth Actors in the 1980s' in Stephen Chan and Vivienne Jabri (eds), *Mediation in Southern Africa*, Macmillan, London and Basingstoke 1993, pp.34–5.

19 *Mission to South Africa* (as cited in note 16), pp.61–2.

20 *Ibid.*, p.135.

21 *Agenda for Peace: An Independent Survey of the Violence in South Africa by the International Commission of Jurists*, International Commission of Jurists, Geneva 1992, p.22.

22 Quoted in *Anti-Apartheid News* (London), May/June 1992.

23 *South Africa: State of Fear – Security Force Complicity in Torture and Political Killings, 1990–1992*, Amnesty International, London 1992.

24 *The Independent on Sunday* (London), 21 June 1992.

25 *The Star* (Johannesburg), 24 June 1992.

26 *Ibid.*

27 *Cape Times* (Cape Town), 1 July 1992.

28 *The Argus* (Cape Town), 2 July 1992.

29 *The Argus*, 3 July 1992.

30 *Sunday Times* (Johannesburg), 5 July 1992.

31 Quoted in paragraph 1 of Boutros Boutros-Ghali, *Report of the Secretary-General on the Question of South Africa*, United Nations S/24389, New York (7 August) 1992.

32 Ken Owen, 'Kings Rule, or Barons, or the Upstarts Take Over', *Sunday Times* (Johannesburg), 26 July 1992.

33 Boutros-Ghali, *op. cit.*, paragraphs 58–59.

34 *The Argus*, 8 August 1992.

35 *Ibid.*

36 Boutros-Ghali, *op. cit.*, paragraph 76.

37 Anthea Jeffrey, *Spotlight on Disinformation about Violence in South Africa*, South African Institute of Race Relations, Johannesburg 1992.

38 Lawrence Schlemmer, 'Violence – What is to be done?', *South Africa International*, Vol. 23, October 1992, pp.60–4.

39 Landsberg, *op. cit.*, p.287.

40 Quoted in Steven Friedman (ed.), *The long journey: South Africa's quest for a negotiated settlement*, Ravan Press, Johannesburg 1993, p.157.

41 Landsberg, *op. cit.*, p.289.

42 *Ibid.*, p.292.

43 Geldenhuys, *op. cit.*, p.35.

44 Greg Mills (ed.), *From Pariah to Participant: South Africa's evolving foreign relations, 1990–1994*, South African Institute of International Affairs, Johannesburg 1994, p.v.

45 *Mail and Guardian* (Johannesburg), 24 April 1998.

46 *Business Day* (Johannesburg), 3 February 1997.

47 See, for example, Ben Turok, '"Feudal attitudes" of wineland farmers are called into question', *Business Day*, 28 May 1997.

48 *The Irish Times* (Dublin), 9 May 1998.

CHAPTER 8

The New Domestic Dispensation

The holding of local elections and the drawing up of a new constitution completed the process of South Africa's democratisation that had begun with the national and provincial elections in April 1994. They are examined in this chapter, along with the government's formulation of its economic policies, its approach to reconciliation, epitomised by the establishment of the Truth and Reconciliation Commission, and the issue of crime. Strictly speaking the period from 10 May 1994 to 30 April 1999 might be considered part of the transition, since the interim constitution in respect of power sharing remains in force to 30 April 1999. If this line of argument is followed, the whole of the Mandela Presidency has to be seen as forming part of the transition. But whether or not this perspective is accepted, it is important that consideration be given as to how the political system is likely to develop after Mandela steps down. In this context, Mandela's speech to the ANC conference in December 1997, widely interpreted as indicating the direction policy is likely to take under Thabo Mbeki, will be examined as a pointer to future developments.

From an early point in the transition, it was envisaged that there would be local elections on the basis of a universal adult suffrage as part of the process of South Africa's democratisation. Elections to the national assembly and to provincial legislatures had been held in April 1994. Local elections were held in the seven ANC-run provinces on 1 November 1995, as well as for 95 transitional councils in the Western Cape. However, as a result of disputes over the demarcation of the boundaries of the local authorities, elections to the Western Cape Transitional Metropolitan Council and its substructures and for the province's rural areas were delayed. So were the local elections throughout KwaZulu-Natal. The remaining local elections in the

Western Cape took place on 29 May 1996; those in KwaZulu-Natal were further delayed to 26 June 1996 as a result of ongoing political violence in the province.

The holding of democratic local elections in South Africa as a whole was the outcome of a process that can be traced back to the establishment at the end of September 1992 of a task group to prepare the ground for negotiations on the structures of local government. It consisted of representatives of the central government, provincial administrations, local government and the South African National Civic Organisation. This followed the signing in the same month of the Record of Understanding between President de Klerk and Nelson Mandela. The meetings of the task group led to the establishment of the Local Government Negotiating Forum on 22 March 1993. Its mission was described as being 'to contribute to the bringing about of a democratic, non-racial, non-sexist and financially viable local government system'.[1] The Forum's membership of 60 was drawn equally from the representatives of statutory and non-statutory authorities. In July 1993, the Forum resolved that the transformation of South Africa's local government should take place in three stages. The first involved the replacement of all existing apartheid-based local authorities by nominated transitional local and metropolitan councils. The second stage would be elections to the newly agreed local authorities. The third stage would take place when the country's final constitution came into effect. The Forum's recommendations formed the basis for the passage of the Local Government Transition Act of 1993.

Implementation of the first stage, the creation of new non-racial local government structures, primarily took place after agreement was reached at local level by local negotiating forums set up for the purpose. After the country's first non-racial elections in April 1994 and the establishment of the Government of National Unity, President Mandela issued a proclamation giving the country's nine provincial governments the authority to implement the Local Government Transition Act. The speed with which new transitional local authorities were established varied from province to province. But as a result both of the complexity of the process and of the emphasis placed on getting local acceptance of proposals for the new authorities, progress was slower than had originally been envisaged, forcing the postponement of plans for the second stage, the holding of elections. It had been originally been intended that these should be held throughout the country in October 1994. They had then been put back to April 1995, before the setting of the end of October 1995 as a final deadline for the holding of the elections. In October 1994, the Minister for

Provincial Affairs and Constitutional Development, Roelf Meyer, announced the appointment of Frederik van Zyl Slabbert and Khehla Shubane as co-chairpersons of a task group to oversee the holding of the local elections, while at the end of November President Mandela issued a proclamation permitting provincial governments to impose transitional councils on areas where local forums had failed to reach agreement.

Both the requirement of voter registration and the failure of the political parties to generate much interest in their outcome through their campaigns ensured that the main difference between the local elections which took place on 1 November 1995 in seven of the country's nine provinces and parts of the Western Cape was a much lower turn-out than in the elections of 1994. The Election Task Force estimated that registered voters constituted 76.7 per cent of those eligible to vote on 1 November, while the numbers who turned out to vote on the day constituted 48.7 per cent of registered voters.[2] The ANC entitled its manifesto for the local elections, *A Better Life: Let's Make it Happen Where We Live*. Crime was the most visible issue in the campaigns of the political parties. For example, the ANC made wide use of a poster with the slogan: 'tough on crime, tough on the causes of crime'.[3] Comment on the outcome of the local elections on 1 November focused on the extent of the ANC's successes across the country, unsurprising though these were in the light of the outcome of the 1994 elections. Initially, much was made of breakthroughs by the party in dramatically increasing its share of the vote among Coloured voters,[4] but the final totals presented a more muted picture, of relatively little change in party percentages compared to 1994. The ANC won 61.7 per cent of seats across the country; the National Party 15.7 per cent.[5]

The two cases where polling was delayed, most of the Western Cape and the whole of KwaZulu-Natal attracted far greater interest, since these two provinces had non-ANC governments. In the Western Cape voters outside Cape Town and its environs had two votes; one for a direct election of a ward representative by a plurality of the total votes of the ward and another for the party list to elect further members by proportional representation. There were 95 transitional local councils, voting for which occurred on 1 November 1995 and seven rural services councils, elected on 29 May 1996. Cape Town and its environs, encompassing most voters in the province, was covered by the Western Cape Transitional Metropolitan Council, which was broken down into seven substructures. Voters in this case had three votes; one for a ward representative; another for the party list for the substructure; and a third for the party list for the Metropolitan Council as a whole. Wards were distributed between suburb and township according to a formula agreed in the multi-party negotiations in 1993.

The perception of an ANC challenge to the National Party's dominant position in the Western Cape was very much in voters' minds when polling took place at the end of May 1996. In contrast to the other provinces in South Africa, the majority of the population in the Western Cape (constituting approximately 60 per cent of the electorate) were Coloureds, making the contest a test of the ANC's capacity to demonstrate its non-racial appeal. The political context of the National Party's decision to leave the Government of National Unity gave added importance to the contest, with the outcome being seen as a judgement on this party's adoption of a new role.[6] In the event, the National Party won the elections to the Western Cape Transitional Metropolitan Council, with the ANC coming a strong second.. For the National Party, its victory was a vindication of its decision to leave the Government of National Unity. The results of the proportional vote for party lists to the Metropolitan Council are set out in Table 8.1. The most striking aspect of the results was the extraordinarily poor showing of the Democratic Party, the party identified with English-speaking white opposition to apartheid. In the context of Cape Town it was closely identified with the city's liberal traditions. Throughout the apartheid era the city had been a bastion of opposition to the imposition of social segregation and returned a number of MPs for the Democratic Party in elections to the country's white parliament during the 1980s.

Table 8.1

Proportional vote for party lists for Western Cape Transitional Metropolitan Council

National Party	358,365	48.53%
African National Congress	282,247	38.23%
Democratic Party	29,739	4.03%
African Christian Democratic Party	17,391	2.36%
Pan Africanist Congress	12,552	1.70%
Freedom Front	7,332	0.99%

Source: *Local Government Elections Western Cape: 1996 Results at a glance*, Project Vote, Cape Town 1996, p.63.

The Star reported the outcome of the elections under the headline: 'Nats' Cape victories spark fears of racial polarisation'.[7] Commentary on the outcome focused on the polarisation of opinion in the city and of the failure of the Democratic Party in its heartland of the Cape peninsula. The *Cape Times* editorial on the elections was headed 'The Cape's flight to the laager':

> The National Party may have changed a few of its spots since 1987, the last time it frightened whites en masse into its right-wing fold, but the same sort of tactics again proved successful last week when it campaigned to turn the Cape metropole into a white/coloured laager as a bulwark against black control. Only in one of six substructures, the central city, was it significantly outnumbered by the ANC, a party supported by blacks even more overwhelmingly than the NP was by whites. This polarisation suggests that the voters still approach their politics largely on ethnic lines, in spite of the attempt of some leaders, notably Nelson Mandela, to calm white fears and curb black impatience. Trust is clearly still in short supply on both sides. It is also clear that the great majority of voters see South African politics as a two-party fight, and have little confidence in the smaller parties to protect their interests.[8]

In fact, the pattern of party support proved somewhat more complex than this editorial suggested in the elections in KwaZulu-Natal.

The delayed local elections in KwaZulu-Natal took place in fraught circumstances. The IFP's participation in the elections of April 1994 had been based on an accord with the ANC and the National Party, which provided that any outstanding issues of disagreement among the parties in relation to the transitional constitution should be submitted to international mediation. Disagreement over the interpretation of the accord led to the IFP's withdrawal in April 1995 from the Constituent Assembly responsible for the drafting of the final constitution. At the same time, the IFP attempted to use its position as the majority party in the KwaZulu-Natal provincial assembly to secure greater powers for the province. To this end, the IFP drew up its own draft constitution for the province, which it submitted to the legislature in October 1995. The IFP draft called among other things for the Kingdom of KwaZulu-Natal to be a 'federate' province of South Africa with its own citizenship, constitutional court, and militia. The ANC condemned the draft as amounting to secession and as unconstitutional. Passage of the constitution required a two-thirds majority in the provincial assembly. The IFP attempted to put pressure on the other parties to make concessions to its viewpoint by raising the possibility that it might go back to the electorate to get a mandate for its proposals. However, the IFP still failed to muster the necessary majority and was forced ultimately to make substantial modifications to its proposals so as to secure passage of the constitution by the deadline of 15 March 1996.

These constitutional disputes inevitably affected the progress on the province's preparations for the local elections. By July 1995 it was evident that the province would not be ready to hold the local elections by 1 November because of continuing disputes over the boundaries and composition of a number of authorities. In fact, it was as a result of a report on the situation in the province that the government was forced to choose between the option of delaying elections everywhere or of amending the legislation that required that the local elections should be held on the same day throughout the country. It opted for the latter course of action. All the parties in KwaZulu-Natal accepted the necessity for this delay. The further delay from 29 May to 26 June proved much more contentious. The ANC in the province had demanded a delay of three months on the grounds that the continuing violence in the province and the existence of no-go areas prevented the holding of free and fair elections. The IFP disputed this.

The dispute between the ANC and the IFP over the date for the KwaZulu-Natal elections was resolved by a special meeting of the Cabinet in early May 1996. The decision that there should be a delay of four weeks was a compromise. Concern over the security situation in the province had been heightened by a series of violent episodes, including an attack on a royal palace, a shoot-out in central Durban following a march by IFP supporters armed with traditional weapons in defiance of the law, and the violent deaths of several candidates. Delay made possible the deployment of extra security forces during the elections. It also made possible an extension of the period for voter registration during which time the number of those on the voters' rolls was raised to over three quarters of those eligible to register. A factor that helped to defuse political tensions during the prolonged election campaign was a fresh peace initiative by the leadership of the two main parties, the IFP and the ANC.

In the campaign IFP leaders presented the party as the only political force in the country capable of resisting the ANC's 'mad drive to totalitarianism'.[9] They contrasted the IFP's commitment to federalism and free enterprise with the centralist tendencies of the ANC, while also making much of the ANC's alliance with the South African Communist Party. The IFP Secretary General, Ziba Jiyane, declared that 'the true home of minorities is the IFP because we are the only party strong enough to protect their community interests'.[10] The distinctive aspect of the ANC's manifesto for the local elections in KwaZulu-Natal was its emphasis on bringing peace to the province, which took the place of the priority that the party had given in its campaigns in the other provinces to combating crime.[11] Fears that polling day would be marred by violence on a large scale were not realised. There were seven deaths in the province as a result of political violence in the week before the elections. However, conditions remained far from ideal for the holding of fair and free elections. The Human Rights Committee identified the existence of 52 no-go areas in the province, 28 belonging to the IFP and 24 to the ANC.

Most of the early results came from the urban areas and this played a large role in shaping the initial perceptions of the outcome. This was of a large swing to the ANC. It was only when the rural returns came in that it became apparent that the IFP's share of the poll would remain greater than that of the ANC (see Table 8.2). In fact, the IFP, the ANC, the National Party, the Democratic Party, and the Minority Front were each able to claim a measure of success in the elections. The results had confirmed the IFP as the province's leading party and to the extent that the conduct of the local elections had provided less scope for large scale electoral fraud helped to lend legitimacy to the party's unexpected victory in 1994. The ANC could point to its successes in winning control of the province's most important councils, including the Durban Metropolitan Council, Pietermaritzburg, Ladysmith, and Newcastle. Indeed, the main political significance of the local elections in KwaZulu-Natal was that the outcome cemented the ANC's domination of the South African political system. In particular, it reduced any possibility that the IFP could bring about the secession of the Kingdom of KwaZulu-Natal from South Africa, the threat of which had played a part in the party's efforts to force the central government to devolve greater power to the provinces. The result was a lowering of political tensions in the province and a reduction in the level of political violence. After the elections, the IFP even sought to establish cooperation with the ANC on particular councils. By the time of the ANC's national conference in December 1997, relations between the two parties had improved to such a degree that the possibility of their eventual merger was being raised.

The National Party, the Democratic Party and the Minority Front each increased their share of the proportional vote compared to the elections to the provincial assembly in 1994. Their success underlined the failure of the IFP to attract support from the province's white and Indian minorities. Indeed, the party's generally poor showing in the urban areas, which largely accounted for its lower share of the overall

Table 8.2

Percentage vote of 'main parties' (parties gaining representation at national or provincial level in 1994) in local elections in KwaZulu-Natal in June 1996 and in the provincial and national elections in KwaZulu-Natal in April 1994

	1996 local	1994 provincial	1994 national
IFP	44.50	50.32	48.59
ANC	33.22	32.23	31.61
NP	12.69	11.21	15.76
DP	3.33	2.15	1.61
MF	2.29	1.34	0.17
ACDP	0.51	0.57	0.46
FF	0.32	0.51	0.46
PAC	0.14	0.73	0.62

Abbreviations of parties: IFP = Inkatha Freedom Party; ANC = African National Congress; NP = National Party; DP = Democratic Party; MF = Minority Front; ACDP = African Christian Democratic Party; FF = Freedom Front; PAC = Pan Africanist Congress of Azania.

Sources: For 1996, figures issued on 2 July 1996 by the KwaZulu-Natal Member of the Executive Council for housing and local government, Peter Miller. For 1994, the Independent Electoral Commission, Johannesburg.

vote in the province, appears to have been due in part to a loss of support among white and Indian voters. The relative success of the Democratic Party contrasted sharply with that party's performance in the Western Cape where the contest between the National Party and the ANC had increased electoral polarisation. R.W. Johnson suggested the following explanation for the difference:

> Among whites the DP . . . is the cultural expression of this most English-speaking of the provinces, giving the party a new strength and significance. From the 1960s on the Progressives and the other forbears of the DP were always stronger in Gauteng and the Western Cape than in Natal. Now the national conference of DP councillors has to take place in KwaZulu-Natal because the province has more of them than anywhere else: the turnabout is striking.[12]

The turnabout is ironic considering Natal's association with the origins of segregation in South Africa and its reputation as a bulwark of English-speaking white conservatism. Johnson argued that the local elections in South Africa in 1995 and 1996 were 'maintaining elections' in contrast to the general and provincial elections of April 1994 which he described as:

'a critical election', that is one in which the universe of political behaviour is given a definite stamp and shape which future elections are likely merely to replicate, with mere short-term fluctuations occurring round that central norm for some time to come.[13]

The outcome of the local elections in all the provinces provides broad support for this thesis, with the important implication that the racial polarisation which was evident in the 1994 elections is unlikely to prove to be of merely passing significance.

The National Party government had originally wanted a constitution to be agreed among the parties before the holding of democratic elections, whereas the ANC's position was that the country's constitution should be drawn up by a democratically elected constituent assembly. What was ultimately agreed in the Multi-Party Negotiating Forum was that the elections would take place under the interim constitution, which came into force on 27 April 1994. The final constitution was to be drawn up by a constituent assembly consisting of the National Assembly and Senate (with ten representatives from each province) sitting together. The procedure for the drawing up of the final constitution was set out in the interim constitution. In particular, it laid down that the final constitution had to conform with a set of 34 constitutional principles. The precise content of these had been the subject of intensive negotiation among the parties. The Multi-Party Negotiating Forum reached agreement on the interim constitution on 18 November 1993. That agreement was embodied in legislation in December. However, it was amended in February 1994 in an effort to secure the participation of members of the Freedom Alliance.

In particular, it was at this point that the 34th constitutional principle was added. The first principle stated that the constitution should provide for the establishment of South Africa as one sovereign state, a common South African citizenship and a democratic system committed to equality between genders and races. The 34th principle stated that this did not preclude a right to self-determination of any community sharing a common cultural and language tradition. It was inserted to allow the extreme right to argue the case for a *volkstaat* and the IFP that for a Zulu kingdom. Further changes were made to the interim constitution as a result of the agreement on 19 April 1994 under which the IFP agreed to participate in the elections. In summary, the constitutional principles provided that the main political parties would be entitled to a share in government at least until April 1999, that the final constitution could not be amended by ordinary legislation, that discrimination would be prohibited except for the purposes of affirmative action, that the final constitution would contain a justiciable bill of rights and that the separation of executive, legislative and judicial powers would be entrenched.

An elaborate procedure existed for the approval of the final constitution. The Constituent Assembly was required to complete its work in two years, establishing a deadline of 8 May 1996 for the passage of the final constitution. To secure passage the text required the support of two-thirds of all members of the Constituent Assembly (with the further requirement that provisions relating to the boundaries, powers and functions of the provinces needed the approval of two-thirds of all members of the Senate). If the text failed to clear these hurdles, after further deliberation on the text involving a panel of experts and certification of the text by the Constitutional Court, there was provision for a text that had secured the support of a simple majority of members of the Constituent Assembly to be submitted to a referendum. Passage by referendum required the support of 60 per cent of votes cast.

In the 1994 elections the ANC failed to win a two-thirds majority in the Constituent Assembly. It won 312 seats, 15 short of a two-thirds majority. Further, the difference could not be made up with the support of any one of the four minor parties (the Freedom Front, the Democratic Party, the PAC and the African Christian Democratic Party). This outcome provides part of the explanation why the world's leading authority on consociational arrangements should have harboured the illusion that 'prospects for a stable power-sharing equilibrium' had been enhanced as a result of the 1994 elections.[14] In fact, the ANC had no intention of accepting power sharing as a permanent feature of government, though it was concerned that the process of drawing up the final constitution should be seen as inclusionary so as to give the outcome as much legitimacy as possible. To this end, the public was invited to submit written submissions on the content of the constitution, while a series of meetings were held around the country to allow members of the public to make their points verbally. Approximately two million submissions were made and distributed to the six theme committees given the task of drafting particular sections of the constitution.

A clause of the Agreement for Reconciliation and Peace of 19 April 1994 under which the IFP agreed to take part in the elections provided that 'any outstanding issues in respect of the King of the Zulus and the 1993 constitution as amended will be addressed by way of international mediation'.[15] The ANC regarded this provision as having no applicability to the drawing up of the final constitution, while the IFP regarded it as giving the party the right to revisit the whole basis for the drawing up of a final constitution. After the 1994 elections the IFP demanded that the ANC and the National Party honour their pre-election agreement to international mediation. A complicating factor was that because the IFP had fallen out with King Zwelithini, this demand did not have his support. Eventually, in Feburary 1995 negotiations took place among the three parties to see whether they could reach agreement on the terms for international mediation. These ended in failure and in April 1995 the IFP withdrew from the Constituent Assembly.

A working draft text of the final constitution was published on 22 November 1995. It included a number of options at points where differences remained among the parties. In particular, the National Party continued to argue for the entrenchment of power sharing. It eventually conceded defeat on this issue in February 1996. As the deadline approached a number of outstanding issues between the two major parties remained in relation to content of the bill of rights. These were resolved after the ANC made it clear that it was willing to make use of the deadlock-breaking mechanisms provided for in the interim constitution and seek approval in a referendum if the constitution failed to secure the two-thirds majority needed. Agreement on the outstanding differences between the ANC and the National Party was reached on 7 May and the final constitution was adopted on 8 May by an overwhelming majority. This was by no means the end of the constitution-making process.

Under the terms of the interim constitution, the draft agreed by the Constituent Assembly had to be submitted to the Constitutional Court for certification that it was in compliance with the 34 constitutional principles laid down in the interim constitution. The Constitutional Court gave its judgement on 6 September 1996. It did not certify the draft in its entirety and as a consequence some of the provisions of the constitution had to be amended by the Constituent Assembly. A revised draft received certification by the Constitutional Court on 4 December. President Mandela formally signed the new constitution in a ceremony on 10 December 1996 and it came in force on 4 February 1997. The most obvious differences between the new constitution and the interim constitution were the replacement of the Senate as the second chamber of the parliament by the National Council of Provinces and the removal of the provisions for power sharing.

On 9 May 1996, the day after the Constituent Assembly approved the draft text of the final constitution, the National Party leader, F.W.

de Klerk, announced that his party would be withdrawing from the Government of National Unity on 30 June 1996. His announcement prompted a sharp fall of the South African currency in foreign exchange markets. The sudden ending of power sharing had not been expected as the National Party was entitled to maintain its place in the Government of National Unity until April 1999. The rationale for the party's decision was that going into Opposition would enable the party to prepare for the coming of adversarial politics. It was also a recognition of the party's limited influence on policy-making under the Government of National Unity. It underlined the fact that South Africa's transition did indeed entail a passage from white minority rule to African majority rule, even if the ANC's domination of the political system remained tempered by white domination of the economy.

The economic policies of the Mandela government have been powerfully affected by two major constraints on its freedom of action in this field; the prevailing neo-liberal international economic consensus and the legacy of the country's relative economic stagnation since the boom of the 1960s. A recognition that the confidence of the markets could only be maintained by a commitment to financial orthodoxy and the belief that such confidence was vital to the country's ability to attract inward investment have underpinned the government's economic policies. This approach had been clearly signalled before the 1994 elections by the ANC's dropping of its long-standing commitment to a policy of nationalisation. It was reflected in government by the adoption of a programme of privatisation. Annual growth in *per capita* incomes from 1960 to 1996 at constant prices is shown in Table 8.3. It is striking that *per capita* incomes in 1996 are in real terms below the level achieved in 1967. (Some adjustment may be made to these figures in due course as a consequence of the results of the 1996 census, but the overall picture of a decline in *per capita* incomes since the mid 1980s is unlikely to be challenged.)

The centrepiece of the government's economic policies in its first two years was the Reconstruction and Development Programme (RDP). The aim of the RDP was 'to meet basic needs' through extending universal 'access to ..services like electricity, water, telecommunications, transport, health, education and training' and thereby to 'open up previously suppressed economic and human potential'.[16] A special ministry was established to promote the RDP and a RDP fund was set up to finance projects under the RDP. Among initiatives of the RDP was the extension of free health care to pregnant women and children under six, school feeding programmes and a major programme of

Table 8.3

Gross Domestic Product *per capita*, 1960–1996, at constant 1990 prices

Year	GDP per head	Year	GDP per head	Year	GDP per head
1960	R5717	1973	R7765	1986	R7517
1961	R5780	1974	R8033	1987	R7495
1962	R5974	1975	R7969	1988	R7631
1963	R6245	1976	R7946	1989	R7633
1964	R6559	1977	R7733	1990	R7434
1965	R6770	1978	R7755	1991	R7192
1966	R6876	1979	R7848	1992	R6879
1967	R7171	1980	R8163	1993	R6816
1968	R7270	1981	R8380	1994	R6854
1969	R7408	1982	R8138	1995	R6938
1970	R7587	1983	R7790	1996	R7007
1971	R7704	1984	R7987		
1972	R7625	1985	R7700		

Source: Elizabeth Sidiropoulus, Anthea Jeffrey, Shaun MacKay, Herma Forgey, Cheryl Chipps and Terence Corrigan, *South Africa Survey 1996/97*, South African Institute of International Affairs, Johannesburg 1997, p.654.

electrification of homes by the state utility. However, in general the results proved disappointing. In particular, many RDP programmes fell far short of meeting the targets that had been set, such as the aim of building of 200,000 new housing units per year. There were complaints of poor communications and long delays in implementation. The difficulties encountered prompted the closure of the RDP office in 1996.

In June 1996 the government unveiled a new macro-economic strategy, *Growth, Employment and Redistribution* (GEAR).[17] Its aims include the achievement of sustainable growth of 6 per cent a year, the creation of over 800,000 new jobs by 2000 and a 13 per cent rise in exports. It envisages that these aims can be achieved through a combination of low inflation, a reduction in the budget deficit, increased foreign investment, trade and exchange rate liberalisation, an acceleration of privatisation, fiscal reform and labour flexibility. The overall purpose of GEAR is to tackle the problem of the persistence of low economic growth, while retaining (and in some respects regaining) the confidence of the markets. This course has been forced on the government by the fact that, unlike the Zimbabwean economy which enjoyed a boom in the years immediately following independence as the result of the ending of the conflict and the removal of economic sanctions, the South African economy did not achieve high growth rates after 1994, despite the benefits of political stability, the ending of remaining sanctions and goodwill towards South African products abroad.

It is important to emphasise that the major constraints on the government's economic policies do not stem from the nature of the transition, as they are not constraints originating in the political system. Nevertheless, it is understandable that left-wing critics of the new order in South Africa have sought to connect the government's new macro-economic strategy, the persistence of very high levels of inequality in incomes and wealth and white acquiescence in the passage to African majority rule.[18] It may reasonably be argued that a general appreciation of the economic constraints under which *any* government would have to operate played a part in the readiness of both De Klerk to pursue a negotiated settlement and of white opinion to support him in the referendum of 1992. In other words, the economic climate of the 1990s, including the impact of globalisation, the demise of the Communist economic model and the dominance of a neo-liberal economic agenda, arguably made it easier for whites to accept political change. However, the evidence does not support the proposition that the ANC entered into an explicit deal with the old regime to safeguard white economic privilege in return for political power.

In fact, the downward pressure on white living standards from the mid-1980s has meant that the further threat posed to white living standards in the future by affirmative action has tended to loom larger in white perceptions of the new order than the notion that their privileged position is being safeguarded by the government's macro-economic strategy. What is more, affirmative action has tended to be associated in white minds with perceptions that the efficiency of all manner of services has been declining, with consequent pessimism about the country's future economic prospects. These considerations, along with that of the high level of crime, provide the most common reasons given by whites for emigration.[19] A consequence of the constraints on the adoption of policies directed at the redistribution of wealth has been increased reliance by the government on affirmative action or employment equity, as it is now being called, to overcome the legacy of apartheid.

A popular yardstick for the implementation of affirmative action in the public sector has been the principle articulated by the Black

Management Forum that companies should reflect the racial composition of the country in their composition. Movement in this direction has substantially increased the number of blacks in the higher income groups. According to the Bureau of Market Research at the University of South Africa, the real disposable income of whites declined by 2.5 per cent in the period 1985 to 1994, while that of Africans increased by 35.6 per cent.[20] At the same time, South Africa has remained one of the most unequal societies in the world in terms of income distribution, with the richest 20 per cent of households earning in 1993 more than 19 times the income of the poorest 20 per cent of households.[21] Since 1994 the size of the African elite has expanded rapidly, pointing to a further sharp reduction in the disparity between white and African disposable income. However, there is little to indicate that there has been any substantial reduction in the overall level of inequality between rich and poor since 1993.

Although the unwillingness of the Mandela government to pursue radical policies of redistribution can readily be explained in terms of ministers' calculations of the detrimental economic consequences of such policies, there was also a political dimension to the course followed by the government after 1994. The ANC was very conscious that it needed the cooperation of the civil service in implementing its policies and of the security forces in maintaining law and order. It was acutely aware of the threat that racial polarisation might pose to that cooperation. To defuse this threat Mandela committed the government to the pursuit of a policy of reconciliation. This also formed the basis on which the government handled the issue of violence from the era of white minority rule. The interim constitution agreed among the parties in November 1993 provided that in order to advance reconciliation 'amnesty shall be granted in respect of acts, omissions and offences associated with political objectives and committed in the course of the conflicts of the past'.[22] However, the mechanism that the government established for this purpose after the 1994 elections, the Truth and Reconciliation Commission (TRC), proved contentious from the moment it was first proposed. In particular the preference of the National Party was for a mechanism that did not in De Klerk's words '[tear] the stitches from the wounds'.[23]

The hostile attitude of the National Party and of the IFP to the setting up and operation of the TRC stands in marked contrast to the overwhelmingly positive international reaction to this dimension of South Africa's transition. Indeed, the TRC has served to underpin the international legitimacy of the transition, with the fading of the favourable impression made on world opinion by the 1994 elections.

The TRC was established through the Promotion of National Unity and Reconciliation Act of 1995. Its 17 members were appointed by President Mandela in November 1995, with Archbishop Desmond Tutu as its chairman. At its first meeting in December 1995, three committees were established to carry out its different tasks; the Committee on Human Rights Violations; the Committee on Amnesty; and the Committee on Reparation and Rehabilitation. A function of the TRC as a whole is to produce a comprehensive report on the nature, causes and extent of human rights violations during the conflict of the past, which has been taken to cover the period from 1 March 1960 to 5 December 1993.

While the TRC has subjected the actions of all sides of South Africa's various conflicts of the past to scrutiny, by reason of the lack of legitimacy of apartheid and the outcome of the transition, the actions of the supporters of apartheid and its allies have tended to appear in a far worse light than the actions of those seeking the demise of the system, regardless of the nature of the acts involved. In particular, those on the winning side are in a position to plead that their actions, however regrettable they may have been in some of their consequences, were undertaken as a means to a legitimate end. The inevitable asymmetry in responses to the different sides of the conflict has led the ANC's opponents to cry foul and to accuse the TRC itself of bias. While the attacks on the TRC have not succeeded in undermining its legitimacy, the disputes surrounding its functioning have tended to obscure the role that agreement among the parties on amnesty played in the transition.

This is encapsulated in the concept, justice without ashes. This recognises that justice needs to be pursued only so far as it does not encourage the losers in a conflict to fight to the bitter end. The aim is to avoid violence being carried out solely with a view to escaping retribution and not for any larger political purpose. The promise of amnesty is intended to allow the losers an exit from conflict. In the South African context, it was also designed to provide all the parties with a measure of reassurance about their position, regardless of the outcome of the 1994 elections. From the ANC's perspective, the TRC has provided a means to make good on the promise of amnesty in a way most acceptable to its supporters' wishes for the crimes of the apartheid era to be accorded public recognition. In practice, the TRC has not fully met these wishes since it has had limited success in uncovering the whole story of the National Party government's actions against those fighting against apartheid inside or outside the country. This is because by and large only members of the security forces already convicted of serious offences or facing the near certainty of conviction have felt any compelling need to provide information to the TRC.

The constitutional nature of the South African transition has entailed a survival into the new era of a number of institutions of the old order, including, most obviously, those for the maintenance of law and order. In particular, both the courts and the police reflect legal continuity in the midst of radical political change, with mainly symbolic change in the manner of their functioning. The problems encountered in this area have been made worse by the priority that was given during most of the apartheid era to the political function of the police over the combating of ordinary crime. While a high level of crime predated the transition, the years since 1990 have been characterised by especially high levels of crime, with the consequence that South Africa numbers among the most crime-ridden societies in the world, particularly in relation to crimes of violence, such as murder and robbery. The persistence of very high levels of crime since the 1994 elections has become a source of political contention, despite numerous initiatives by government to tackle the issue. The most important of these was the National Crime Prevention Strategy launched in May 1996 and aimed at addressing the failings of the criminal justice system, mobilising community opinion against criminality, improving cooperation among government departments and enhancing regional cooperation to fight cross-border crime. Passage of legislation such as the Proceeds of Crime Act of November 1996 enlarging the courts' powers of confiscation illustrates another aspect of the government's approach to the issue.

Among aspects of the crime wave that have caused especial concern have been the operation of crime syndicates and gangs particularly in relation to vehicle hijacking, drug trafficking and arms smuggling. Also of major concern have been the large numbers who have lost their lives in taxi wars, a by-product of fierce economic competition in a poorly regulated industry and high profile heists that have netted armed robbers huge sums of money. Causes of the crime wave can be found in the country's extreme inequalities, the conspicuous consumption of a new elite, widespread unemployment in the urban areas and the ready availability of guns as a legacy of past conflicts. Fear of crime has led to a mushrooming of private security firms in the suburbs. It has also prompted the formation of vigilante organisations, the most prominent of which has been People Against Gangsters and Drugs (PAGAD), which came to national attention in August 1996 when its members killed a gang leader outside his home in the

Western Cape. Although most of the victims of crime come from the African majority and surveys have shown it to be an issue of major concern to the township residents, politically the issue has tended to take on a racial coloration that has cast whites in the suburbs as the principal victims. In this context it reflects a widespread fear in the white community that the crime wave is, in part, an expression of a demand for racial redistribution of the country's wealth, as well as of disappointment at the economic fruits of liberation.

The response of the ANC to the issue of crime has primarily been to argue that its high level is a legacy of apartheid. However, in the long run this approach has disadvantages to the party as an explanation of the continuance of a crime wave, since it suggests the failure of its efforts in government to lay the foundations of a new society. The issue of crime was prominent in President Mandela's lengthy report to the 50th national conference of the ANC. Part of his five-hour address to the conference explained the high level of crime with reference to 'desperate socio-economic conditions'. At the same time, he stressed his government's inheritance of a very high level of violent crime and pointed out that the figures for murder, attempted murder and culpable homicide in Johannesburg had been steadily declining since 1994 and, further, that of the different parts of the city the wealthy suburbs were the least affected. However, other parts of his speech put a totally different gloss on the crime wave. Mandela also placed the problem of crime in the context of the existence of a counter-revolutionary conspiracy by elements of the former ruling group to destabilise the country's democracy through practical activities such as:

- the encouragement and commission of crime;
- the weakening and incapacitation of the state machinery, including the theft of public assets, arms and ammunition being among these;
- the hiding of sensitive and important information from legal organs of state; and
- the building of alternative structures, including intelligence machineries as well as armed formations.[24]

The theme of crime was also present in his savage attack on the United Democratic Movement (UDM), a new political party formed by Bantu Holomisa, the former military ruler of Transkei and Roelf Meyer, the National Party's chief negotiator during the multi-party negotiations in 1993. He described Holomisa and Meyer as 'former bed-fellows as functionaries of the apartheid system and its security forces', while declaring that 'the presence of leaders of criminal gangs at its founding conference was no accident'.

Mandela's address was also remarkable for what it had to say about other political parties. Its main theme was the need for the transformation of South African society. He accused the main white political parties of seeking to protect white privileges through the interpretation they placed on reconciliation. He went on: 'Accordingly, during the last three years, the opponents of fundamental change have sought to separate the goal of national reconciliation from the critical objective of social transformation.' He strongly attacked the National Party for failing to cooperate with the TRC. He suggested that the reason why the former ruling establishment had failed to tell the truth about the operation of the National Security Management System during the final years of white minority rule was because it harboured the ambition, if the opportunity arose, to reactivate the machinery for counter-insurgency in the future to prevent progress towards a more equal society. He also accused the National Party of fomenting fears of Africanisation among Coloureds and Indians, as well as whites. He acknowledged the impact of this campaign:

> It is clear that the majority within these national minorities continue to believe that the ANC represents the interests of the African majority and that their own perceived interests stand opposed to those of the African majority. . . . As we can expect, among the Coloureds and Indians, the view that the non-racial democracy constitutes a threat would be most prevalent among the working class and lower middle class, who would be the first to feel the pressure of African competition in the context of a deracialised labour market. It is among these sectors of the population that we find the greatest fear of the impact of our policy of affirmative action.[25]

His criticism of the Democratic Party was scarcely any less savage. He described it as engaged in a race with the National Party to convince the white minority that it was the more reliable and better defender of white privilege. By contrast, Mandela had kind words for the IFP referring to its cooperation with the ANC 'in a joint effort to consolidate peace in the country and to encourage a culture of tolerance and non-violent political competition among our respective members and supporters'. He also emphasised historical ties between the two parties and the fact they shared the same constituency of the rural and urban poor. At the same time, Mandela was dismissive of critics within the ANC of the oppressive character of African traditional authority within the rural areas, describing their position as 'infantile radicalism'. A further dimension of the Africanist flavour of the speech was a section on the African renaissance. Mandela argued that the ending of the Cold War, the impact of globalisation, the bankruptcy of neo-colonialism and South Africa's liberation created a favourable set of circumstances for a revival of the continent's political and economic fortunes. Other elements of the speech to attract attention were attacks on the media and on foreign funded non-governmental organisations. Virtually the only uncontentious part of the speech was Mandela's criticism of careerism and corruption within the ANC's own ranks.

A common explanation of what came to be dubbed 'the enemies of change' speech was that it had been deliberately tailored to suit the agenda of Thabo Mbeki, elected President of the ANC in succession to Mandela at the conference and, barring accident, certain to be the ANC's candidate for the Presidency of the country in 1999. As an editorial in the *Mail and Guardian* explained:

> Perhaps it was really Thabo Mbeki's words in the mouth of Mandela to lend a retrospective sense of continuity to a more radical ANC agenda on its way, supplanting the 'reconciliation' era. Given our history, we are still sorely in need of a leadership that emphasises reconciliation and not racial division. Those ANC leaders who insist on pursuing the language of racial identity and stereotypes are playing with fire. And the fire might start where least expected – for instance, on the street, where xenophobia against foreign nationals is becoming odiously apparent. And why is transformation seen as anti-thetical to reconciliation? Mandela has always had us believe they are two sides of the same coin of building a successful nation. Does he see enemies of transformation under every bed because the ANC is itself vulnerable to the charge that it has not done enough for real transformation?[26]

While there are a few references to the ANC's achievements in government in the speech, the overall tone is one of disappointment that more had not been achieved since the elections in 1994. The most obvious reason for such disappointment was that the government's tailoring of economic policies to the financial markets had failed to deliver the country from low economic growth and the continuing stagnation of living standards which that implied.

In this respect, virtue has gone unrewarded, as even some of the government's fiercest critics have been willing to concede.[27] One explanation that is often given for the failure of foreign investors to respond to the opportunities that GEAR presented to them has been concern over the high level of crime. The country seems trapped in a vicious circle, since the most promising antidote to the high level of crime would appear to be the jobs that would come with the very investment that the crime wave has been driving away. The emphasis on transformation in the 'enemies of change' speech can best be interpreted as a promise on the part of the ANC to deliver better lives to its supporters even in the absence of gains being delivered to the whole society through higher economic growth rates. The drafting of new legislation to promote affirmative action can be seen in a similar light. If these developments constitute a reliable guide to the future direction of policy after the ending of the Mandela era, then the polarisation of South African politics on the basis of race seems set to continue.

Notes to Chapter 8

1   Carole Cooper, Robin Hamilton, Harry Mashabela, Shaun MacKay, Elizabeth Sidiropoulos, Claire Gordon-Brown, Stuart Murphy and Julia Frielinghaus, *Race Relations Survey 1993/94*, South African Institute of Race Relations, Johannesburg 1994, p.564.

2   Elizabeth Sidiropoulus, Anthea Jeffrey, Shaun MacKay, Rory Gallocher, Herma Forgey and Cheryl Chipps, *South Africa Survey 1995/96*, South African Institute of Race Relations, Johannesburg 1996, p.454.

3   As witnessed by the author while he was living in Johannesburg in 1995.

4   See, for example, 'No apathy, but plenty of poll errors', *Weekly Mail and Guardian* (Johannesburg), 3 November 1995.

5   *South Africa Survey 1995/96*, p.456.

6   See, for example, 'De Klerk faces city vote test', *Financial Times*, 30 May 1996.

7   *The Star* (Johannesburg), 1 June 1996.

8   *Cape Times*, 31 May 1996.

9   Mangosuthu Buthelezi, *Launch of the IFP's campaign for local government elections*, Inkatha Freedom Party, Durban 30 March 1996, taken from the IFP's web site at http://www.ifp.org.za.

10   Ziya Jiyane, *Secretary General calls on IFP key organisers for final push to victory*, Inkatha Freedom Party, Durban 13 June 1996, taken from the IFP's web site at http://www.ifp.org.za.

11   *A Better Life: Let's make it happen where we live – ANC Kwa-Zulu Natal local government election manifesto 1996*, African National Congress, Durban 1996, taken from the ANC's web site at http://www.anc.org.za.

12   R.W.Johnson, 'Understanding the Elections', *KwaZulu-Natal Briefing* (Helen Suzman Foundation), No. 3, August 1996, pp.18–19.

13 *Ibid.*, p.18.

14 Arend Lijphart, 'Prospects for Power Sharing in the New South Africa' in Andrew Reynolds (ed.), *Election '94 South Africa: The campaigns, results and future prospects,* James Currey, London 1994, p.230.

15 Quoted in Dirk Kotze, 'The New South African Constitution' in Murray Faure and Jan-Erik Lane (eds), *South Africa: Designing New Political Institutions,* Sage Publications, London 1996, p.48.

16 *The Reconstruction and Development Programme: A policy framework,* African National Congress, Johannesburg 1994, p.6.

17 For a full description of GEAR see Elizabeth Sidiropoulus, Anthea Jeffrey, Shaun MacKay, Herma Forgey, Cheryl Chipps and Terence Corrigan, *South Africa Survey 1996/97,* South African Institute of Race Relations, Johannesburg 1997, pp.710–5

18 See, for example, John Pilger, 'The betrayal of South Africa's revolution', *Mail and Guardian,* 17 April 1998. See also Martin J.Murray, *The Revolution Deferred: The Painful Birth of Post-Apartheid South Africa,* Verso, London and New York 1994.

19 See, for example, the debate on emigration in the letters pages of the *Electronic Mail and Guardian,* 8–13 May 1998.

20 *South Africa Survey1996/1997,* p.380.

21 The World Bank, *World Development Report 1997,* Oxford University Press, New York 1997, p.223.

22 Quoted in Alex Boraine and Janet Levy (eds.), *The Healing of a Nation?,* Justice in Transition, Cape Town 1996, p.124.

23 *Ibid.*, p.xviii.

24 *Report of the President of the ANC, Nelson Mandela to the 50th National Conference of the African National Conference,* text taken from ANC web site at http://www.anc.org.za.

25 *Ibid.*

26 *Mail and Guardian,* 19 December 1997.

27 See, for example, the editorial, 'History repeats itself', *Frontiers of Freedom* (South African Institute of International Affairs, Johannesburg), No.11, First Quarter 1997.

CHAPTER 9

Conclusion: the Misunderstood Miracle

The completely literal meaning of miracle is an event of such a nature as to be attributable only to the intervention of the Almighty. There are quite a number of people in South Africa who do literally believe that God intervened to ensure that the elections took place peacefully. Some of Archbishop Tutu's comments on the first anniversary of the 1994 elections, celebrated as Constitution Day, a public holiday, were in this spirit.[1] The IFP leader, Chief Mangosuthu Buthelezi, played up to such religious sentiments by suggesting that his meeting with a Kenyan mediator, paving the way to the IFP's participation in the elections, was due to divine intervention. The meeting had only taken place because Buthelezi's plane had been forced to turn back because of engine trouble. Buthelezi suggested this was not a coincidence.[2] Leaving aside believers in such divine providence, the use of the term miracle conveys to most people simply an outcome that is both highly benign and contrary to expectations.

In practice, it is possible to detect a difference between the external application of the term miracle to the South African transition and its internal application. From outside South Africa, what appeared most surprising was not merely that whites should have given up power without a fight, but the apparent ease of the transition of South Africa from a society governed by apartheid to one governed by the principle of non-racialism. From inside South Africa, a narrower view of the miracle tended to be taken so that it was often applied simply to the closing months of the transition, in particular, the resolution in rapid succession of a whole series of crises that threatened the 1994 elections – the problem of the incorporation of the independent homelands of Bophuthatswana and Ciskei, the violence in the East

Rand townships and Natal, and the related issue of the IFP's participation in the elections.

In applying the concept of a miracle to the South African transition, the term, transition, also merits reflection. It begs the questions of what state of affairs it is a transition from and what a transition to. At the outset this book adopted a radical view of this issue characterising the transition as a passage from white minority to African majority rule. Of course, how one characterises the transition has a bearing on one's explanation of it. A disadvantage of the characterisation in this book is that it actually compounds the problem of explanation since it takes the view that what has to be explained is not a compromise between two sides as a result of a hurting stalemate, but the victory of one side over the other. Even more remarkable than there being such a definitive outcome to the process was the fact that this change took place constitutionally and without a blood-bath, even if it would be inaccurate to describe the transition as peaceful.

To assist the task of explanation, the approach taken in this book has been to disaggregate the problem into two discrete questions. Firstly, why did President de Klerk embark on the liberalisation of the South African political system in 1990? Secondly, why did the ANC emerge from the transition in such a politically dominant position? It is necessary to separate the two issues, since a significant factor in bringing about the liberalisation of the polity was a belief that this would not have the outcome of majority rule, at least as that term was conventionally understood in an African context. Thus, the possibility of a different outcome was an important element in debates during the 1980s on South Africa's future. These were strongly influenced by the notion that South Africa had more in common with deeply divided societies in other parts of the world than it did with the rest of Africa. Another factor in De Klerk's readiness to embark on his trek to an uncertain destination was the end of the Cold War, which appeared to place the ANC at a major strategic disadvantage at a critical juncture in the establishment of new political dispensation.

A major difficulty for accounts of the transition in terms of a pact between elites is the one-sided nature of the outcome of the process of negotiations. Another difficulty is the extent of popular mobilisation that took place during the course of the transition, a circumstance militating against the capacity of the elites to deliver the support of their followers for such a pact. In reality, the consociational or power sharing aspects of even the interim constitution were relatively weak. Thus, when the National Party left the Government of National Unity following the adoption by the Constituent Assembly of the text of a new constitution, one of the justifications that its leaders advanced for this decision was the party's lack of influence on government policy during the two years that they had held office as ministers. The absence of any provision in the interim constitution for the exercise of a minority veto at any point placed the ANC in a position to dominate the decision-making process in the Government of National Unity.

A further difficulty for attempts to explain the transition as a compromise among elites is accounting for the high level of political violence during the transition. While one reason for the violence was opposition to the negotiations, that provides at best only a partial explanation. It makes altogether more sense to place the violence in a much wider context of conflict over the rules of political competition among all the contending parties, including parties engaged in the quest for a negotiated settlement. Three chapters in this book have examined the role of violence during the transition, giving support to the proposition that it was a significant factor in the outcome of the process. In particular, the violence created an opening for the international community to play a part in the transition, in a manner that tended to favour the ANC since it was seen as representative of a majority of the population and accorded legitimacy on that assumption. That assumption was vindicated by the results of the 1994 elections; arguably, it also made a contribution to that outcome.

But while political violence and the actions of the international community during the course of the transition have found a place in the narrative of the transition, neither has been treated as a factor in the explanation of its outcome. Other propositions have been advanced to explain the miracle or to deny that the transition was a miracle. Among writers taking a positive view of the transition, two kinds of general explanations have predominated. The first may be called the myth of non-racialism; the second the myth of the South African model. The reason for labelling them as myths is that they gloss over the substance of the changes, while exaggerating the significance of some of the symbolic trappings of the transition. The centrepiece of the myth of non-racialism is that change came about because South Africans discovered that they had a common identity that overrode racial differences. In Archbishop Tutu's phrase, a rainbow nation was born. In this account of events, in the past South Africans had been blinded by racial prejudice, but the scales had fallen from their eyes making political accommodation possible.

There are both collective and individual versions of this line of argument. That is to say, there are accounts that stress the change in the attitudes of whole communities as paving the way for the miracle and accounts that stress the role of key power holders in the process. A rich source for the latter is the journalist Allister Sparks's book, *Tomorrow is Another Country*, sub-titled 'The Inside Story of South Africa's Negotiated Revolution'.[3] Chapter Two of the book is called 'Tennis Court Diplomacy'.[4] Piet de Waal and Kobie Coetzee were students together at the University of the Orange Free State. They became close friends through tennis. In the 1980s Kobie Coetzee became Minister of Justice, Police and Prisons. By this time his friend, Piet de Waal was a lawyer in the small town of Brandfort. It was to a township on the edge of Brandfort that Winnie Mandela was exiled in 1977. As the only lawyer in town, Piet de Waal was obliged to take on Winnie Mandela as a client. In the event, a close friendship developed between the de Waal family and Winnie Mandela, and particularly between Winnie Mandela and Adele de Waal, Piet's wife. As Sparks tells the story, it was the de Waals who persuaded the Minister of Justice, Police and Prisons Kobie Coetzee to initiate talks between the government and the prisoner Nelson Mandela. That led to four years of secret talks between the government and Mandela, beginning in 1985.

The prologue to Sparks's book contains another story in a somewhat similar vein. This is 'The Tale of the Trout Hook', a story of male bonding.[5] In the spring of 1991, Roelf Meyer, the Deputy Minister of Constitutional Development and a key government negotiator, and Cyril Ramaphosa, a leading figure in the African National Congress (ANC) were invited to a holiday lodge by a wealthy Johannesburg stockbroker. Cyril Ramaphosa was a trout-fishing enthusiast and took Roelf Meyer fishing. The inexperienced Meyer managed to get a hook deeply embedded in one of his fingers. After the failure of gentler efforts to dislodge the hook, Cyril told Roelf that yanking it out was the only solution. To prepare him for this ordeal, Cyril sedated him with whisky before fetching a pair of pliers to do the job. The friendship that developed between the two men as a result of this episode laid the basis of their relationship as the two key negotiators of the transition, or so the legend goes.

Patti Waldmeir's book, *Anatomy of a Miracle*, contains a number of similar anecdotes arising of contacts between the white establishment in South Africa and the ANC from 1985. She tells how a senior official of the ANC, Seretse Choabe, embraced the chairman of the *Broederbond*, Pieter de Lange, as a way of apologising to him after threatening to shoot him when the two men first met at a conference in New York in June 1986. 'Such impossible moments of reconciliation' say Waldmeir 'were to be repeated thousands and thousands of times in the years to follow.'[6] She also recounts the story of Thabo Mbeki's present of a lighter he had been given as gift in North Korea to the same *Broederbond* chairman, when De Lange's own pipe-lighter broke down in the course of hours of discussions in a New York hotel. A stately home near Bath, Mells Park House, was made available through the mining company, Goldfields, for a series of meetings between ANC officials headed by Thabo Mbeki, and members of the Afrikaner elite between November 1987 and May 1990. Here, according to Waldmeir, 'the real work was done over Glenfiddich at the fireside'.[7] Other small luxuries that the participants particularly appreciated were grapes and wine from the Cape, despite the anti-apartheid movement's boycott of such South African products.

Engaging as these stories are, they put overwhelming emphasis on changes in the attitudes of the elites through such contacts as the key to creating the basis for a negotiated settlement. In other words, they treat the contacts themselves as providing the basis for changes in the attitudes of the participants in such meetings. However, it is evident that the reason why such meetings took place in the first place was because the parties were seeking a negotiated way out of South Africa's political impasse. Even if it is accepted that personal interaction between key power holders played a part in overcoming prejudices that remained an obstacle to the initiation of negotiations, it does not explain how the elites were able to overcome prejudice in the wider community. A strong argument for contending that such prejudice was overcome in the course of the transition was that the racial conflagration which many writers had predicted would be the outcome of the conflict was averted.

This provides the basis for a thesis advanced by Rupert Taylor that by constructing a non-racial alternative to apartheid, the mass-based opposition to the government during the 1980s changed the nature of the conflict.

> This calculated construction of non-racial democratic politics worked to transform the terms of the conflict away from a 'black'/ 'white' racial dynamic, by exposing the presumed 'objective facts' of the conflict situation as variable values – such that the real and imagined risks of breaking with apartheid did not prove as great as many 'white' South Africans had foreseen. Projecting such an image of the future worked to pull the present toward the future, it undercut the fear of a racially conflictual future, and created the possibility for a non-zero sum outcome.[8]

Taylor argues that one of the reasons why analysts did not anticipate the nature of the transition was a failure to take account of 'the fluidity of identity politics' and the ability of people to transform themselves through 'constructing a new identity and a new nation'.[9]

The main weakness of this thesis is that it ignores an important reality of the new South Africa. This is that the country has remained electorally polarised on racial lines, though not admittedly, as might have been expected, given the discrimination that Coloureds and Indians suffered under the policies of apartheid between whites and blacks (meaning in this context, Africans, Indians, and Coloureds), but between whites and Africans. This is apparent both from the polarisation of the voters along racial lines in the April 1994 elections, as discussed in Chapter 6, and its persistence in the local elections in 1995 and 1996, as discussed in Chapter 8. Admittedly, precise information on the contours of racial electoral polarisation is lacking because of weaknesses and gaps in the survey material available for analysing the correlation between race and support for particular parties. But what the survey evidence does unequivocally refute is the thesis that the racial identities established under apartheid have dissolved. For example in IDASA's post-election survey, as noted in Chapter 7, a small minority of respondents identified themselves simply as South Africans (13.6 per cent), while race was the most common basis for respondents' self-descriptions, commoner than ethnicity, language or religion.[10]

In his edited book on the 1994 elections, Andrew Reynolds estimated that the National Party won between 3–4 per cent of the African vote and the ANC between 2–3 per cent of the white vote.[11] It is an indication of how deep-rooted the appeal of the myth of non-racialism is that, despite the fact that his own estimates underlined the reality of a racially polarised electorate, Reynolds's preface focused on an African domestic servant who voted for the National Party and an Afrikaner who voted for the ANC, an anecdote utterly untypical of the behaviour of the electorate as a whole.[12] In reality, the two groups most divided in their political loyalties were Coloureds and Indians. Despite the way they were treated under apartheid, a majority of both these groups supported the National Party in the 1994 elections. However, the ANC did secure the support of a significant minority of both groups. Although both the ANC and the National Party made an effort to project themselves to the electorate as non-racial parties in their campaigns for the 1994 elections, in practice their ability to appeal across the white-African dividing line was very limited, if for rather different reasons.

It may be objected to this line of argument that the outcome of the 1994 elections bore the imprint of the racial minorities' fears of African majority rule, as a result of the divisions created by apartheid, and that with the dissipation of their fears, such polarisation will diminish. However, there is little evidence of that as yet in any of the elections held since 1994. Further, political discourse has continued to be dominated by race. A common theme of a number of prominent political commentators in the South African press has been the survival of racism in new guises in the Mandela era. The flavour of this writing is well conveyed in the following extract from a May 1998 column by William Makgoba entitled 'The strategies of the new racists':

> Because new racism is couched in the vocabulary of equal opportunity, colour-blindness, race neutrality and, above all, individualism and individual rights, it has managed to escape the experts and the general public. The new racists have played on the emotions of minority populations to promote instability, social disharmony and lack of focus and common purpose. By repackaging such slogans as 'let's not judge people by the colour of their skin but by the content of their character' to defeat the genuine redressive effects of affirmative action, new racists are out to protect their ill-gained power and fan the flames of racial disharmony.[13]

The particular context of these comments was the success of the Democratic Party in a series of local by-elections in suburban areas in 1998. The massive swing among white voters to the Democratic Party from the National Party was attributed to the former's aggressive championing of white interests, including strong opposition to affirmative action, as well as to the latter's unpopularity, partly as a result of the low standing of the party's new leader, Marthinus van Schalkwyk, elected in September 1997 after De Klerk resigned from the post, but also as a consequence of white disenchantment with the transition negotiated by the party.

Racial polarisation has also been a very evident feature of debates on subjects such as crime, transformation and the operation of the Truth and Reconciliation Commission (TRC). There has been particularly sharp criticism of the TRC in publications of the South African Institute of Race Relations. An editorial in its quarterly *Frontiers of Freedom* accusing the TRC of attempting to saddle whites with feelings of collective guilt for the crime of apartheid unless they made a confession to the TRC complained:

If part of the history of this country is that a majority of whites kept sup-porting apartheid at the polls despite all the hideous things that were known about it, another part is the long history of opposition among whites to that very system. The liberal voice among whites, now singled out for stigmatisation previously reserved for Inkatha, has a history of opposition to racism as proud as that of anyone in the country.[14]

A factor that has arguably contributed to such bad feelings on both sides of the racial divide has been the failure of the political miracle of 1994 to produce an economic bonanza for the country that might have softened the conflict of white and African interests in the new era.

A second common view of the transition is what may be called the myth of the South African model. This was the notion that in reach-ing a settlement the country came up with a political model new to Africa, to a degree original, and arrived at by South Africans themselves. Among enthusiasts there was the further belief that the model had applicability to other African conflicts; and particularly to the case of Angola. Writers varied in what they included in the South African model, but for most its main element was the Government of National Unity. Under the interim constitution all parties that received more than 5 per cent of the votes cast for the National Assembly were entitled to places in the Government of National Unity in proportion to their electoral success. But the focus on the element of power sharing under the interim constitution actually simply underscored the weakness of the case that South Africa had come up with a new model.

In particular, power sharing is only a temporary arrangement and as an entitlement of parties securing more than 5 per cent of the vote disappears after April 1999. It was designed to smoothe the path to majority rule, not to be an alternative to it. Indeed, looked at from this angle, the trajectory of South African change is not new at all, but follows the broad lines of what has happened in a number of other instances of the ending of white minority rule in Africa. The cases where the parallel with South Africa is most apparent are those of Kenya, Zimbabwe, and Namibia. Admittedly, the transitional arrangements in these cases were somewhat different from South Africa's. For example, in the case of Zimbabwe, they provided for separate and disproportionate representation of whites in the National Assembly for the first seven years of independence, while in the case of Namibia they required that decisions in the Constituent Assembly should be by a two-thirds majority.

However, while the particular sunset mechanisms varied, the rhetoric of racial reconciliation that accompanied the transitions in Kenya, Zimbabwe, and Namibia was much the same as in South Africa. In their day, each of the first three was hailed as a miracle of accommodation, much as South Africa is now. Take, for example, this description of Namibia's transition:

> As one of the last colonies in Africa to attain independence, Namibia has attracted interest both in terms of its special history of *apartheid* and the difficulties which the country must overcome as a result, but also regarding the promise the country holds as a stable and democratic society. The relatively smooth transition from colony to independent state, following the long overdue implementation of United Nations Security Council Resolution 435/1978 in 1989–90, gave rise to optimism. The Namibian constitution, forged through inter-party negotiation and consensus, has been widely heralded as a model for other burgeoning democracies in Africa. And the policy of *national reconciliation*, spearheaded by the former liberation movement, South West Africa People's Organisation (SWAPO), now in government, has, in a somewhat paternalist fashion, been lauded as a mark of political maturity. Despite the prognosis for a healthy political future, Namibia still bears the scars of both its recent and distant pasts. The tasks of transforming an ethnically fragmented society, redressing extreme economic imbalances in access to resources and building a more diversified and equitable economy, as a consequence, remain formidable.[15]

With only minor changes, this could double as a description of South Africa's transition. In Namibia, the ground for its new politics was laid during the campaigning for the country's internationally supervised general election in 1989, most notably in the conciliatory speeches of the SWAPO leader, Sam Nujoma. In the light of the close links between Namibia and South Africa, it is not surprising that the path Namibia took was seen by some as providing a precedent for South Africa itself.[16] In the case of Kenya and Zimbabwe, the lustre of their example disappeared with the passing of their transitional phase, apart from relatively rare instances where their policies of racial reconciliation in the years immediately after independence were referred to, generally by those advocating accommodation with the forces of African nationalism. Apart from references to Namibia as a possible model for South Africa, coverage of Namibian politics has been slight, even in South African newspapers, since the country's independence.

In the case of Zimbabwe, the shift from conflict to reconciliation took place immediately after the outcome of the country's internationally supervised general election in February 1980 was announced. The moment was described by William Spring:

As suddenly as it began, though, the panic subsided. An extraordinary television broadcast by Robert Mugabe on the evening of 4 March did much to re-establish confidence. He revealed his new policy of 'reconciliation': "We will ensure that there is a place for everyone in this country. We want to ensure a sense of security for both the winners and losers ... Let us forgive and forget. Let us join hands in a new amity." It was not only the content of Mugabe's speech, which turned things round, but its style, Mugabe's general appearance and its presentation. After years of being portrayed as a bogeyman, the absolute antithesis of truth and righteousness, he now emerged, on television anyway, in his true colours; urbane, sophisticated, fluent, an extraordinarily intelligent politician, with the gift of saying soothing words at the right time. His apparent magnanimity in victory struck a chord in the white community: Christians began to question their own motives and perceptions.[17]

Similarly, in Kenya's case, it was a statement by Jomo Kenyatta following the electoral victory of the Kenya African National Union (KANU) in May 1963 that launched Kenya's policy of racial reconciliation.[18]

Of these three cases of racial reconciliation following majority rule, it is the case of Zimbabwe that has been subjected to the most careful critical analysis. In an article published in *International Affairs* just over a year before the unbanning of the African National Congress in South Africa, Jeffrey Herbst examined the policy in Zimbabwe in depth, while drawing conclusions about its possible implications for South Africa. Herbst argued that the foundation of racial reconciliation in Zimbabwe rested on a bargain.

The bargain, which is never discussed publicly but is understood by almost everyone, is essentially that the whites who are now economically active can stay, continue to operate their businesses and farms, and lead the colonial life they are accustomed to for the rest of their lives. Their children, with two exceptions, must leave.

The exceptions were commercial farming and wildlife tourism. Herbst went on:

The racial bargain rests on the idea that Zimbabwe will not need to Africanize the economy by force because in a generation or so [there] .. will be very few whites in the country, and they will not pose a political or economic threat to the government.[19]

However, what Herbst called a bargain is perhaps more accurately described simply as the consequence of a situation in which the white minority lost political power, while retaining a measure of economic leverage. Herbst contended that the Zimbabwean experience was of limited relevance to South Africa because of the much larger size of the white population and because whites in South Africa had fewer opportunities for emigration than their counterparts in Zimbabwe. He also maintained that whites in South Africa were in a better position to forge alliances with other ethnic groups to sustain their position. He concluded: 'The prospects for easy reconciliation in South Africa therefore appear to range from the dim to the non-existent.'[20]

What Herbst failed to anticipate, along with most other observers of South African politics, was the speed with which the political power of the white community would diminish in the 1990s, along with its shrinking share of the total population. The erosion of white economic power has taken place more slowly. The basis of it has been affirmative action rather than Africanisation, but the end result of the process is not likely to be very different. This is not to discount the importance of the many differences among the cases of Kenya, Zimbabwe, Namibia and South Africa. Nevertheless, it is striking how at the time of the transition in each case, a great deal was made of their exceptionalism. Yet the broad political outcome in the four cases has been similar. It seems likely that with the passage of time South Africa will look less and less different from the other cases.

It is rather ironic, given the ANC's interest in the concept of an African renaissance, that the ANC should have pressed the relevance of the South African model to the Northern Ireland peace process in the course of 1997 and 1998, while the similarities between its own transition and the transfer of power in a number of other African countries have been overlooked. The irony is compounded by the role that the case of Northern Ireland played in the thinking of those advocating consociationalism as a way out of South Africa's impasse, in opposition to the ANC's quest for majority rule. The South African model was also invoked as a solution in the cases of Angola and Mozambique, but in relation to ending their post-independence civil wars, rather than their transitions from colonial rule, which of course preceded the South African transition. The analogy between Angola and South Africa attracted interest during the transition, because of similarities in the strategies of Jonas Savimbi and Mangosuthu Buthelezi. However, the fear of an Angolan-type debacle in South Africa greatly diminished once the IFP decided to take part in the elections, accepted the results and entered the Government of National Unity. A strong basis for the analogy is the role that regional cleavages have played in underpinning the political positions of both Savimibi and Buthelezi, though also placing a ceiling on the support they are able to secure nationally.

A further reason for rejecting the notion of a South African model, besides the precedents that existed elsewhere in Africa for such a transfer of power accompanied by policies of reconciliation, is that it understates the role that international norms played in shaping the outcome. Indeed, the debt South Africa owes to the international community has been invoked in debates on how the country should deal with its past. A striking example is a speech by Justice Richard Goldstone at a conference to discuss the establishment of the TRC in July 1994. Speaking in support of the setting up of the TRC, he said that South Africa was under international legal and moral obligations to act:

> We have a legal duty because international human rights conventions oblige us to bring human rights abuses to light and to punish those responsible. But we also have a moral duty because the installation of a democratic government in South Africa is substantially due to the contribution of the international human rights movement in the form of the Anti-Apartheid Movement. South Africa is unique in that it is the only country to achieve change as a result of an international human rights endeavour – and we owe a moral duty to pay our dues.[21]

However, this perspective is also compatible with the view that South Africa has a special mission to fulfil as a paragon of change. Projection of South Africa's negotiated revolution as an example to other countries also has obvious appeal as a way of legitimising South Africa's own transition in the rest of the world.

Mandela's extraordinary speech to the 50th national conference of the ANC in December 1997 made reference to a third perspective on the transition to be found in positive accounts of South Africa's transition, though one somewhat less prevalent than either the myth of non-racialism or the myth of a South African model. This was a view of the transition as a deal between the races on reconciliation and transformation. In other words, whites were offered reconciliation and forgiveness for their complicity in the crime of apartheid in return for their support for a programme of transformation designed to ensure that those who had been most disadvantaged under apartheid would receive the help they needed to avail themselves of the opportunities that South Africa had to offer. In this way the racial disparities of the past were to be overcome. The notion of the transition as a compact that benefited both black and white is most clearly conveyed in Peter Hain's account of the transition.

> It was as if a great millstone had been lifted. Whites could for the first time be themselves, at ease with the world. I was reminded of their friendliness

and old-fashioned courtesy: it was always there, but obscured by complicity in the brutality of apartheid. The old South Africa that we had left had been descending relentlessly into the pit of human depravity. The new one was buoyed by infectious optimism from whites and blacks alike – though they too were caught by the same sense of wondering whether it was actually true.[22]

There remain, of course, many different possible interpretations of the contents of the reconciliation/transformation deal or of who is responsible for its implementation. Thus, the actual context of Mandela's reference to this view of the transition was criticism of the country's white political parties for seeking to frustrate transformation, thereby reneging on their side of the bargain.

Negative views of the South African transition are relatively rare. They tend to arise out of the proposition that the transition has produced little or no change in the living conditions of the majority of the population. A relatively soft version of this perspective, which does not blame the ANC for this situation, is that the Mandela government has been hamstrung by the protection for property rights written into the constitution from taking radical steps to benefit the majority. For example, Jon Qwelane has argued in his South African newspaper column that the constitution remains a serious obstacle to fundamental change.

> For example, land distribution will never be fairly and fully addressed unless the constitution gives the Government strong muscle to do so, instead of protecting whites' ill-gotten land as it does at present. And until the land question is honestly addressed, millions of black South Africans will remain 'squatters' in the land of their birth, while there is not a single white 'squatter' or white 'squatter camp' in this country.[23]

The context of Qwelane's argument was controversy over the ANC's ambition to secure a two-thirds majority in the national elections in 1999 to give the party the power to amend the constitution.

A harder version that the ANC has betrayed the South African revolution has been put forward by the journalist John Pilger and a similar case that the revolution has been deferred has been made by Martin J. Murray.[24] In an article entitled 'The betrayal of the South African revolution', Pilger argues that the people of the townships brought about the transition of 1994 through their struggles.

> It follows that they ought not to have merely an expectation of a better life, but a right to one. The truth is that this right is still denied and South Africa is still not theirs. What is clear is that 'reconciliation', to which

Mandela has devoted himself to the applause of most of the world, provides little more than a facade behind which apartheid continues by other means. For the question remains: reconciliation for whom?[25]

According to Pilger, economic apartheid remains almost untouched by the transition.

[E]nclaves like Sandton are apartheid's unchallenged bastions, from which 5 per cent of the population control 88 per cent of the nation's wealth. This grotesque imbalance of power has not changed since democracy and is not likely to. They, not the majority, have been rewarded by democracy and 'reconciliation'.[26]

However, Pilger does acknowledge that there has been change within this structure of inequality as a result of the rise of a new black (African?) elite. Pilger's analysis contains echoes of Colin Leys's characterisation of Kenya's economic policies after independence as the Africanisation of colonial structures of inequality. In this context, Leys quotes the manifesto of the New Kenya Group before independence as showing an acute understanding of the potential for such a neo-colonial solution.

The inherent problem of Kenya lies in the wide gulf between the living and cultural standards of the well-to-do and those of the poorer majority but this is magnified into a racial problem by the fact that in our country racial and economic difference lie together. The usual historical economic conflict is thus, in our case, exacerbated by race. The only solution, in our view, is vigorously to tackle the basic problem of low living standards, so that there may rapidly emerge from the poorer majority people having similar interests and similar ideals, to those economically more advanced.[27]

This analysis was borne out in practice by the emergence of an African elite after independence with a stake in the survival of many of the social and economic institutions the country had inherited from the colonial era.

Pilger blames the government's adoption of a neo-liberal macro-economic strategy for the existence of a similar state of affairs in South Africa. He suggests that this was the price that the ANC had to pay for securing the support of both business and the international community prior to the transition. He posits the existence of a gentlemen's agreement to this effect as a result of the secret meetings that preceded 2 February 1990. Martin Murray develops a similar case.

The bargain that the white oligarchy has struck is to trade exclusive political power for continued economic advantage. The survival and adaption of political and economic elites goes hand-in-hand with the containment of the aspirations of the working class and the poor. . . . . . The striking paradox that casts its long shadow over the slow and painful birth of post-apartheid South Africa is that, for all that has happened, not much has changed.[28]

The main weakness of such arguments lies in the absence of a credible left-wing economic strategy that the ANC might otherwise have pursued on coming to power. For the ANC to have continued in its adherence to commitments to nationalisation would have required the party to have ignored the experience of the rest of the world in the 1990s and to have stuck to an agenda that left-wing parties aspiring to govern in other liberal democracies everywhere else in the world had abandoned. Of course, these circumstances did make easier the ANC's relations with big business in South Africa, but it is overstating the case to suggest that contacts with business leaders were a more important factor in influencing the evolution of the ANC's economic policies than the global economic environment in which it came to power.

It is important that the case against presenting the South African transition as a genuinely benign set of events should not be overstated. In particular, changing attitudes among whites on race did help to facilitate the process of change in South Africa. Further, the agreement late in 1992 between the ANC and the National Party on power sharing, even if it was for a limited period, was a crucial turning point in the transition, breaking an impasse between the two sides that threatened to plunge the country into chaos. That agreement represented a recognition of the power realities on both sides. In the case of the ANC, it was the recognition that without the cooperation of white civil servants it would be unable to govern effectively. Power sharing with the National Party was a way of securing their cooperation, as was the commitment to safeguard their jobs. In the case of the National Party, the agreement represented the recognition that it was not in a strong enough position to insist on power sharing on a permanent basis, as well as reflecting an appreciation that if it was to project itself effectively as a non-racial party in the future, it would have to free itself from commitments to maintaining ethnic minority vetoes. Further, in so far as the cases of Kenya, Zimbabwe and Namibia can be seen as providing precedents for the South African transition, it must also be acknowledged that South Africa avoided the fate of other settler colonies, such as Algeria, Angola and Mozambique. The traumatic transitions to majority rule of these three countries constituted precedents for a far more catastrophic outcome than occurred in South Africa.

However, without denying the skill of the parties in negotiating the path from minority to majority rule, it is important not to lose sight of the larger picture. This is the reality that change came to South Africa, as it did in other cases of white minority rule in Africa, because of a shift in power that made it impossible for whites to maintain their rule and stability and order at the same time. Once the white rulers started to make concessions to African nationalists in an attempt to stabilise the situation, they found themselves in a position that required further concessions. Even the extreme white right were influenced by the power realities. Thus, one of the surprising aspects of the South African transition was the relative quiescence of the extreme white right. As explained in Chapter 4, a partial explanation is to be found in the fact that the most significant violent actions of the extreme white right during the transition all backfired. Another reason why there was relatively little extreme white right-wing violence was that a sizeable section of this strand of opinion placed their faith in a constitutional approach to securing concessions from the ANC. The ANC sensibly encouraged such a strategy in the knowledge that it could rely on the predominance of Africans in the rural areas to show that a *volkstaat* would not be feasible in practice.

Analysis with the benefit of hindsight is of course relatively easy. Just as most political scientists failed to predict the fall of Communism in Eastern Europe, so most failed to anticipate the political accommodation of whites and blacks (in this context, Africans, Coloureds, and Indians) in South Africa. One reason was that South Africa tended to be compared not with other situations of white minority rule in Africa, but with deeply divided societies elsewhere in the world such as Northern Ireland and Israel/Palestine, where the potential for shifts in power (in so far as they existed at all) were rather different. This is not to reject such comparisons, which this author has frequently made himself, but to underline the danger of overemphasising similarities and underplaying differences when making such comparisons. Another reason was that a number of South African political scientists were mesmerised by the writings of Arend Lijphart when constructing scenarios of political change in South Africa.

Lijphart suggested that the following created favourable conditions for the establishment of power-sharing in deeply divided or multi-ethnic societies.

[1] a multiple balance of groups
[2] no majority group
[3] groups of roughly equal size
[4] a relatively small population
[5] external threats perceived as a common danger by the different groups
[6] the presence of some society-wide loyalties
[7] the absence of extreme socio-economic inequalities
[8] the relative isolation of the segments from each other
[9] prior traditions of political accommodation.[29]

At a pinch, one might argue that two of the conditions existed in the South African case, '[6] the presence of some society-wide loyalties', since there was widespread identification with South Africa as a territory, and '[8] the relative isolation of segments from each other', in so far as residential segregation remained a legacy of the apartheid era. But the other conditions did not apply. It was wishful thinking on the part of apologists for apartheid in the 1980s and a misreading of the significance of the conflict between the ANC and Inkatha by others, including Lijphart himself, that led some to conclude that South Africa could be characterised as a land of minorities and that consequently '[2] no majority group' could be applied to the South African case.

In these circumstances the fact that South Africa appeared to have achieved a settlement apparently based on consociational principles did indeed seem a miracle. The differences between power-sharing in the Government of National Unity and Lijphart's requirements for a consociational system were glossed over. As long as there was a possibility that power sharing might remain an enduring feature of the system, the proposition that the South African transition was a triumph for Lijphart's ideas could be defended . Its credibility disappeared with the adoption of the final constitution, which discarded any vestige of power sharing. In fact, it can be argued that the South African transition refutes the proposition that in deeply divided or multi-ethnic societies, political accommodation is only possible by the permanent entrenchment of power sharing. Further, there is little likelihood of power sharing arising voluntarily out of a multiple balance of power in the National Assembly.

If what has happened in Kenya, Zimbabwe, and Namibia is taken as a precedent for likely political developments in South Africa, then circumstances are hardly likely to favour a revival of power sharing in the near future. In Kenya a year after independence, the Official

Opposition, the Kenya African Democratic Union, crossed the floor to join the government. In Zimbabwe there was also a merger of the two main rival nationalist parties, on the terms of the major and increasingly dominant party of Robert Mugabe. In Namibia SWAPO substantially increased its majority in the National Assembly in the country's second democratic elections in December 1994. Its share of the vote went up from 57.3 per cent to 73.9 per cent. This has proved to be a very common pattern in Africa. A party's status as the country's liberation movement forms the basis of its victory at the first democratic elections, while in the second, it does even better because it has the advantage of being the government with patronage at its disposal, in addition to still being seen as the country's liberator. On this precedent the ANC's dominance seems likely to grow as well. If South Africa does become increasingly dominated by the ANC in the years ahead, it will of course underline how large the shift in power ultimately has been and make it appear still more remarkable that it occurred with relatively little racial violence or political upheaval.

For a number of writers, the essence of the South African miracle is to be found in the disaster that was avoided, the fact that, as Christopher Saunders puts it, 'white rule ..ended, not with the Voortrekker Monument and Union Buildings in ruins, but .. with Nelson Mandela speaking in the ballroom of Johannesburg's lead-ing hotel'.[30] Conceiving of the miracle as a moment rather than a process has advantages, though also presenting problems. The most trivial of these is which moment to choose; 27 April 1994 the first day of general voting in the country's first non-racial elections; 2 May 1994, when Mandela claimed victory in those elections at the Carlton Hotel (the choice made by Saunders); or 10 May 1994 when Mandela was inaugurated as President of South Africa. An advantage of conceiving of the miracle as a moment is that it captures the mood of euphoria that existed at the time. Of course, it is inevitable that people's memories of how they felt during those remarkable days from the start of polling for special voters on 26 April to Mandela's inauguration on 10 May will themselves change in the light of contemporary developments. However, it seems likely that regardless of South Africa's future development, they will be looked back to as among the country's finest hours.

Treating the miracle as a moment brings out another connotation of the concept. This is the implication that miracles are by nature short lived. They are fragile like bubbles and like bubbles miracles do not last. This sense is conveyed by Steven Friedman who entitled the afterword to a 1994 book on the South African transition, 'A Brief

Miracle?'.[31] The title of the book itself was *The Small Miracle*. This was an allusion to Mandela's victory speech at the Carlton Hotel on 2 May 1994 in which he referred to the birth of democracy in South Africa as 'a small miracle'. Amidst the euphoria of those days that seemed a modest claim. However, what is striking from the perspective of the late 1990s is the extent to which the expectations of a much brighter future that the 1994 elections inspired, have been disappointed. Apartheid's legacy of low economic growth and of massive inequalities of income and wealth has proved much more difficult to shake off than white minority rule. Further, racial political polarisation has also persisted in the new South Africa, contrary to the image of the 1994 elections as the birth of non-racial politics in the country. And in so far as this is what the outside world has contrived to read into the South African transition, the miracle has been misunderstood.

Notes to Chapter 9

1   *The Irish Times* (Dublin), 28 April 1995.

2   *Sunday Times* (Johannesburg), 24 April 1994.

3   Allister Sparks, *Tomorrow is Another Country: The Inside Story of South Africa's Negotiated Revolution*, Struik Book Distributors, Sandton 1994.

4   *Ibid.*, p.15.

5   *Ibid.*, p.3.

6   Patti Waldmeir, *Anatomy of a Miracle: The End of Apartheid and the Birth of the New South Africa*, Viking, London 1997, p.64.

7   *Ibid.*, p.79.

8   Rupert Taylor (with Jacklyn Cock and Adam Habib), 'Projecting Peace in Apartheid South Africa', paper for Special Session No. 46, 'Conflict and Order in South Africa', International Political Science Association's 17th World Congress, Seoul, Korea 1997, p.8.

9   *Ibid.*

10 Robert Mattes, *The Election Book: Judgement and Choice in South Africa's 1994 Election*, Institute for Democracy in South Africa, Cape Town 1995, p.41.

11 Andrew Reynolds (ed.), *Election '94 South Africa: The campaign, results and future prospects*, David Philip, Cape Town 1994, p.193 and p.190.

12 *Ibid.*, p.xiii.

13 *Mail and Guardian*, 15 May 1998.

14 'Analogies and apologies', *Frontiers of Freedom*, No. 16, Second Quarter 1998.

15 Leif John Fosse, 'Negotiating the nation: ethnicity, nationalism and nation-building in independent Namibia', *Nations and Nationalism*, Vol. 3, No. 3, November 1997, p.427.

16 See, for example, Christopher Saunders, 'Namibia holds hopeful lessons for the SA transition', *Business Day* (Johannesburg), 22 January 1993.

17 William Spring, *The Long Fields: Zimbabwe since Independence*, Pickering Paperbacks, Basingstoke 1986, p.18.

18 The text of Kenyatta's statement is reproduced in C.J.Gertzel, Maure Goldschmidt and Don Rothchild (eds), *Government and Politics in Kenya: A Nation Building Text*, East African Publishing House, Nairobi 1969, p.21.

19 Jeffrey Herbst, 'Racial reconciliation in southern Africa', *International Affairs*, Vol. 65, No. 1, Winter 1988/89, p.46.

20 *Ibid.*, p.51.

21 Alex Boraine and Janet Levy (eds), *The Healing of the Nation?*, Justice in Transition, Cape Town 1995, pp.121–2.

22 Peter Hain, *Sing the Beloved Country: The Struggle for the New South Africa*, Pluto Press, London 1996, p.206.

23 Jon Qwelane, 'White parties up to their old tricks', *The Star and SA Times* (London), 20 May 1998.

24 Martin J.Murray, *The Revolution Deferred: The Painful Birth of Post-Apartheid South Africa*, Verso, London 1994.

25 John Pilger, 'The betrayal of South Africa's revolution', *Mail and Guardian*, 17 April 1998.

26 *Ibid.*

27 Colin Leys, *Underdevelopment in Kenya: The Political Economy of Neo-Colonialism 1964–1971*, Heinemann, London 1975, p.43.

28 Murray, *op. cit.*, pp.4–5.

29 Arend Lijphart, 'Consociation' in Desmond Rea (ed.), *Political co-operation in divided societies*, Gill and Macmillan, Dublin 1982, p.183.

30 Christopher Saunders, 'Reflections on the South African transition' in Peter F.Alexander, Ruth Hutchison and Deryck Schreuder (eds), *Africa Today: A Multi-Disciplinary Snapshot of the Continent in 1995*, Humanities Research Centre, Australian National University, Canberra 1996, p.55.

31 Steven Friedman and Doreen Atkinson (eds), *The Small Miracle: South Africa's negotiated settlement*, Ravan Press, Johannesburg 1994, pp.331–7.

Chronology

Some Significant Dates in South Africa's Transition

1976

16 June – Start of Soweto uprising arising out of protests against the imposition of the use of Afrikaans in African secondary schools.

1977

12 September – Death in detention of Black Consciousness activist Steve Biko.

4 November – UN Security Council imposes mandatory arms embargo on South Africa.

1983

20 August – Formation of the United Democratic Front (UDF).

2 November – Majority of whites back tricameral constitution in referendum (66 per cent voting 'Yes').

1984

22 August – Low turn-out in elections for (Coloured) House of Representatives

28 August – Low turn-out in elections for (Indian) House of Delegates

1985

21 March – Langa (Uitenhage) massacre.

20 July – Declaration of state of emergency.

30 November – Formation of COSATU.

1986

19 May – EPG mission ended by SAAF bombing raids on Botswana, Zambia and Zimbabwe.

2 October – Congress overrides President Reagan's veto on sanctions legislation

1987

9 July – Meeting between ANC and Afrikaner intellectuals in Dakar, Senegal.

5 November – Release of senior ANC figure, Govan Mbeki.
1988
24 February – Restrictions placed on 17 anti-apartheid organisations.
1989
5 July – Meeting between prisoner Nelson Mandela and President P.W.Botha.
14 August – P.W.Botha resigns and is succeeded by F.W. de Klerk.
21 August – Adoption of Harare Declaration setting out ANC's terms for negotiations with the South African government.
15 October – Senior ANC leaders released, including Walter Sisulu.
1990
2 February – In speech opening parliament President de Klerk announces unbanning of the ANC and other prohibited organisations.
11 February – Release of Nelson Mandela from prison.
2–4 May – Meeting between government and ANC resulting in Groote Schuur Minute.
6 August – Further meeting between government and ANC resulting in Pretoria Minute; ANC suspends all armed actions.
1991
31 January – Mandela and Buthelezi meet.
15 February – D.F.Malan Minute between government and ANC.
14 September – Signing of National Peace Accord.
20 December – Start of formal multi-party talks in CODESA.
1992
17 March – Whites vote by large majority (69 per cent 'Yes') to support continuation of reform process in referendum on negotiations.
17 June – Boipatong massacre.
15 July – UN Security Council debate on situation in South Africa.
7 September – Bisho massacre
26 September – Record of Understanding between government and ANC.
1993
10 April – Assassination of Chris Hani.
25 June – Attack by extreme right on World Trade Centre, venue of multi-party negotiations.
2 July – Confirmation of 27 April 1994 as date for South Africa's first non-racial general election.
7 December – Installation of TEC.
1994
12 March – Bophuthatswana reincorporated into South Africa.
28 March – Shell House killings during Zulu protests in centre of Johannesburg.
19 April – Agreement for Reconciliation and Peace under which the IFP agreed to participate in the elections

26–29 April – Voting in country's first non-racial general election.

2 May – De Klerk concedes victory to ANC.

10 May – Inauguration of Mandela as President of South Africa.

1995

1 November – Local elections in most of South Africa.

1996

29 May – Local elections in most of Western Cape.

26 June – Local elections in KwaZulu-Natal.

30 June – National Party withdrawal from the Government of National Unity.

1997

4 February – Final constitution comes into force.

9 September – Marthinus van Schalkwyk succeeds De Klerk as leader of the National Party.

16–20 December – 50th ANC National Conference.

1999

30 April – Power-sharing provisions interim constitution to expire.

Select Bibliography

Adam, Heribert, Frederik van Zyl Slabbert and Kogila Moodley, *Comrades in Business: Post-Liberation Politics in South Africa*, Tafelberg, Cape Town 1997.

Barber, James, *Forging the New South Africa*, Royal Institute of International Affairs, London 1994.

Boraine, Alex and Janet Levy (eds), *The Healing of the Nation?*, Justice in Transition, Cape Town 1995.

Brewer, John D. (ed.), *Can South Africa Survive?: Five Minutes to Midnight*, Macmillan, Basingstoke 1989.

Brewer, John D. (ed.), *Restructuring South Africa*, Macmillan, Basingstoke 1994.

Carlsnaes, Walter and Marie Muller (eds), *Change and South Africa's External Relations*, International Thomson Publishing, Johannesburg 1997.

Cohen, Robin, *Endgame in South Africa?*, James Currey, London 1986.

Ellis, Stephen and Tsepo Sechaba, *Comrades against Apartheid*, James Currey, London 1992.

Etherington, Norman (ed.), *Peace, Politics and Violence in the New South Africa*, Hans Zell Publishers, London 1992.

Faure, Murray and Jan-Erik Lane (eds), *South Africa: Designing New Political Institutions*, Sage Publications, London 1996.

Friedman, Steven (ed.), *The long journey: South Africa's quest for a negotiated settlement*, Ravan Press, Johannesburg 1993.

Friedman, Steven and Doreen Atkinson (eds), *The Small Miracle: South Africa's negotiated settlement*, Ravan Press, Johannesburg 1994.

Gann, L.H. and Peter Duignan, *Hope for South Africa?*, Hoover Institution Press, Stanford 1991.

Gann, L.H. and Peter Duignan, *Why South Africa Will Survive*, Croom Helm, London 1981.

Giliomee, Hermann, 'Democratization in South Africa', *Political Science Quarterly*, Vol. 110, No. 1, Spring 1995.

Giliomee, Hermann and Jannie Gagiano (eds), *The Elusive Search for Peace: South Africa, Israel and Northern Ireland*, Oxford University Press, Cape Town 1990.

Giliomee, Hermann and Lawrence Schlemmer (eds), *Negotiating South Africa's Future*, Southern Book Publishers, Johannesburg 1986.

Gutteridge, William and J.E.Spence (eds), *Violence in Southern Africa*, Frank Cass, London 1997.

Hain, Peter, *Sing the Beloved Country: The Struggle for the New South Africa*, Pluto Press, London 1996.

Hanf, Theodor, Heribert Weiland and Gerda Vierdag, *South Africa: the Prospects for Peaceful Change*, Rex Collings, London 1981.

Herbst, Jeffrey, 'Racial reconciliation in southern Africa', *International Affairs*, Vol. 65, No. 1, Winter 1988/89.

Horowitz, Donald L., *A Democratic South Africa?: Constitutional Engineering in a Divided Society*, Oxford University Press, Cape Town 1991.

Jeffrey, Anthea, *The Natal Story: 16 Years of Conflict*, South African Institute of Race Relations, Johannesburg 1997.

Johnson, R.W. and Lawrence Schlemmer (eds), *Launching Democracy in South Africa: The First Open Election, April 1994*, Yale University Press, London and New Haven 1996.

Kane-Berman, John, *Political Violence in South Africa*, South African Institute of Race Relations, Johannesburg 1993.

Lee, Robin and Lawrence Schlemmer (eds), *Transition to Democracy: Policy Perspectives 1991*, Oxford University Press, Cape Town 1991.

Mandela, Nelson, *Long Walk to Freedom: The Autobiography of Nelson Mandela*, MacDonald Purnell, Randburg 1994.

Mare, Gerhard, *Ethnicity and Politics in South Africa*, Zed Books, London 1993.

Mattes, Robert, *The Election Book: Judgment and Choice in South Africa's 1994 Election*, Institute for Democracy in South Africa, Cape Town 1995.

Mayall, James and Mark Simpson, 'Ethnicity is not Enough: Reflections on Protracted Secessionism in the Third World', *International Journal of Comparative Sociology*, Vol. 33 (1–2), 1992.

Murray, Martin J., *The Revolution Deferred: The Painful Birth of Post-Apartheid South Africa*, Verso, London 1994.

O'Meara, Dan, *Forty Lost Years: The apartheid state and the politics of the National Party, 1948–94*, Ravan Press, Randburg 1996.

Reynolds, Andrew (ed.), *Elections '94 South Africa: The campaign, results and future prospects*, James Currey, London 1994.

Sisk, Timothy D., *Democratization in South Africa: The Elusive Social Contract*, Princeton University Press, Princeton, New Jersey, 1995.

Slabbert, F. van Zyl and David Welsh, *South Africa's options: Strategies for sharing power*, David Philip, Cape Town 1979.

Sparks, Allister, *The Mind of South Africa: The Story of the Rise and Fall of Apartheid*, Mandarin, London 1991.

Sparks, Allister, *Tomorrow is another country: The inside story of South Africa's negotiated revolution*, Struik, Sandton 1994.

Sunter, Clem, *The High Road: Where are we now?*, Tafelberg, Cape Town and Human and Rousseau, Cape Town 1996.

Sunter Clem, *The World and South Africa in the 1990s*, Human and Rousseau, Pretoria and Tafelberg, Cape Town 1987.

Taylor, Rupert, 'The End of Apartheid as part of "the End of History"?', *The South African Journal of International Affairs*, Vol. 3, No. 1, Summer 1995.

Van Rooyen, Johann, *Hard Right: The New White Power in South Africa*, I.B. Tauris, London 1994.

Waldmeir, Patti, *Anatomy of a Miracle: The End of Apartheid and the Birth of the New South Africa*, Viking, London 1997.

Index